AFRICANS IN BRITAIN

AFRICANS
IN
BRITAIN

Edited by
DAVID KILLINGRAY

FRANK CASS

First published in 1994 in Great Britain by

FRANK CASS & CO. LTD.
2 Park Square, Milton Park,
Abingdon, Oxon, OX14 4RN

and in the United States of America by
FRANK CASS
270 Madison Ave,
New York NY 10016

Transferred to Digital Printing 2005

British Library Cataloguing in Publication Data

Africans in Britain – (Special Issue of
"Immigrants & Minorities", ISSN 0261-9288;
Vol.12, No.3)
 I. Killingray, David   II. Series
 305.896041

 ISBN 0-7146-4571 0 (hb)
 ISBN 0-7146-4107 3 (pbk)

Library of Congress Cataloging-in-Publication Data

Africans in Britain / edited by David Killingray
       p.   cm.
    "Special Issue of the journal Immigrants & minorities, vol.
12, no. 3, 1993"—CIP data sheet.
    Includes bibliographical references and index.
    ISBN 0-7146-4571-0 (hbk) : $32.50. — ISBN 0-7146-4107-3 (pbk) :
$15.00
    1. Africans—Great Britain—History. 2. Great Britain—Race
relations. I. Killingray, David.
    DA125.N4A4 1994
    941'.00496—dc20   93-50944
                                                        CIP

This group of studies first appeared in a Special Issue on 'Africans in Britain' of *Immigrants and Minorities*, Vol.12, No.3, published by Frank Cass & Co. Ltd.

Typeset by Vitaset, Paddock Wood, Kent

Printed and bound by Antony Rowe Ltd, Eastbourne

Contents

Editor's Note

In December 1991 the African Studies Association of the United Kingdom and The Royal African Society jointly sponsored a conference on 'The African Presence in the United Kingdom'. Appropriately it was held in the Africa Centre in London's Covent Garden, where between 80 and 90 people, including representatives of African communities, social workers, school and university teachers, met for two days to discuss the experience of African immigrants and settlers in Britain. Those discussions were focused by nearly 20 papers which were largely historical in content and dealt with African communities; Africans in business, politics, and the armed forces; African students, writers, and musicians; African refugees; African religious expressions in Britain; art and representation of Africans; and Africans in show business.

The organizers were only too aware that there were gaps in the programme. Certain topics and themes important to contemporary African communities in Britain were not addressed by specific papers or speakers, although that absence was a good deal compensated for during the vigorous discussions. The record of African experiences and activities in Britain, both past and present, is of great interest to Africans and also those of African descent living in Britain. But the history of African and 'Black' people in Britain is not exclusive and it belongs to all who live in these islands and thus needs to be given greater prominence in the school curriculum as well as the market-place. It was in that spirit that a final session of the conference discussed how the two sponsoring bodies could more closely work with and lend support to African peoples in the United Kingdom. It is hoped that this volume of essays will convey to a wider audience something of the rich contribution that has and is being made by Africans, as well as people of African descent, to the cultures of Britain.

The study of Africans in Britain has suffered a serious loss in the death of two participants in the conference. Paul Edwards who, before most thought it had any significance, helped to focus attention on the whole topic of Africans in Britain, specially Equiano and the literate Africans in the eighteenth century, died in 1992. Ray Jenkins, of Staffordshire University died suddenly in April 1993 aged 54. Ray's research was primarily on the colonial Gold Coast and modern Ghana; he made major contributions to the study of the 'talented minority' who came from that area of West Africa to Britain in the nineteenth and early twentieth centuries. This volume of essays is dedicated to their memory with gratitude and thanks for friendship and encouragement.

DK

Africans in the United Kingdom:
An Introduction

DAVID KILLINGRAY

*Since the sixteenth century there has been a small African minority
in Britain. British historians have largely ignored the presence of
both African and 'Black' people. This introductory article looks at
the experiences of African immigrants, settlers, and those of African
parentage in Britain during a period of over 400 years and suggests
a number of themes and topics which merit further research.*

The decennial census in 1991 recorded that there were more than 207,000
Africans in the United Kingdom. This was the first census in which people
were invited to indicate their ethnic origin; in earlier censuses the only
means of identifying possible ethnicity was from a person's place of birth
and this did not necessarily indicate ethnic origin.[1] The ethnic origin that
individuals subscribe to on a census form may not in fact be a true indication
of their geographical origin. Defining Africa as the place of ethnic origin
and birth may be a political or emotive statement about an indirect origin
by people who are 'Afro-Caribbean' or 'African-American'. The earlier
census suggests the following estimated figures for Africans living in the
United Kingdom: 1911 – 4,540, 1921 – 4,940, 1931 – 5,202, 1951 – 11,000.
Most came from West Africa, were male, and lived mainly in London or
the other major port cities of Liverpool, Bristol and Cardiff.[2]

   The subject of the essays in this collection, and of this introductory
article, is Africans born in the continent who came as visitors and
residents to Britain and also those born in this country of African parentage. It is not the intention here to recount in detail the history of the
presence in Britain of African people; that has been admirably done by
Peter Fryer and others.[3] This contribution looks at a number of themes,
suggests possible areas for research and in the process surveys some of the
existing literature.

The Early Presence of African Peoples

There is archaeological and literary evidence of an African presence in
Romano-Britain, and some evidence that discharged African ex-soldiers
settled near York. 'It would be a nice irony against racist opinion', wrote
Paul Edwards, 'if it could be demonstrated that African communities

were settled in England before the English invaders arrived from Europe centuries later.'[4] And in the early Middle Ages a small number of Africans, principally from the north, journeyed along the trading, raiding and slaving sea routes to British shores. From the sixteenth century onwards Europe's expanding maritime trade, specially in slaves, brought Africans to Britain in a variety of servile roles, as seamen, manual labourers, and also children as aristocratic 'pets'. The majority of people of African origin lived in the major slaving ports of London, Liverpool and Bristol, although they were to be found all over the country. Contrary to the often stated claims for the Mansfield decision, it was not until the early nineteenth century that slavery was finally made illegal in the United Kingdom.[5]

Much more needs to be known about the African, and indeed the Black, population of Britain in the nineteenth century, their individual biographies, networks and communities. There is some evidence to indicate that the Black population may have been less noticeable than it had been in the previous century, although not the 'disintegration' suggested by Walvin.[6] It may well be that intermarriage between black and white blurred the black British population except in certain parts of London and the major ports where black people were always in evidence both in transit and as settlers. Certainly Africans were commonly seen in major ports, especially those serving the West African trade; but there is increasing evidence that although black people might excite comment in the shires their presence there was less unusual than once was thought to be the case. In the latter part of the century, as the African empire grew, the African presence in Britain increased. Most Africans coming to Britain were seamen or in manual employ, or 'natives' brought over for display at one or other of the regular international fairs and colonial exhibitions staged in London. In addition there was a new class, principally the West African coastal elite using the receipts of trade, sending their young people to Britain for education, and making regular visits to the metropole in pursuit of their professional interests as clergy, doctors, lawyers and traders.

This process continued through the twentieth century as more Africans came to Britain to study and in official capacities integral to the infrastructure of Empire. Africans from the colonies, with few exceptions, could enter Britain without let or hinderance.[7] Ironically the great increase of African immigration to Britain followed the end of colonial rule c.1960 and the introduction of new laws to restrict entry to the country. As in the past Africans came into Britain for a variety of reasons. Involuntary movement was central to the slave trade and to many capitalist enterprises that took Africans from the West coast of the continent. More recently a steadily growing number of Africans have arrived in

Britain as political refugees from harsh regimes and revolutions. And as African economies declined in the 1960s and 1970s they have been joined by economic refugees. For many African states this slow diasporic haemor-rhage, particularly of skilled people, has fuelled economic decline. For example, Ghana has spent a considerable part of its wealth in training young people in schools and universities only to see them leave to live in London, Paris, New York, or even Palermo. Medical doctors driving taxis in foreign cities is not a good human investment. In London alone there are probably more than 10,000 Ghanaians, many with professional skills.

Why Study Africans in Britain?

This is a question well worth asking and attempting to answer. What is the significance of the African presence in Britain that makes it worthy of study? There are several justifications. First of all, Africans are an immigrant minority, distinctive from, although often confused with, Afro-Americans by people in the host community. Along with Black people in general Africans have been marginalized or ignored in the writing of British history; many well-informed people express surprise that Britain has had an African presence during the past 400 years and that there is a sizeable African minority living in the country at the present. Secondly, Africans, in common with Black people and many immigrant minorities, have been exploited and subject to racial harass-ment and discrimination in employment, housing and social provision. Racial antipathy to foreigners and outsiders is endemic in most societies; Africans' distinctiveness, and their often servile status or position, exposed them more readily to abuse. By the mid-nineteenth century racial ideas and attitudes in Britain were being comforted by pseudo-scientific theories which cast a long shadow over racial relations and continued for much of the next century.[8] Those racial attitudes and expressions are an unfortunate part of British intellectual and cultural history. We cannot study and attempt to understand how such ideas and images were fashioned without also looking at the people who were observed. And trying to pierce the gloom of popular perceptions of race also means looking at the way in which Africa and African people have been represented in various forms of art and entertainment, in novels and films.[9]

Thirdly, the African presence is central to the history of Britain as an Imperial power. Africans who came to Britain for education received more than merely academic schooling. Many were also politically shaped by the experience and returned to play an active part in nationalist movements and to become future rulers. In part the destruction of empire and the transfer of power lay in the language, legal lessons and political skills acquired by younger anti-colonial-minded Africans in British institutions and exercised in their small pan-Africanist circles in London and elsewhere.

And perhaps a fourth, and minor, reason for looking at Africans in Britain is because their response and adaptation to British society and institutions provides lessons about human versatility and endeavour. Fortunately there are also a few accounts written by Africans who looked with curious and critical eyes at British society and institutions and which provide that helpful outsider's view much needed by unconscious, confident, or insular people.[10]

Whose History? History from Above and from Below

For the rest of this article I want to address and expand upon the themes and ideas raised in the essays in this collection and then to suggest other themes that might form an agenda for historians of the African presence in Britain.

The vast majority of Africans who came to Britain over the last 400 years were either non-literate or left no personal written record. In most cases their personal history is lost. By contrast a considerable amount is known about the few Africans who wrote memoirs or accounts based on their experiences of the slave trade which were published in the late eighteenth century[11] while the letters of Philip Quaque and some less well-known writings have also been rescued from relative obscurity by historians.[12] Africans who did not write in English but gained patrons or prominence have also been more easily retrieved from the dust of the past.[13] However, for the overwhelming majority of Africans in Britain, the records are slender and diffused. It is only comparatively recently that historians have begun to try to use systematically the scattered and often brief references to Africans and black people in parish registers, probate papers, medicity and criminal records, and newspapers. Ian Duffield's meticulous use of court and transportation records provides a sterling example of what can be done to discover a dimension of British Black history that was little known.[14]

The history of Africans in Britain who were from the elite (students, businessmen, and so on) is important, although even their lives are often difficult to reconsruct from the fragmentary records that they left or that mentioned their activities. A good example is the rescuing from obscurity by Hakim Adi of the Nigerian nationalist Bandele Ominiyi, a man who was unknown to most of the specialists on pan-Africanist politics.[15] Marika Sherwood's endeavours to reconstruct the vital London years of

Kwame Khrumah (see below) indicate the lacunae in writing about one of Africa's most important modern politicians. Clearly there is a need for more biographies of African leaders, studies which take greater account of the experience of living in Britain.[16] There is also a place for Afro-British family histories, for example the Hutchisons and Bannermans, as well as those families which are being formed today.

The writing of Afro-British history from below has begun, an attempt to place on the map of the past the lives and activities of ordinary African men and women who were slaves, servants, seamen, and invariably poor.[17] Clearly not all were non-literate as Ian Duffield shows in his contribution; for the first half of the nineteenth century British African/Black levels of formal literacy were probably similar to those of other working-class people in Britain. In the eighteenth century the servile origin of many Africans placed them mainly amongst the poor, although sickness, old age and misfortune often propelled people without property or income into poverty. The Afro-British poor concerned philanthropists, including Equiano, and the Committee for the Relief of the Black Poor saw one solution in shipping them back to West Africa as settlers in Sierra Leone.[18]

A good number of the Africans who came to Britain were seamen and therefore a shifting population moving from port to port. They are elusive to the historian unless they had the misfortune to fall sick or into dire need, run foul of the law, or happened to take shore employment, married and settled down. Liverpool, Bristol and London had a small but distinctive Afro-British population in the eighteenth and nineteenth centuries constantly fuelled by a small number of in-coming Africans. And from the 1840s onwards the Bute Town area of Cardiff also gained an African population, mainly from seamen;[19] so did South Shields where, after 1870, a small Yemeni and Somali maritime community developed. African seamen served on both mercantile and Royal Navy vessels[20] and those who fell sick or were unable to find another berth were often forced to beg in British streets.[21] In the mid-1880s, when Gordon fever was at its height, Sudanese seamen employed on British war transports plying between Egypt and the Woolwich arsenal were accused of being spies and barred from employment; in a later 'Great' war the urgent need for labour over-rode such considerations and seamen and dock workers were recruited for British ships and dockyards from various corners of the Empire.[22]

There are some obvious sources which provide information on African seamen, but many of the Africans who came to Britain are only likely to be retrieved from dispersed and isolated references in local records, such as parish registers and census enumerators' returns. An invaluable approach is through family history which can start with the recent present and discrete personal oral evidence, memoirs and photographs, and then be linked to the scattered references in records. Family historians have a great deal to contribute in providing much of the essential data if a full history is to be written of the African presence in Britain.[23]

The Quest for Education

Several of the essays in this collection, particularly the ones by Adi, Hargreaves, Kirk-Greene, are concerned with Africans in twentieth-century Britain for the purposes of higher education. The process is an old one. As early as the sixteenth century European traders saw the value of having a few Africans with some formal education who could serve the interests of commerce on the west coast. By the mid-eighteenth century a few West African chiefs and traders, recognizing the value of formal instruction in literacy and numeracy, were entrusting their European trading partners with the education of their children in Britain.[24] In 1794 Wadstrom recorded that there were 'generally from fifty to seventy [African children] at school in Liverpool'.[25] Following the establishment of the settlement at Sierra Leone an increasing number of local African children, including girls, were sent to Britain for an education provided in Clapham, south-west London, and in 1801 a Society for the Education of Africans was established.[26]

By the middle of the nineteenth century West African coastal elite families had already begun sending their children to Britain for education. This was paid for mainly by family or friends, occasionally by philanthropic organizations, and in a few cases from British or colonial government funds. We know most about the children from Sierra Leone and the Gold Coast and the schools that they attended in Britain, thanks to the work of Christopher Fyfe and Ray Jenkins,[27] but there were also a good number of youngsters sent from the Gambia and southern Nigeria. In some cases a whole family moved to Britain as did the Smiths of Freetown in 1872, settling first in Norwood but moving shortly thereafter to St Helier in Jersey. The Smith children, several being daughters, were educated solely in Britain.[28] African children boarded at English schools and girls were sometimes found a suitable family who would provide accommodation.[29]

The Temne chief Naimbanna, recognizing the value of a European training, had sent two of his sons to Britain for schooling in the late eighteenth century. This example was followed by other African rulers, often at the instigation of missionaries and colonial officials who hoped that African princes would serve as agents to plant European 'civilization' and Christianity in the black continent. Samuel Moroka, son of Moroka II, the Baralong ruler, was sent to study at St Augustine's, Canterbury, while

Lewanika, the Lozi ruler, sent his two sons to Bethany School, Goudhurst in Kent, at the beginning of this century. One of the terms of the British–Asante treaty of 1831 was that two sons of the royal family, Owusu Kwantabisa and Owusu Ansah, should be taken as hostages and educated in Britain at the expense of the British government. Both young men returned to the Gold Coast in 1841 and John Owusu Ansah, as he had been baptized, served the Wesleyan Methodists, the colonial government, and the Asante state in various capacities.[30] Following the British defeat of Asante in 1874 the son of the Asantehene, Kofi Nti was sent to England to be educated. He attended the Surrey County School, Cranleigh, for six years but was expelled in 1881 'guilty of immoral conduct with a servant girl here'.[31]

In the late nineteenth century the West African elite unsuccessfully demanded a West African university to complement Fourah Bay College in Freetown. Failing this provision the only source of higher education and professional training was in Europe or North America. Philip Quaque, from the Gold Coast, in the mid-eighteenth century studied in England and was ordained in the Anglican church before returning to his native land as chaplain at Cape Coast castle, but the training of African clergy was not resumed until nearly the mid-nineteenth century.[32] Besides ordination training, the study of law and medicine attracted a good many West Africans to Britain. In the 1850s the War Office paid for three Sierra Leoneans to study medicine in Britain with the purpose of returning them to West Africa as army doctors. One of those men was James Africanus Horton who graduated from King's College, London, and Edinburgh, and later wrote medical studies on West African topics and *West African Countries and Peoples*.[33] The list of those, principally West Africans, coming to study in British universities in the nineteenth and early twentieth centuries is impressive. It represented, as it still does for many Africans going overseas to study, the severe sacrifice of long years of absence from family, friends and familiar surroundings. And for the West African elite in the late nineteenth and early twentieth centuries, the impressiveness of this list is compounded by the high quality of the 'talented minority' and the several qualifications in law, medicine and theology that many individuals gained.[34]

The record of African student achievement given in the essays in this collection represents but a part of the story of the last 150 years of the African quest for higher education. A full account since 1850 would embrace many of the great names in recent African history, Pixley Seme, Kenyatta, Nkrumah, Nyerere as well as lesser-known figures such as George Ekim Ferguson, the Gold Coast surveyor, and Kofoworola Aina Moore, the first African woman to enter Oxford in 1933.[35] That account would also have to analyse the academic interests and activities of the greatly increased African student body in Britain which reportedly numbered up to 2,000 in 1947, and is many times more than that now.[36]

The Colonial Office during the 1920s–40s took an active interest in the political activities of African students, as both Hakim Adi and Marika Sherwood show in their contributions. It is clear that that great department of state, along with Scotland Yard and MI5, was monitoring individual African students – some might call it 'collecting the dirt' on them – early in the century. Duse Mohamed Ali's activities were closely watched; Bandele Ominiyi and Theodore Alex Hlabagani, at Edinburgh, were spied upon by members of the National Vigilance Society and Colonial Office officials saw fit to record with few questions their scurrilous letters; while the sexual behaviour of C.E. Reindorf, studying medicine at Durham, was also known in Whitehall.[37]

Obviously we need to know more about the changing attitudes and responses of the Colonial Office to African student politics, as well as other student activities in Britain, in order to assess the significance of the various pan-African bodies and how they sought to fashion public opinion and influence official policies.[38] In that process there is also a need for an assessment of the role of the late Ivor Cummings, the British-Sierra Leonean who was Warden of Aggrey House from 1935 and appointed just after the outbreak of war to the Colonial Office as the liaison officer with colonial students.[39]

African Political Agendas in Britain

A solid literature has steadily appeared over the past 30 or so years to lay the foundations for a better understanding of the roots and dimensions of pan-Africanist politics and activities in Britain to 1946.[40] In addition there have been a number of studies on specific pan-Africanist organizations, but a more detailed examination is required of the individuals involved, the networks that they formed and their sources of finance and support.[41] Hakim Adi has already indicated with his study of Ominiyi that it is possible to resurrect little-known pan-Africanist activists,[42] while his essay on the WASU (and his forthcoming London Ph.D.) along with Marika Sherwood's research on Nkrumah's London years indicate the complexities as well as the rich rewards involved in such research. The League of Coloured Peoples, non-radical in politics but the major pressure group representing mainly middle-class Caribbean and African people in Britain which served as a watchdog against racial discrimination through the 1930s and 1940s, certainly deserves a full-scale study;[43] so do those smaller and less well-recorded working-class organizations such as the Coloured Workers' Association created by Ernest Marke, and the Colonial Peoples' Defence Association set up in Liverpool in the late 1940s to resist government proposals to repatriate African seamen.

An Indian, Dadabhai Naoroji, entered the House of Commons in 1892 but it was not until 1987 that the first MP of immediate African origin, Paul Boateng, was elected for Brent South. The significance of national politics should not divert attention from the more pronounced African involvement at various levels in provincial politics about which we need to know a great deal more. There are many Africans active in local politics all over the country, from Kofi Appiah, the mayor of Tower Hamlets, to the rather unpredictable electoral strategies of Nkechi Amalu-Johnson and Poline Nyaga who in early 1991 switched from Labour to give the Conservatives a majority in the London borough of Brent.[44]

Many Africans in Britain, particularly students, had political agendas which were only partly to do with British politics. The early pan-African organizations attempted to influence official policy in London but they also had an eye to political change in the African colonies. Indeed, one or two African political organizations had their origins in Britain; for example, the British Somali Society formed in the mid-1930s and the Somali Youth League in the next decade;[45] also the London-based Egbe Omo Oduduwa, a Yoruba cultural organization, formed by Chief Awolowo and fellow students in 1946 which two years later functioned as a political party in Nigeria.[46] At present in Britain a good number of expatriate Africans continue to participate in their home domestic politics, as parties in exile or as overseas branches of national and regional parties. A glance at the 'Noticeboard' page at the end of the weekly *West Africa* gives some indication of the extent of those activities.

African affairs have occasionally had an impact on British politics. Gordon besieged in Khartoum, the Suez crisis, and the outcry against the Hola camp atrocities are but reminders of the resonating influences that colonial events can have on British politics. One of those instances, although never a crisis, was Seretse Khama's exile to Britain, which is examined in Neil Parson's essay. That affair was an important political benchmark in Britain's national and international politics for it helped to focus a growing British public awareness and political opposition to apartheid in South Africa.

Africans in the Armed Forces

Rather surprisingly more is known about Africans and black men in the British Army in the eighteenth than the nineteenth century. African and black musicians were employed in several regimental bands in the eighteenth century and freed blacks, some of whom were African-born, formed loyalist troops during the American war of independence. By the mid-1840s 'Blackamoor' bands had disappeared from the British Army and there is little evidence of Africans serving in the Army throughout the Victorian period. Kru and other Africans were accepted by the Royal Navy but only for non-continuous service as stokers, coopers and carpenters and at lower wages than British able seamen.[47] Army officers were required to be of 'pure European descent', although exceptions were made for J.A. Horton and W.B. Davies, both from Sierra Leone, who were trained in Britain and then commissioned as medical officers in 1859 but specifically for service in West Africa, and also in the unusual case of the hostage son of Emperor Tewedros of Ethiopia who briefly attended RMA Sandhurst in 1878.

Official policy up to the First World War was to exclude men of African origin from the Army. But policy could be bent – as in the case of James Durham, a child picked up from a Sudan battlefield in 1885 by soldiers of the Durham Light Infantry, who became first the Regiment's mascot and then an enlisted boy bugler.[48] During the First World War some Africans resident in Britain succeeded in enlisting while others were rejected because of their colour.[49] Most African recruits originated form the West coast,[50] although two men from central Africa are also known to have served in the Army.[51] African soldiers and sailors were among the victims of the race riots that occurred in seven British towns in 1919.[52] Compared to the First World War relatively little has been written on Africans serving in British home regiments in the Second World War,[53] although Roger Lambo's essay on Africans in the Royal Air Force reverals another forgotten contribution. Ethnic monitoring on a self-classifying basis, introduced into the armed forces in April 1987, will provide future researchers with a better idea of the African complement in each service.

Men from the locally recruited constabularies in the West African colonies between 1875 and the end of the century were sent to Britain for several months at a time for specialist training. Infantrymen came to the School of Musketry at Hythe, to Shorncliffe and Woolwich, while bandsmen went to Kneller Hall.[54] Military courses for African soldiers were increased after 1945 as colonial forces slowly adopted Africanization policies. Many of the coup leaders in post-independence anglophone African states saw service either at RMA Sandhurst or the Infantry School at Mons. State occasions also brought African troops to London for the Victorian Jubilees, various Coronations, and the Peace parade in 1945.

The largest number of African troops recorded in Britain was during the two world wars. Between 1916 and 1918 the South African Native

Labour Contingent, raised for labour service on the Western Front, had rest camps at Shorncliffe and Devonport. And when the S.S. *Mendi*, en route from Plymouth to France with the last contingent of the SANLC, was struck by another vessel and sank in the English Channel off the Isle of Wight on a misty night in February 1917, many of the 615 drowned Africans were washed up on southern English beaches.[55] There is no English memorial to them, but there should be. In mid-1940 African *tirailleurs* were among the French troops evacuated from Dunkirk to south-east England to form the nucleus of the Free French forces. Later in the war, in October 1944, French African troops, many of them former prisoners-of-war, were involved in a minor mutiny at a transit camp at Huyton, near Liverpool.[56] A similar camp was established near Horsham, Sussex, for repatriated Black South African prisoners-of-war in 1944, who were then taken on sight-seeing visits to London and other towns.[57]

So far the themes touched on are those that have been addressed in this collection of essays. I now want to discuss topics and themes that are not mentioned and to suggest their significance for any future programme of research into Africans in Britain.

Communities and Networks

African communities and associational networks in Britain have increased in the last 30 years as the expatriate African population has grown. Older, smaller communities existed in Liverpool, Bristol, Cardiff, parts of East London, and Somalis in South Shields – where communal interests based on origin and race were additionally stimulated by an often hostile host society. The Afro-Caribbean networks also brought together black people of different social backgrounds and interests into associations and political organizations such as the African Progress Union and The League of Coloured Peoples.

Since the 1960s African communal associations in Britain have proliferated. An idea of the range of West African meetings alone, although not the number of people involved, is conveyed by the events advertised in two issues of *West Africa* in September 1992: meeting of Edo State Union in Great Britain; Akwa Ibom Community UK dance; Asante Kotoko Society dance, dance of Ika Union of UK; Ga Danme Homowo Festival; inauguration of Akyemfo Nkusukum Mba Kuw; Ghanaian Presbyterian Church at Christ Church and Upton Chapel, Lambeth North; Keta Secondary School – 40-year celebration for old pupils in the UK; Nigerian National Union dance at the London Hilton; dances of the Esan Progressive Union, the Ghana National College, and the New Patriotic Party which will be attended by Professor Adu Boahen; Nzema

Association UK – annual Kundum festival at Camden Centre; St Augustine's Cape Coast – Past Students' Union; Opoku Ware Old Students' Association; and Prempeh College Old Boys' Association. There was also a programme of meetings and lectures held at the Africa Centre in Covent Garden.[58] This selection is randomly chosen and limited to London and largely focused on the activities of people from merely three West African states.

A great deal of further research is required on the pre-1950 communities and networks of Africans in Britain, while the post-1960 scene is overwhelming in weight and potential richness. One piece of work in preparation on Ghanaian migrants in London suggests that community associations can be grouped into four categories: Village/Town Associations, for example, the Wenchi Association, the Oguaa Akoto Kuv (Cape Coast Welfare and Cultural Association); Ethnic and Clan Associations, bodies that bring together Asante or Ga-Adangbe people, or those from Larteh; Regional Unions such as those representing people from Northern Ghana or from Brong-Ahafo; and finally, Old Boy/Girl Associations drawing together former pupils of particular schools. Many of these Ghanaian associations have a social welfare role for members, but some, particularly the village/town associations, help to organize and channel resources to assist development projects in the home village or town. Ethnic and clan associations, linked to cultural and feudal interests, often serve as a political base for individuals, while old school associations largely focus on the specific needs of the school.[59] The linkages between these various associations, churches, ex-patriate political groupings, credit unions and welfare societies, commercial activities, and the African newspapers and magazines published in Britain, offer a vibrant and constantly shifting scene for study. One important task would be to collect the material and ephemera generated by these bodies and to interview participants involved in the various associations.

African Commercial Activities

One of the early written accounts by an African in Britain is by the Gold Coast merchant John E. Ocansey.[60] There was nothing uncommon in West African 'merchant princes', some of whom owned ships, coming to Britain in the second half of the nineteenth century to conduct business. It seems to have been a regular activity and more particularly so with the 'booms' in timber, rubber, gold and cocoa after 1880.[61] There is a good deal more to be known about the commercial interests of West African merchants not only in West Africa itself but also their business connections in Britain and elsewhere.[62]

Business interests were frequently combined with other activities. Dusé Mohamed Ali, the Egyptian journalist, together with John Eldred Taylor, launched the *African Times and Orient Review* in July 1912 following the Universal Races Congress held in London. It was, as Ali wrote in the first issue, to be 'a Pan-Oriental, Pan-African journal at the seat of the British Empire which would lay the aims, desires and intentions of the Black, Brown, and Yellow Races – within and without the Empire – at the throne of Caesar'.[63] John Eldred Taylor from Freetown, and long resident in London, had various business interests which Ian Duffield has called 'a string of inter-connected and dubious companies with slender assets and extravagent aspirations'.[64] In 1918 he set up the *African Telegraph*, a short-lived newspaper which did not effectively advance his business interests or financial welfare.[65]

The history of African business activity in Britain will remain on the agenda but contemporary commercial roles should also be added. Journals such as *African Business*, *West Africa*, and the *Weekly Journal* offer some basic information which might suggest a research strategy, although a systematic account of modern Afro-British business might go some way towards amending current popular ideas about the low levels of African entrepreneurial activity and skill.

Spectacle and 'Entertainment'

European travellers to sub-Saharan Africa often saw Africans as exotic. The exploitation of black slaves for profitable labour was paralleled by the exploitation of the African body as profitable spectacle. From the early sixteenth century onwards Africans were employed or used in Europe for 'entertainment'; as 'pageant performers',[66] on the stage, in ethnographic shows, the circus and the music hall. Africans were presented as exotic, as grotesque caricatures, freaks, and also as bestial stereotypes. Much of the impressario-organized employment of Africans for purposes of spectacle was in the context of African powerlessness and victimization. Undoubtedly some Africans willingly engaged in such displays but for many there was a high degree of direct exploitation.

African entertainers were used by the wealthy in England in the early sixteenth century, but the age of African spectacle and display appears to have been the hundred years after 1810. In that year Saartjie Baartman, a San woman from Southern Africa, was widely displayed in London chained in a cage and labelled the 'Hottentot Venus'. Because of her steatopygia she was treated as a freak and an object of curiosity to be gawped at and poked by fee-paying crowds.[67] In the 1840s and 1850s the display of San people ('Bushmen'), including children, in travelling public shows in Britain and Europe was not uncommon.[68] As popular leisure increased after 1870, and also public interest in Africa, so did the demand for African spectacle. 'Bushmen' appeared in staged shows in London in 1884 (when popular interest was excited by the idea of the 'missing link'), and as late as 1915 a Khoisan 'wild dancing bushman' was performing in south-east English towns.[69]

From mid-century, Africans were often exhibited in ethnographic shows, or what might more accurately be described as anthropological zoos. For example, in 1853 a group of Zulu people, the 'Caffirs at Hyde-Park-Corner' as they came to be called, were displayed in acts which were reported to be typical of the daily life of 'this wild and interesting tribe of savages in their domestic habits, their nuptial ceremonies, the charm song, finding the witch, hunting tramp, preparation for war, and territorial conflicts'.[70] Following their defeat at the hands of British armies, Asantes and Zulus proved to be popular exhibits in ethnographic shows. Africans were also brought to Europe for the regular international exhibitions and fairs, sometimes housed in mock villages and performing their supposed indigenous daily tasks. For example, there were Nubians with tents and animals at Alexandra Palace, London, in 1877.[71] Ten years later West Africans were on display at the Indian and Colonial Exhibition in London, while there was a Senegalese village at the Franco-British Exhibition, Earls Court, London, in 1908. These ethnographic shows raise a number of pertinent questions about the recruitment and inducements offered to Africans as well as their own experience as objects of popular curiosity in strange surroundings. And to what extent were images of savage Africa fostered in the British public mind by these displays?[72]

The appeal of exotic Africa drew large crowds who flocked to see Frank Fillis's show 'Savage South Africa', which ran in London in 1899–1900. The cast arrived by chartered liner from the Cape and included Peter Lobengula, self-claimed son of Lobengula the 'last King of the Matabele'.[73] Also popular were the six short statured people from central Africa, the 'Ituri pygmies', brought to Britain by Colonel James Harrison and exhibited in London and provincial towns in 1905–07. Apart from living in the grounds of the Harrison's East Riding home, these people also had the distinction of making five gramophone records, the first British commercial recordings by Africans.[74]

Afro-Americans sporting regal titles and fancy clothes, pretending to be Africans from exotic backgrounds, traded on sensation-hungry British crowds. From the scanty information on some of these entertainers whose major theatre was the minor music hall, small travelling circus, or the street and public park, it is difficult to determine whether or not they were indeed African. One example of these pseudo-Africans is Amgoza LoBagola who claimed to have been brought up in Scotland; he appeared variously as an 'Arab cyclist', African chief and a Dahomean fire-eater, but was, in fact, Joseph Howard Lee, born in Baltimore in 1887[75]

Occasionally Black and African people were sought for stage shows and films. In 1923 Sol Plaatje, the first secretary of the South African Native National Congress, then living in London, was driven by financial circumstances to play the part of a spear-carrying African chief in 'The Cradle of the World', at the Philharmonic Hall, a role in contrast to all his arguments about African advancement.[76] Stage entertaining was but a short walk to the film set. Johnson (Jomo) Kenyatta, for example, had a minor part in Korda's *Sanders of the River* filmed at Shepperton in 1934, in which Paul Robeson played Chief Bosambo. Robeson in this film, in *King Solomon's Mines* (1937), and in various stage roles provided the British Public with a new and powerful image of African-ness. More importantly for many Africans and Black people, Robeson's prominence as well as his political radicalism (he was patron of the WASU in 1934) provided them with a new sense of self-esteem.[77]

The contribution by Africans in Britain to the whole range of musical expression is reasonably well-documented. It stretches over 400 years: African musicians employed in the London pageants of the seventeenth century; distinguished composers and performers such as Coleridge-Taylor and Fela Sowande, and singers of the quality of Evelyn Dove; the important influence of African musicians on ragtime, jazz, and popular dance music of the 1920s–40s; and the great surge of interest in African music and African performers in bands, in stage shows, recordings, and in broadcasting since 1950, as well as promising African orchestral players.[78]

Sport is one area where many young people are likely to identify African players, not only the progress of teams through the World Cup (the popularity of the Cameroons squad, for example) but the role of individual African and black players and athletes in British teams. Here television and a host of sports magazines aimed at the young, exert a powerful influence in fashioning favourable images. Large numbers of British youngsters know about the footballers John Fashanu and Peter Ndlovu, and their African counterparts who play for Marseilles and Anderlecht, while to many the Nigerian rugby players Martin Offiah, Victor Ubogu, Steve Ojomoh, Adebayo Adebayo, Francis Emeruwa, Chris Oti and Andrew Harrison are household names.[79] So also are African boxers and athletes such as Kriss Akabusi.[80] But how many sports-mad young people, or their elders, have heard of Arthur Wharton, from the Gold Coast, who was the first person to run 100 yards in ten seconds at the British Amateur Athletics Association meeting in London in 1886? He surely needs to be better known![81]

Imperial Crossroads

As the centre of an expanding Empire Britain inevitably became for many Africans a crossroads to be visited in transit, a place of petition, settlement and exile. Certain European travellers in Africa, and a few missionaries, returned home with African servants in tow some of whom settled in Britain. Mungo Park's companion, the Manding speaker Johnson; Gabre Mariam from Ethiopia, a maSotho known only by his English name of William John Thomas, Dorugu and Abbega the young slaves from nothern Nigeria liberated by Heinrich Barth; Jacob Wainwright the Nasik Yao who acted as a pall-bearer at Livingstone's funeral; H.M. Stanley's 'My Kalulu'; and Jacko, the companion of Verney Lovett Cameron, are just some of the Africans who came to live in Britain in the second half of the nineteenth century.[82]

African Women

African women in Britain is an obvious theme for research within the context of both black and gender studies.[83] Joan Grant's ongoing work hopefully will tell us more about African women in Britain,[84] while Adelaide M. Cromwell's biography of Adelaide Smith Casely Hayford offers a helpful if less than thorough biography of a member of one of the major inter-colonial dynastic families of coastal West Africa.[85] The experience of African women in Britain offers distinctive insights into ideas about family and social relationships, work, politics, and many of the pressures rarely felt by men.[86] The life of Sally Forbes-Bonetta, taken as a child from Dahomey by Commodore Forbes of *H.M.S. Bonetta*, brought to Britain and 'adopted' by Queen Victoria, sent to the CMS School in Freetown, married to the Sierra Leonean merchant Captain James Davies in Brighton, and then settled into the elite of Lagos, is a subject for a fascinating biography. All too often written records, invariably produced by men, focus on activities dominated by men, so that research on women is additionally difficult.[87]

In a contemporary context African women in Britain have made their mark in publishing (for example Margaret Busby), athletics and music (for example Chichi Nwanoku), film directing and arts administration. On the dark side it is reported that one in five of all women in British prisons are Nigerians who have been arrested for drug-smuggling offences,[88] while unfortunate African women are among the victims of a system of 'domestic slavery'.

Churches and Clergy

This seems to be a theme worth pursuing not only because it is concerned with some remarkable individuals but because it also addresses a range of cultural and communal activities and religious expressions in Britain which are distinctively African.

For over 200 years mission churches sent Africans to Britain to train as clergymen. Nearly 100 years after Philip Quaque was ordained as an Anglican minister, a small number of West Africans, mainly from Freetown, began to come to Britain to study as teachers and clergy, principally under the auspices of the Church Missionary Society.[89] A lesser-known name is that of Thomas Jenkins, son of a coastal trader, brought to Scotland to receive an education who became a school teacher, first in Teviotdale and then a teacher/missionary for the British and Foreign School Society in Mauritius where he died in 1859.[90] In 1857 Tiyo Soga, the first black South African to be ordained, after two periods of study in Scotland returned home as a United Presbyterian missionary accompanied by his Scottish wife.[91] The work of the Universities' Mission to Central Africa, in the 1870s, resulted in several Africans being sent to England for ordination training at St. Augustine's Canterbury and at Dorchester.[92]

By the latter part of the nineteenth century there was an increasing disregard by European missionaries of African church leaders and a trend towards training African Christians at institutions in Africa. One exception was the Colwyn Bay African Training Institute in North Wales, founded by the former Baptist missionary William Hughes. During the life of the Institute, from 1889 to 1912, more than 100 Africans passed through it including the distinguished Nigerian church leader Dr Mojola Agbebi.[93]

African Christians worked in 'darkest England', for example, Salim Wilson, a Dinka ex-slave, whose main mission work was in Yorkshire and Lincolnshire from the late 1890s until his death in 1939, earning him the soubriquet of 'the Black Evangelist of the North',[94] and Revd. Daniel Ekarte, one of several West Africans who from the early 1920s to the 1950s, served in Liverpool at the African and West Indian Mission.[95] Today there are a good number of African clergy working in British churches, not necessarily those with African congregations, and also in para-church organizations.[96]

Perhaps of much greater importance than the role of scattered individuals is the work of African churches in Britain seeking to minister mainly to African congregations, although some, such as the Church of the Cherubim and Seraphim, have a missionary purpose to attract white people. These churches are centred on London but also have groups in other major cities with large African minorities. They are, for the most part, branches of predominantly West African Churches, sometimes syncretic in theology, charismatic in leadership, pentecostal in worship and with an emphasis on prophetism and healing. The Church of the Cherubim and Seraphim, an Aladura or prayer church, first started in Britain in 1965 and by the early 1990s had 12 branches with between 12,000 and 20,000 members.[97] At the 26th anniversary celebrations of the church, attended by 2,000 people at the headquarters in Forest Gate, East London, it was reported that

> the choir, backed with African drums, sang moving and spiritually inspired songs in Yoruba and other Nigerian languages. From the huge crowd came an overwhelming response. The congregation danced in a file, joyfully and rhythmically moving round the inside of the church led by the Choirmaster Evangelist T.J. Browne and Senior Apostle Pastor E.A. Sobo, the Church Secretary.[98]

For African churches finance is often a problem and worship is in borrowed churches or hired buildings; nearly all church leaders earn their living from secular employment. In several African churches women play an important role as evangelists and in healing and prophetic ministries. The Musama Disco Christo Church, which originated from and mainly caters for people from Ghana, is currently led by the Revd. Jerisdan Jehu-Appiah, grandson of the founder, who came to Britain in 1979. The Church, as with many other African Christian fellowships, also serves in a welfare and pastoral role for members, finding jobs, counselling over health, marriages and child care.[99] A regular feature of many African churches is revival meetings and campaigns, often involving visiting preachers, prophets and healers from the African home churches.[100] A good deal of work has been undertaken on African churches in Africa and also on Black churches in Britain. However, the African churches in the United Kingdom, with the added fascination of an Afro-centric theology and practice in a post-industrial society, have not yet received the scholarly attention that they deserve.

African Refugees in Britain

Today Africa has the largest number of refugees relative to its population of any of the continents. The mid-1970s saw a great increase in displaced people as a result of war, drought and famine. A small but growing number were able to find refuge in Britain and Europe or the United States, invariably people who had received a formal education, possessed some modern skills, had overseas contacts and a knowledge of English or another foreign language.

One or two Africans, usually rulers, went into enforced exile or found refuge in Britain from the mid-nineteenth century onwards;[101] in the 1960s dissident politicians and students formed the bulk of African exiles and refugees. But in the 1970s the number grew. For example, there were between 400 and 550 Eritreans in Britain in 1974, but with the Ethiopian revolution and war the number increased to 7,000 by 1991. Refugees from African anglophone states, most notably Uganda, Ghana and South Africa had strong cultural reasons for coming to Britain, but they were also joined by people from troubled non-English speaking states such as Somalia, Zaire, Angola, and Ethiopia. By 1989 it was estimated that there were more than 34,000 exiles from West Africa alone in the United Kingdom. Three years later, an increasingly concerned Home Office stated that there were 25,000 outstanding applications for asylum, and ministers were seeking means to further tighten entry requirements.

African refugees arriving in Britain have tended to settle in areas where there are already members of their community. Thus Somalis have gone to east London, Cardiff and Yorkshire, and Ugandans to south London. Settlement of refugees in poorer inner city areas, such as Haringey and Newham in east London, added to the existing problems of boroughs which already were short of cash, had a poor stock of housing and overburdened welfare services. The small African self-help organizations which grew out of the refugee communities, for example, the Eritrean Relief Association and the Relief Society of Tigray, sought to deal with problems of immigration and settlement as well as providing instruction in the mother tongue, but their activities were constrained by limited funds and dependence on volunteer help.[102]

Conclusion

Fifty years ago Africans, and people of immediate African origin were a small minority in Britain. From a few thousand in 1940, the African population has increased to more than 200,000 in the early 1990s. On balance the majority have come from West Africa and that, and my own interests, may account for the overly West African bias of this essay. The names of Africans in Britain are now relatively commonplace, particularly in sport but also in the world of letters (for example, Ben Okri, winner of the Booker Prize in 1991) and in the media and design. Their presence has enriched British social and cultural life and, with the rapid growth in communications and travel, hopefully made an island population slightly less insular in attitude. The history and experience of African people in Britain requires its chroniclers, historians and sociologists. Africans in particular are urged to turn their hand to this important task.

NOTES

1. Maire Ni Brolchain, 'The Ethnicity Question for the 1991 Census: Background and Issues', *Ethnic and Racial Studies*, Vol.13, No.4 (1990), pp.542–67. Census enumerators' returns are closed for 100 years. *The Times*, 30 Nov. 1992, p.5. *The Independent*, 23 March 1991, p.3, reported that 7,700 Africans lived in the London borough of Lambeth.
2. See M.P. Banton, *The Coloured Quarter: Negro Immigrants in an English City* (London, 1955), pp.66–8.
3. Peter Fryer, *Staying Power: The History of Black People in Britain* (London, 1984). The first book about the African presence is by Edward Scobie, *Black Britannia* (Chicago, IL, 1972). See also James Walvin, *Black and White: The Negro and English Society, 1555–1945* (London, 1973); F.O. Shyllon, *Black People in Britain 1555–1833* (London, 1977); Nigel File and Chris Power, *Black Settlers in Britain, 1555–1958* (London, 1981); Paul Edwards and James Walvin, 'Africans in Britain 1500–1800', in Martin L. Kilson and Robert I. Rotberg (eds.), *The African Diaspora: Interpretive Essays* (Cambridge, MA, 1976), pp.173–204; F.O. Shyllon, 'Blacks in Britain: A Historical and Analytical Overview', in Joseph E. Harris (ed.), *Global Dimensions of the African Diaspora* (Washington, DC, 1982) pp.170–94. Another useful source is H.W. Debrunner, *Presence and Prestige: Africans in Europe: A History of Africans in Europe before 1918* (Basel, 1979).
4. Paul Edwards, *The Early African Presence in the British Isles*, Occasional Papers, No.26, Centre of African Studies, Edinburgh University, 1990, p.2; also in Jagdish S. Gundara and Ian Duffield (eds.), *Essays on the History of Blacks in Britain* (Aldershot, 1992), pp.9–29; and David Keys in *The Independent* (London), 20 March 1989, p.7.
5. See F.O. Shyllon, *Black Slaves in Britain* (Oxford, 1974).
6. Walvin, *Black and White*, Ch.12.
7. On immigration to the UK see Colin Holmes, *John Bull's Island: Immigration and British Society, 1871–1971* (London, 1988); and James Walvin, *Passage to Britain* Harmondsworth, 1984).
8. Christine Bolt, *Victorian Attitudes to Race* (London, 1971); Douglas A. Lorimer, *Colour, Class and the Victorians: English Attitudes to the Negro in the Mid-Nineteenth Century* (Leicester, 1978).
9. Annie Coombes, 'Art and Representation of Africans', paper given to the conference on 'The African Presence in the UK', Africa Centre, Covent Garden, London, Dec. 1991. A number of popular novels, *c*.1890–1910, portrayed Africans who had received a university education in Britain as having but a thin veneer of 'modern civilization'. For example, in Frank F. Moore, *Dr. Khoomahdi of Ashantee* (London, 1896), 'a nigger remains a nigger, and remains on speaking terms with a baboon even though he has a college degree and wears tweeds' (p.16). Mary Gaunt and J.R. Essex were prolific writers of popular fiction; in *The Arms of the Leopard; A West African Story* (London, 1904), and *The Silent Ones* (London, 1909), 'the "educated" nigger', Dr Craven, an Asante, who, despite his MB from Cambridge and study at Heidelburg, remains at heart a savage. In *The Arm of the Leopard*, a British-educated African clergyman who speaks French and has read most of the classics, says to Craven: 'My English education . . . has not made me forget the customs of my fathers. My abstinence [from human flesh] has rather whetted my appetite for them. Don't you find it so? They tie you up a bit in England, you know' (p.258). John Buchan's famous *Prester John* (London, 1910), is about an insurrection in South Africa led by the British-

educated Revd John Laputa who combines his Christian ideas with African religious beliefs and practices; see David Daniell, 'Buchan and "The Black General"', in David Dabydeen (ed.), *The Black Presence in English Literature* (Manchester, 1985), pp.135–53. Henry Hesketh Bell, 'His Highness Prince Kwakoo', in *Love in Black* (London, 1911), is the tale of a British-educated African con-man. Cullen Gouldsbury, *The Tree of Bitter Fruit* (London, 1910), deals with an improvement-minded colonial official's failure to 'civilize' Mkonto, an African boy who he brings to Britain to be educated. In several of these novels the educated African falls in love with a white girl, to the outraged horror of other Europeans, but rescue from miscegenation is at hand usually by a noble white suitor.

10. For example, Ham Mukasa's *Uganda's Katikora in England* (London, 1904, reprinted as *Sir Apolo Kagwa Discovers Britain*, edited by Taban lo Liyong (London, 1975)); A. Falorin, *England and the English: Personal Impressions During a Three Year's Sojourn* (London, n.d.); A.B.C. Merriman-Labor, *Britons Through Negro Spectacles* (London, 1909).

11. Ukawsaw Gronniosaw, *A Narrative of the Most Remarkable Particulars of the Life of James Albert Ukawsaw Gronniosaw, An African Prince* (Bath, n.d. *c.*1770); Ignatius Sancho, *The Letters of the late Ignatius Sancho, an African to which are prefixed Memoirs of His Life by Joseph Jekyll, Esq., M.P.*, (London, 1782); Ottobah Cugoano. *Thoughts and Sentiments on the Evil and Wicked Traffic of the Slavery and Commerce of the Human Species* (London, 1787); Olaudah Equiano, *The Interesting Narrative of the Life of Olaudah Equiano, or Gustavus Vassa, the African*, 2 vols. (London, 1789).

12. For example, John Jea, *The Life, History and Sufferings of John Jea, the African Preacher* (Portsea, n.d., *c.*1815). See Paul Edwards' contribution below, and also Paul Edwards and David Dabydeen, *Black Writers in Britain 1760–1800* (Edinburgh, 1991).

13. Douglas Grant, *The Fortunate Slave: An Illustration of African Slavery in the Early Eighteenth Century* (London, 1968), is an account of Job Ben Solomon, a Gambian Muslim, literate in Arabic, who was taken as a slave to the West Indies but freed, brought to England where he was feted before returning home in 1734.

14. See Ian Duffield's contribution below. The task of gathering such references is vital before an adequate locational, occupational, marital analysis of Africans in Britain can be undertaken. A single collecting points seems obvious.

15. Hakim Adi, 'Bandele Ominiyi – A Neglected Nigerian Nationalist', *African Affairs*, Vol.90, No.361 (1991), pp.581–605.

16. There are a few. For example, some of the essays in Margery Perham (ed.), *Ten Africans* (London, 1936), Jeremy Murray-Brown, *Kenyatta* (London, 1972), Philip Short, *Banda* (London, 1974), Adelaide M. Cromwell, *An African Victorian Feminist: The Life and Times of Adelaide Smith Casely Hayford 1868–1960* (London, 1986), Joseph Appiah, *Joe Appiah: the Autobiography of an African Patriot* (Westport, CT, 1990), and the biography of Seretse Khama being written by Neil Parsons and Willie Henderson. Two other autobiographies of Africans who lived extensively in Britain are: Ernest Marke, *Old Man Trouble* (London, 1975), and R. Wellesley Cole, *An Innocent in Britain: Or the Missing Link* (London, 1988).

17. See Norma Myers, 'Reconstructing the Black Past: Blacks in Britain, circa 1780–1830', unpublished Ph.D thesis, University of Liverpool, 1990.

18. Stephen Braidwood, *The Black Poor and White Philanthropists: Foundation of the Sierra Leone Settlements 1786–91* (forthcoming).

19. Little, *Negroes in Britain*, Chs.3 and 4; Neil Evans, 'Immigrants and Minorities in Wales, 1840–1990: A Comparative Perspective', *Llafur: Journal of Welsh Labour History*, Vol.5, No.4 (1991), pp.5–26; Dilop Hiro, 'Three generations of Tiger Bay', *New Society*, 21 Jan. 1967, pp.385–7.

20. See Myers, 'Reconstructing the Black Past', p.109. *Parliamentary Papers*, 1816, Vol.10, 'Report Relating to East Indian Affairs', 349, p.15, refers to John Dennis, 'a native of Mocambique in Africa; was shipped in the *Minerva* as an able seaman, and as such was paid and victualled at the full rate, the same as if he had been an Englishman. Till now it was never thought that African seaman, like Dennis, of which description

there are hundreds in the navy and mercantile service . . .'

21. Myers 'Reconstructing the Black Past', p.107. *Parliamentary Papers*, 1910, Vol.XXII. Cd.5134. 'Report of Committee on Distressed Colonial and Indian Subjects. Minutes of Evidence and Appendices'. The Dreadnought Seaman's Hospital, Greenwich, admitted sick African seamen; see National Maritime Museum, Greenwich, London. Dreadnought Seaman's Hospital registers. DSH 16 and subsequent, 1862–92; also J. Salter, *The East in the West or Work Among the Asiatics and Africans in London* (London, 1895), Chs.IX, XI and XII. See also Shamis Hussein, 'Somalis in London', in N. Merriman (ed.), *The Peopling of London* (London, 1993), pp.163–8.

22. See *Sevenoaks Chronicle and Kentish Advertiser*, 17 April 1885, p.8. Howard Bloch, 'African, Caribbean and Asian Seamen in the Royal Docks, 1914–1919', paper given to the conference on Ethnic Seafarers in the UK, Liverpool, Dec. 1992.

23. Augustus Casely Hayford, 'Black Oral History and Methodology', *The Local Historian*, Vol.20, No.2 (1990), pp.59–64. Paul Hair, 'African Ancestry in Britain', *Local Population Studies*, 48 (1992), pp.60–61.

24. *The Royal African, or Memoirs of the Young Prince of Annamaboe* (London, 1749); Wylie Sypher, 'The African Prince in London', *Journal of the History of Ideas*, 2 (1941), pp.237–47; Thomas Thompson, *An Account of Two Missionary Voyages* (London, 1758), p.35.

25. C.B. Wadstrom *An Essay on Colonization*, 2 vols. (London, 1794), Vol.1, pp.94–5.

26. Wadstrom, *Essays on Colonization*, Vol.2, pp.11 and 124; Little, *Negroes in Britain*, pp.186ff; Lorimer, *Colour, Class and the Victorians*, p.217.

27. Christopher Fyfe, 'Sierra Leoneans in English Schools in the Nineteenth Century', in Lotz and Pegg, *Under the Imperial Carpet*, Ch.2. Ray Jenkins, 'Gold Coasters overseas, 1880–1919; With Specific Reference to Their Activities in Britain', *Immigrants & Minorities*, Vol.4, No.3, (1985), pp.5–52.

28. Cromwell, *An African Victorian Feminist*, Ch.3.

29. For example, James Godfrey Wilhelm, an Igbo recaptive and Freetown merchant, sent his 14-year-old daughter Christiana to lodge with the retired CMS missionary J.F. Schön near Chatham; PRO HO107/1611, 1851 Census, Brompton, Kent.

30. Ivor Wilks, *Asante in the Nineteenth Century* (Cambridge, 1975), Ch.14.

31. PRO CO 6/136/3124, Rev J. Merriman to Colonial Office, 19 Feb. 1881.

32. F.L. Bartels, 'Philip Quaque of Cape Coast, 1742–1816', *Transactions of the Gold Coast and Togoland Historical Society*, 1955, pp.153–77; Edwards and Dabydeen, *Black Writers in Britain*, pp.101–16.

33. Published in London in 1868; reprinted with an introduction by Christopher Fyfe, Edinburgh, 1969. Another Sierra Leonean doctor, with a brief practice in Croydon, was Daniel Taylor, the father of the distinguished composer Samuel Coleridge-Taylor. See Paul McGilchrist and Jeffrey Green, 'Some Recent Findings on Samuel Coleridge-Taylor', *The Black Perspective in Music*, Vol.13, No.2 (1988), pp.151–78, and Jeffrey Green, '"The Foremost Musician of His Race"; Samuel Coleridge-Taylor of England, 1875–1912', *Black Music Research Journal*, Vol.10, No.2 (1990), pp.233–52.

34. Ray Jenkins, 'A Talented Minority: Enterprising Gold Coaster in Britain, 1880–1920', paper given to the conference on 'The African Presence in the UK', Africa Centre, London, Dec. 1991.

35. Perham, *Ten Africans*, Ch.X.

36. *WASU Magazine*, Vol.XII, No.3 (1947), p.12, 'Table of West African Student Interests in Britain and Ireland'.

37. Adi, 'Bandele Ominiyi', pp.599–600; PRO CO 96/517/15441, 1912.

38. Paul Rich, 'The Black Diaspora in Britain: Afro-Caribbean Students and the Struggle for a Political Identity, 1900–1950', *Immigrants & Minorities*, Vol.6, No.2 (1987), pp.151–73.

39. Ivor Cummings, was born in West Hartlepool in 1913, of a Sierra Leonean father and a British mother, and died in October 1992; see Bankole Timothy's appreciation, *West Africa*, 2–8 November 1992, pp.1872–3, and the obituary by Val Wilmer, *The Independent*, 4 Dec. 1992, p.15.

40. George Shepperton, '"Pan-Africanism" and "pan-Africanism": Some Historical Notes'. *Phylon*, Vol.XXXIII, No.4 (1962), pp.346–58; Imanuel Geiss, *The Pan-African Movement* (1968; Eng. trans. London, 1974); J. Ayodele Langlye, *Pan-Africanism and Nationalism in West Africa 1900–1945* (Oxford, 1973); Ras Makonnen, *Pan-Africanism from Within* (Nairobi, 1973); P. Olisanwuche Esedebe, *Pan-Africanism. The Idea and Movement 1776–1963* (Washington, DC, 1982). See also Paul B. Rich, *Race and Empire in British Politics* (Cambridge, 1986).

41. For example, Samuel Rohdie, 'The Gold Coast Aborigines Abroad', *Journal of African History*, Vol.VI, No.3 (1965) pp.389–411; W.F. Elkins, 'Hercules and the Society of People of African Origin', *Caribbean Studies*, Vol.2, No.4 (1972), pp.50–56; Jeffrey Green, 'The African Progess Union of London 1918–1925', paper given at the Institute of Commonwealth Studies, University of London, 5 Feb. 1991.

42. Adi, 'Bandele Ominiyi'.

43. See Roderick J. Macdonald, 'Dr Harold Moody and the League of Coloured Peoples, 1931–1947; A Retrospective View', *Race*, Vol.XIV, No.3 (1973), pp.291–310; Fryer, *Staying Power*, pp.326–334; Ron Ramdin, *The Making of the Black Working Class in Britain* (Aldershot, 1987), Ch.5; and the LCP journal *The Keys* July 1933–September 1939, reprinted with an introduction by Roderick J. Macdonald (Millwood, New York, 1976).

44. *West Africa*, 9–15 Sept. 1991, 16–22 Nov. 1992; *The Independent Magazine*, 26 Oct. 1991, pp.38–42.

45. Marika Sherwood, 'Racism and Resistance: Cardiff in the 1930s and 1940s, *Llafur*, Vol.5, No.4 (1991), pp.63–5.

46. S.O. Arifola, 'Obafemi Awolowo and the Egbe Omo Oduduwa, 1945–1948', in U.O. Oyelarin and Toyin Falola *et al.* (eds.), *Obafemi Awolowo: The End of an Era?* (Ile-Ife, 1988), pp.97–101.

47. Theophilus E. Samuel Scholes, *Glimpses of the Ages or the 'Superior' and 'Inferior' Races, so called, Discussed in the Light of Science and History*, Vol.2 (London, 1908), pp.250–51.

48. I owe this information to Jeffrey Green.

49. David Killingray, 'All the King's Men? Blacks in the British Army in the First World War', in Lotz and Pegg, *Under the Imperial Carpet*, pp.164–81.

50. Ernest Marke, *Old Man Trouble*, p.25, joined up with his friend Tommy McCarthy, also from Freetown. PRO CO 96/619/55527, 11 Nov. 1920, details officials attempts to try to prevent Pte. Jacob Amnah Sam, of Accra, taking his British wife with him to West Africa. Several poignant files record the repatriation of mentally-ill soldiers, for example, PRO CO 368/22/17024, Pet. John Fleo, RASC, to Freetown, 31 March 1920; PRO CO 368/22/27352, Pte. John Morrison, Duke of Wellington's (W. Riding) Regt., to Freetown, 12 Jan. 1920.

51. Frederick Njilima, whose father was hanged following the Chilembwe rising in Malawi, 1915: see John McCracken, '"Marginal Men": The Colonial experience in Malawi', *Journal of Southern African Studies*, Vol.15, No.4 (1989), pp.551ff; and Bulaya, the servant of Stewart Gore-Brown: see Robert Rotberg, *Black Heart – Gore-Brown and the Politics of Multiracial Zambia* (Berkeley, CA, 1977), p.70.

52. Fryer, *Staying Power*, Ch.10; Jacqueline Jenkinson, 'The 1919 Race Riots in Britain: Their Background and Consequences', unpublished Ph.D. thesis, University of Edinburgh, 1987; and the account by the Somali seaman and poet, Ismaa'il, who was living in Cardiff at the time: Richard Pankhurst, 'An early Somali autobiography', *Africa* (Rome), XXXII (1977), pp.373–4.

53. See Marika Sherwood, *Many Struggles. West Indian Workers and Service Personnel in Britain (1939–45)* (London, 1984), Ch.1; and David Killingray, 'Race and Rank in the British Army in the Twentieth Century', *Ethnic and Racial Studies*, Vol.10, No.3 (1987), p.281.

54. For example, CO 96 files for Gold Coast, 1875–1896, contain frequent references.

55. B.P. Willan, 'The South African Native Labour Contingent, 1916–1918', *Journal of African History*, Vol.XIX, No.1 (1987), pp.61–86. Rhodes House Library, Oxford.

Anti-Slavery Society papers. Mss.Brit.Emp.s.23 H2/60, 'South African Labour Corps, Folkestone Rest Camp'. Norman Clothier, *Black Valour. The South African Native Labour Contingent, 1916–1918, and the Sinking of the Mendi* (Pietermaritzburg, 1987).

56. Myron Echenberg, *Colonial Conscripts: The Tirailleurs Sénégalais in French West Africa, 1857–1960* (London, 1991), p.100.
57. L.W.F. Grundlingh, 'The Participation of South African Blacks in the Second World War', unpublished D.Litt. thesis, Rand Afrikaans University, Pretoria, 1986, p.222.
58. *West Africa*, 14–20 and 21–27 Sept. 1992, pp.1562 and 1663.
59. I owe this information to Nicholas Atampugre of the Panos Institute, London, who is preparing a book on Migrants and Development.
60. Ocansey, *African Trading*.
61. Jenkins, 'Gold Coasters Overseas', pp.16ff; Duffield, 'Pan-Africanism, Rational and Irrational', *Journal of African History*, Vol.XVIII, No.4 (1977), pp.597–620. A.G. Hopkins, 'Economic Aspects of Political Movements in Nigeria and the Gold Coast 1918–1939', *Journal of African History*, Vol.VII, No.1 (1966), pp.133–52; Langley, *Pan-Africanism and Nationalism in West Africa*, Ch.V.
62. For example little is known of the commercial interests and activities of C.F. Hutchison and J.H. Brew from the Gold Coast, both of whom spent several decades in Britain from the 1880s. Brew, resident in London from 1888 to his death in 1915, acted as guide and mentor to the abortive Asante embassy in 1895–96, an intriguing role.
63. Ian Duffield, 'Dusé Mohamed Ali and the Development of Pan-Africanism, 1865– 1945', 2 vols., unpublished Ph.D. thesis, University of Edinburgh, 1971.
64. Ian Duffield, 'John Eldred Taylor and West African Opposition to Indirect Rule in Nigeria', *African Affairs*, Vol.70, No.280 (1971), p.255.
65. Christopher Fyfe and David Killingray, 'A Memorable Gathering of Sierra Leonians in London 1919', *African Affairs*, Vol.88, No.350 (1989), pp.41–6.
66. Fryer, *Staying Power*, pp.25–32.
67. Bernth Lindfors, 'Courting the Hottentot Venus', *Africa* (Rome), 40 (1985), pp.133– 48; and Lindfors, 'Ethnological Show Business: Footlighting the Dark Continent', paper given to the conference on 'The African Presence in the U.K.', Africa Centre, London, Dec. 1991.
68. *Illustrated London News*, 1845: 7, p.160; and 1852: 21, p.372.
69. Neil Parsons, 'Frantz Taibosch, "The Wild Dancing Bushman": The Search for an Enigma', paper given to Department of History Seminar, University of Cape Town, 30 July 1993.
70. *The Times*, 16 May 1853, p.4; Bernth Lindfors, 'A Zulu View of London', *Munger Africana Library Notes*, 48 (1979). Charles Dickens, having observed the show, wrote a biting satire on the ignobility of 'noble savages'; *Household Words*, 11 June 1853, pp.197–202.
71. *Illustrated London News*, 6 Oct. 1877.
72. The Nigerian clergyman James 'Holy' Johnson, was dismayed that the West African exhibits at the Indian and Colonial Exhibition of 1887 were so unrepresentative of African genius; see E.A. Ayendele, *The Missionary Impact on Modern Nigeria 1842 –1914* (London, 1966), p.187. A recent study of international exhibitions, which barely addresses the questions raised here, is by Paul Greenhalgh, *Ephemeral Vistas. The Expositions Universelles, Great Exhibitions and World's Fairs, 1851–1939* (Manchester 1987).
73. Ben Shepherd, 'A Royal Gentleman of Colour', *History Today*, 34 (April 1984), pp.36–41, and 'Showbiz Imperialism: The Case of Peter Lobengula', in John M. MacKenzie (ed.), *Imperialism and Popular Culture* (Manchester, 1986), pp.94–112.
74. Jeffrey P. Green, 'The Ituri Forest Pygmies in Britain: 1905–1907', paper given at the conference on 'The African Presence in the UK', Africa Centre, London, Dec. 1991.
75. Bata Kindai Amgoza Ibn LoBagola, *An African Savage's Own Story* (New York, 1930).
76. Brian Willan, *Sol Plaatje: South African Nationalist, 1876–1932* (London, 1984), pp.287–91.

77. On Robeson's impact on Britain in the late 1920s and early 1930s see Phil Foner (ed.), *Paul Robeson Speaks* (London, 1978), pp.76–94.
78. A useful survey, although focused on London, is by Chris Stapleton, 'African Connections: London's Hidden Music Scene', in Paul Oliver (ed.), *Black Music in Britain. Essays in Afro-Asian Contributions to Popular Music* (Milton Keynes, 1990), Ch.5, and also pp.50–51. On Coleridge-Taylor, see references at note 33 above. Also the various essays in Lotz and Pegg, *Under the Imperial Carpet*: Josephine Wright, 'Early African Musicians in Britain'; Marjorie Evans, 'I Remember Coleridge: Recollections of Samuel Coleridge-Taylor'; Rainer E. Lotz, 'Will Garland's Negro Operetta Company'; and Howard Rye, 'The Southern Syncopated Orchestra'. Stephen Bourne, 'Highflying Spirit of a Dove' (Evelyn Dove), *The Weekly Journal* 1 Oct. 1992. K. Owusu, *The Struggle for Black Arts in Britain* (London, 1986). E. Southern, *Biographical Dictionary of African-American and African Musicians* (Westport, CT, 1982), for Fela Sowande.
79. See *The Times*, 27 Dec. 1989, p.22 (Martin Offiah), *West Africa*, 8–14 Oct. 1990, p.2609 (John Fashanu), 28 Oct.–3 Nov. 1991, p.1823, and 23–29 Nov. 1992, p.2033.
80. Ted Harrison, *Kriss Akabusi on Track* (Oxford, 1991).
81. Ray Kenkins, 'Sportsman Extraordinaire', *West Africa*, 3 June 1985, and 'Salvation for the Fittest? A West African Sportsman in Britain in the Age of the New Imperialism', *International Journal of the History of Sport*, Vol.7, No.10 (1990), pp.23–60.
82. *The Travels of Mungo Park* (Everyman edn., 1907), p.21, for Johnson; Duncan Cumming, *The Gentleman Savage. The Life of Mansfield Parkyns 1823–1894* (London, 1987), pp.107 and 149, for Gabre Miriam who retired to 'Abyssinia Cottage', Ruddington, Notts.; Anthony Kirk-Greene and Paul Newman, *West African Travels and Adventures: Two Autobiographical Narratives from Northern Nigeria* (New Haven, CT, 1971), for Dorugu and Abbega; William John Thomas, the servant and companion of William Cotton Oswell, died in 1864 and is buried in St John's churchyard, Buckhurst Hill, London; Donald Simpson, *Dark Companions. The African Contribution to the European Exploration of East Africa* (London, 1975), pp.103–4, mentions Jacob Wainwright; H.M. Stanley, *My Kalulu, Prince, King and Slave: A Story of Central Africa* (London, 1873; new edn. 1890): Kalulu was at school in Wandsworth 1873–74; Jacko, baptized Jack Francis, lived in the vicarage at Shoreham, Kent, with Cameron's parents: see Malcolm White and Joy Saynor, *Shoreham. A Village in Kent* (Shoreham, 1989) p.146. There is a painting by Charles Cope (1876), hanging in Shoreham church, showing the triumphal return of Cameron with Jacko to the village.
83. For that interest, see Mary Seacole, *Wonderful Adventures of Mrs. Seacole in Many Lands* (London, 1857; new edn. with introduction by Ziggi Anderson, Bristol, 1984); and Mary Prince, *The History of Mary Prince, a West Indian Slave* (London, 1831; new edn. Moira Anderson with preface by Ziggi Anderson, London, 1987).
84. See Joan Grant, 'Abolition, Black Women and Caricature', paper given at the conference on 'The African Presence in the UK', Africa Centre, London, Dec. 1991.
85. Cromwell, *An African Victorian Feminist*.
86. June Ellis (ed.), *West African Families in Britain. A Meeting of Two Cultures* (London, 1978).
87. See Beverly B. Mack, 'Hajiya Ma'daki. A Royal Hausa Woman', in Patricia W. Romero (ed.), *Life Histories of African Women* (London, 1988), pp.60–63; Hajiya Ma'daki, wife of the Emir of Katsina, twice visited Britain, en route to Mecca, in 1921 and 1939.
88. BBC1, 'Inside Story', 7 Oct. 1992.
89. There is a well-known CMS photograph of Bishop Samuel Ajayi Crowther and other African clergy sprawled beneath the 'Wilberforce Oak' at Keston in Kent, taken in 1874; see J.F.A. Ajayi, *Christian Missions in Nigeria 1841–1891: The Making of a New Elite* (London, 1965), plate opp. p.224.
90. Mark B. Duffill, 'New Light on the Lives of Thomas Jenkins and James Swanson', *Transactions of the Hawick Archaeological Society* (1990), pp.31–44, and 'Thomas Jenkins, African farm Servant, Student and School-teacher in Scotland and England,

1803–21', paper given at the conference on 'The African Presence in the UK', Africa Centre, London, Dec. 1991.

91. John A. Chalmers, *Tiyo Soga, a Page of South African Mission Work* (Edinburgh, 1877); Donovan Williams, *Umfundisi: A Biography of Tiyo Soga, 1829–1871* (Lovedale, 1978).

92. Debrunner, *Presence and Prestige*, pp.278–9.

93. William Hughes, *Dark Africa and the Way Out* (London, 1892); Hazel King, 'Mojola Agbebi: Nigerian Church Leader', in Lotz and Pegg, *Under the Imperial Carpet*, pp.84–108.

94. Salim C. Wilson, *I Was a Slave* (London, 1939); Douglas H. Johnson, 'Salim Wilson: The Black Evangelist of the North', *Journal of Religion in Africa*, Vol.XXXI, No.1 (1991), pp.26–41.

95. Carlton E. Wilson, 'Racism and Private Assistance: The Support of West Indian and African Missions in Liverpool, England, during the Interwar Years', *African Studies Review*, Vol.35, No.2 (1992), pp.55–76.

96. For example, Desmond Tutu, now Anglican Archbishop of Cape Town, in the 1960s served curacies in Golders Green and in Bletchingley, Surrey. The Revd. Adeyemi Ladipo, is now vicar of Herne Hill, and neighbour to Revd. John Sentamu in Tulse Hill, south London; Revd. Francis Makambwe is the parish evangelist at St John with St Andrew, Waterloo, London SE1; the Revd. Francis Wainaina, from Kenya, has a parish in the Chester diocese. Julio Mekki, from Zimbabwe, became a London City Missioner in 1993; *Span* (LCM magazine), July–Aug. 1993, p.47.

97. O.A. Abiola, *An Introduction to Aladurism. The Christian Religion of Authority and Power* (Aladura International Church, London, n.d.), and O.A. Abiola, 'The Work of the Aladura Church in Britain', paper given to the conference on 'The African Presence in the UK, Africa Centre, London, Dec. 1991; W.M. Chirwa, *The Establishment of Cherubim and Seraphim Church in the United Kingdom and Overseas* (C. and S. Church London, 1990); C.O. Oshun, *Aladura Romance in Britain* (Selly Oak Colleges, Birmingham, 1990); and an illustrated but inaccurate article by Dorothy Wade, 'Missionaries in a Godless Land', *The Independent Magazine*, 4 May 1991, pp.34–40. Also J. Ashdown (ed.), *Prophets and Prayers. Interviews with Leaders of African Churches in London* (London, 1972).

98. *West Africa*, 16–22 Sept. 1991, p.1561.

99. J.J. Appiah, 'Die Musama Disco Christo Church in London', in *Zeitschrift für Mission*, Vol.XI, No.1 (1985), pp.35–8; Ruth Gledhill, 'Disco Church swings into its Devotions', *The Times*, 26 Dec. 1992, p.6.

100. For example, *West Africa*, 23–29 Sept. 1991, p.1617; Apostle T.O. Olabayo, 'the African Nostradamus' from Nigeria, spoke at the fourth anniversary service of the UK branch of the Evangelical Church of Yahweh Worldwide, St Paul's Church hall, East London.

101. King Dappa Pepple of Bonny was sent into exile, eventually in Tottenham, London, in 1857; see Sylvia L. Collicott, *Connections: Haringey Local–National–World Links* (Haringey, 1986), pp.82–3; Haile Selassie found refuge in Britain in the 1930s. Mutesa II, *kabaka* of Buganda, was deported to Britain in the 1950s (similar to Seretse Khame); in 1966 he fled from independent Uganda to die in poverty in London. The deposed Sultan of Zanzibar went to live in Southend on Sea.

102. Mary Dines, 'African Refugees in the United Kingdom', paper given to the conference on 'The African Presence in the UK', Africa Centre, London, Dec. 1991.

Unreconciled Strivings and Ironic Strategies: Three Afro-British Authors of the late Georgian Period (Sancho, Equiano, Wedderburn)

PAUL EDWARDS

Literary studies of these three Afro-British authors have recognized the ironic strategies used in their anti-slavery writings. But, there are at the same time ambiguities and ambivalences in their under-standings of the moral and economic arguments against slavery, which relate to the social and cultural context of late eighteenth-century Britain.

The first reviewers of Equiano's autobiographical *Interesting Narrative*[1] in June and July 1789 had this to say: in *The Monthly Review*, 'The Narrative wears an honest face, and we have conceived a good opinion of the man, from the artless manner in which he has detailed the variety of adventures and vicissitudes which have fallen to his lot'. A month later another reviewer declared in *The General Magazine and Impartial Review*: 'This is a "round unvarnished tale" . . . The Narrative appears to be written with much truth and simplicity.'[2]

But since the 1960s Equiano has received a growing attention, and his simplicities have come to appear less transparent. His book has fallen from such innocence into the more artful hands of modern literary critics, mostly from the United States – Houston Baker, Henry L. Gates, Robert Stepto, William Andrews, Keith Sandiford, Angelo Costanzo – some of whom see him not only as a precursor of Frederick Douglass and the American genre of slave narrative, but of Ralph Ellison, Richard Wright, and other modern authors. Costanzo writes that Equiano 'set the pattern for countless narratives – both non-fictional and fictional – that have influenced American literature to the present'.[3]

These critics, recognizing the sophistication of *The Interesting Narrative*, have stressed its use of narrative strategies: the subtitle of Sandiford's

The author would like to thank the University of Utah, Ethnic Studies, and Professor Wilfred D. Samuels for the opportunity to read an earlier draft of this article at the Equiano Conference, 'Looking Back with Pleasure', in Salt Lake City, October 1989; and the British Academy, for a research grant. Also Dr David Killingray of Goldsmiths' College, London, for his invitation to offer the paper at the Conference on the African Presence in the UK in December 1991.

book on three early Black British writers, Sancho, Cugoano and Equiano, is *Strategies of Protest*;[4] and Andrews, paying particular attention to recent studies in the theory of autobiography, observes that

> Today our sensitivity to the relativistic truth value of all autobiography and to the peculiar symbiosis of imperfect freedom and imperfect truth in the American autobiographical tradition makes it easier for us to regard the fictive elements of black autobiography as aspects of rhetorical and aesthetic strategy, not evidence of moral failure.[5]

The title of Andrews' book, *To Tell a Free Story*, indicates one of his principal concerns, the manner in which the slave narrator may be constrained by the circumstances in which he tells his tale. There is a delicate line for the reader of slave narrative between seeing authorial inconsistency or uncertainty and recognising strategies either calculated to convey the ironies of an experienced reality or to dramatize the perplexities arising from that experience. He writes:

> When we find a gap in the slave narrator's objective reportage of the facts of slavery, or a lapse in his prepossessing self-image, we must pay special attention. These deviations may indicate a temporary loss of narrative control, or a deliberate effort by the narrator to grapple with aspects of his or her personality that have been repressed out of deference to or fear of the dominant culture.[6]

It might be added that the gap may be between our present perception of what attitudes are appropriate to the tale, and the perception of the narrator in his own time. Thus we need to see slave narrative not necessarily in terms either of credible or unreliable factual records, but possibly more as a dramatization of the authorial self, with all the potential that this must bear for seeming incoherence of self-contradiction, 'a language', says Andrews, 'through which the unknown within the self and the unspeakable within slavery might be expressed',[7] a quality which extends beyond the slave narrative, and might bring to mind Wordsworth's search only a few years after Equiano wrote, for what might be called a rhetoric of inarticulacy in his early narrators (see his note to *The Thorn*: '. . . now every man must know that an attempt is rarely made to communicate impassioned feelings without something of an accompanying consciousness of the inadequateness of our own powers or the deficiencies of language . . .'[8]), a strategic rhetoric pursued in nineteeenth century English narrative from Wordsworth and Coleridge to Conrad, and into modernist literature. So, to quote Andrews' words, slave narratives

Spurred experimentation in narrative modes, metaphors of self and arts of address that challenged other 'perceptions of divisiveness' [Kenneth Burke] between history (fact), literature (fiction) and propaganda (argument) . . . as with any utterance, the way people produce and understand literary works depends upon unspoken, culturally shared knowledge of the rules, conventions and expectations.[9]

For the slave narrator, strategies of discourse were inevitable, but might easily be confused with imprecision, self-contradiction or Uncle Tommery. What Du Bois was to call 'unreconciled strivings'[10] might, in their uneasy ambiguities, bear a resemblance to such deliberately oblique, circuitous or ironic strategies. Andrews comments that 'the perception of [the slave's] narrative as truth depended on the degree to which his artfulness could hide his art'.[11] On the other hand, such appearances of artfulness might distract the reader from finding in the text something less self-consciously disingenuous. The 'truth' being told might be an acknowledgement of the 'unreconciled', if the author were unable to resolve deeply rooted dilemmas. The articulation of 'the truth' would then lie in the contradiction itself, a kind of perplexed candour perhaps, rather than a strategic handling of the material as 'art'.

What I want to examine in this paper is the nature of the strategic ironies that have been found by many critics, including myself, in Equiano's handling of the experience of slavery, and to direct attention to a problem of critical interpretation arising from such readings. To help define this problem, I want first to approach the matter by way of one of the letters of Equiano's Afro-British contemporary, Ignatius Sancho, former butler to the nobility, friend and correspondent of Sterne and Garrick, and fashionable Mayfair shopkeeper. The American critic, Lloyd W. Brown, reviewing my introduction to the 1968 facsimile reprint of Sancho's *Letters*,[12] quotes and discusses the following letter written in 1778 by Sancho to Jack Wingrave, the young son of a friend, who had gone out to India, and had been infected with the racist attitudes of the English community:

I am sorry to observe that the practice of your country (which as a resident I love – and for its freedom and the many blessings I enjoy in it, shall ever have my warmest wishes, prayers, and blessings): I say it is with reluctance that I must observe your country's conduct has been uniformly wicked in the East – West Indies – and even on the coast of Guinea. – The grand object of English navigators – indeed of all Christian navigators – is money, money, money – for which I do not pretend to blame them. – Commerce was meant by the Deity to diffuse the various goods of the earth into every part –

to unite mankind in the blessed chains of brotherly love, society, and mutual dependence: – the enlightened Christian should diffuse the Riches of the Gospel of peace with the commodities of his respective land – Commerce attended with strict honesty, and with religion for its companion, would be a blessing to every shore it touched at. In Africa, the poor, wretched natives – blessed with the most fertile and luxurious soil – are rendered so much the more miserable for what Providence meant as a blessing: the Christians' abominable Traffic for slaves – and the horrid cruelty and treachery of the petty Kings – encouraged by their Christian customers – who carry them strong drink to enflame their national madness – and powder and fire-arms, to furnish them with the hellish means of killing and kidnapping. But enough – it is a subject that sours my blood – and I am sure it will not please the friendly bent of your social affections (Sancho facsimile, p.149, Letter LXVII).

My comment on this was:

We might recognise the two voices of Sancho here, and it is interesting to see which one is dominant. Sancho the former slave emerges in a note of considerable indignation and explicit irony at the greed of 'Christian navigators', drawing the conclusion that their aim had been nothing but 'money-money-money' (the implication might have been different had the word been written only once). At this point, however, Sancho the gentleman-grocer takes over to sing the praises of that excellent blend, religion and commercial advantage. The argument is characteristic of the age . . . (Sancho facsimile, p.xiv).

However, Lloyd Brown reads the letter rather differently. He hears, not two inconsistent voices, but an ironic juxtaposition:

After deploring the depredations of Christian traders, [Sancho] ironically echoes the mercantilist's usual apology for commerce in general and the slave trade in particular . . . it is clear that 'the blessed chains of brotherly love' are not the only kinds of bonds with which Sancho is preoccupied here. He is not being the unquestioning disciple of mercantilism which Paul Edwards supposes him to be in this letter. Indeed, Sancho's ironic insinuations are so effective because his intimate knowledge of his society enables him to subvert its prejudices and ambiguous values from within. The personality of the assimilated African has incarnated one of the basic strategies of the eighteenth century satirist.[13]

I have not suggested that this letter is without irony, nor do I believe that Sancho is such an 'unquestioning disciple of mercantilism' as Lloyd Brown would have it. But I believe that Brown oversimplifies what is going on in the letter, by attempting to explain away conflicts and contradictions by calling them ironies. At the simplest level the ironic tone is only too apparent, in the phrase 'grand object . . . of all Christian navigators', for instance; or outrage, in the triple repetition 'money-money-money', a note of open indignation, hardly to be called 'ironic *insinuation*'. The irony is too plain, and the rage too overt and uncalculated to be called 'strategic', I think. So while Brown understands Sancho's mercantilism as an ironic parody of that of the devious apologists for the slave trade, I would find something more like perplexity and confusion of values here. The doctrine of Christian trade about which the modern reader, such as Lloyd Brown, in a post-colonialist economy might well feel cynical, was in the late eighteenth century broadly acceptable to Sancho, as it was to Equiano who asks in the final chapter of his autobiography, for 'a system of commerce [in which] the native inhabitants will insensibly adopt the British fashions, manners customs &c. In proportion to the civilisation, so will be the consumption of British manufactures' (Equiano II, pp.249–50). The reader might like to find irony in Equiano's use of the words 'insensibly' or 'civilisation', but it would be perverse to argue that such an irony was intended. Equiano is perfectly serious.

Such a view of commerce was in fact a commonplace even of abolitionist argument at this time, when the abolitionist cause was under attack from the West Indian planters and their powerful supporters, as threatening serious economic damage to the nation ('which as a resident I love', declares Sancho, not apparently ironically, 'for the many blessings I enjoy in it'). European traders are seen by Sancho as only partial villains, having reinforced 'the horrid cruelty and treachery of the petty kings . . .'. In warning his friend against 'being too hasty in condemning the knavery of a people who – bad as they may be – possibly were made worse by their Christian visitors', Sancho's hesitant gestures towards placing the blame on barbarous native institutions dissipates the weight of irony carried by the word 'Christian' here. The characteristic note, it seems to me, is less of irony than of moral hesitancy.

We might also bear in mind that the great Adam Smith had argued the economic advantages of a benevolist policy towards slavery and empire, in terms very similar, as we shall see later, to those of Equiano: 'Gentle usage renders the slave not only more faithful but more intelligent, and therefore, upon a double account, more useful.'[14] The mercantiles of Sancho must be seen, as I have suggested, in the context of economic ideas, put forward in all seriousness by Equiano, who would have found them proposed equally seriously in such unimpeachable abolitionist sources as Anthony Benezet's *Some Historical Account of Guinea*, footnoted by Equiano in his *Narrative,* or in the pamphlets of the distinguished Scottish abolitionist James Ramsey, whose war of words with the 'cursory remarker', the planter and slave owner James Tobin, Equiano reviewed in *The Public Advertiser* in 1788.[15] Only a few years before Sancho wrote his letter, the pro-slavery lobby was arguing the case against abolition in such terms as these: 'All our pretended reformers of the age . . . under a cloak of furious zeal in the cause of religion and liberty, do all they can to throw down those essential pillars, commerce, trade and navigation, upon which alone must depend their own enjoyment of any freedom, civil or religious.'[16] These words, published in 1772, seemed still sufficiently influential in 1789 for Wilberforce to quote them in the House of Commons as an illustration of the continuing cruel self-interest of the planters and slavers. But their reception in the Commons is revealing: far from arousing general reproach, we are told, 'A cry of assent was heard in several parts of the House'.[17] Indeed, Wilberforce himself was another of the leading abolitionists who argued that Commerce might indeed satisfy the demands of both economic interest and Christian morality:

> At such an enlightened period as this, when commerce herself adopts the principles of true morality, and becomes liberal and benevolent, will it be believed that the almighty has rendered the depression and misery of the cultivators of the soil in our West Indian Colonies necessary, or even conducive, to their prosperity and safety? No, surely, the oppression of these injured fellow creatures, however profitable in a few instances, can never be generally politic; and in the main, and ultimately, the comfort of the labourer, and the well-being of those who have to enjoy the fruits of his labour will be found to be coincident.[18]

Such faith in Divine Providence is in the spirit of the writings of both Sancho and Equiano. But as late as 1853, the abolition of American slavery was still being seen by the respectable *North American Review* as leading potentially to political and economic disaster: 'It involves property and security, sectional power and party power, and sweeps into its vortex the passions which disturb the repose of society and shake the stability of empires.'[19] In such a climate of economic opinion it was necessary, even for those claiming the purest of humanitarian motives, to demonstrate that Christian virtue might go hand in hand with commercial and political interest. Whatever strategies might be at work, then, in Sancho's letter of 1778, to call them simply ironic is to misinterpret the nature of the contradictory and unresolved impulses on display.

Similarly, in my approach to Equiano's *Narrative*, I shall suggest that the reader needs to recognize a distinction between conscious subversive ironies, and what may be unconscious and contradictory, often more properly to be seen as unresolved dilemma. Though I have no doubt that narrative strategies, often of a subtle kind, are employed by Equiano, which I shall try to define later in the argument, I should like to look at what seems to me a particularly problematic section, the fifth chapter of *The Interesting Narrative*. The first four chapters begin with a prideful account of the Igbo nation and its customs, and Equiano's parents and family. This is followed by a description of his kidnapping by neighbouring African raiders, a brief experience of African slavery which significantly he describes as essentially benevolent, and his fiirst confrontation with monstrous and scarcely human white men 'with red faces and loose hair' aboard a slave ship. He is carried to the West Indies and America and sold to a British naval officer, Pascal, with whom he begins to feel at ease and from whom he comes to expect his liberty after serving him aboard ship for some time. The fifth chapter starts with Equiano's brutal resale into American slavery by Captain Pascal, a man he had come to trust. His new owner, Captain Doran, sells him in turn to a Philadephia merchant, Robert King, and though he is treated with comparative benevolence he has seen enough of the conditions of slavery to evoke powerfully its horrors in America and the West Indies. His account of the ferocious ill-treatment of slaves begins with these comments on those slave owners who claim that the purchase and employment of slaves is a bad bargain:

> . . . if it be true, why do the planters and merchants pay such a price for slaves? And, above all, why do those who make this assertion exclaim the most loudly against the abolition of the slave trade? So much are men blinded and to such inconsistent arguments are they driven by mistaken interest! I grant, indeed, that slaves are some times, by half-feeding and half-clothing, reduced so low, that they are turned out as unfit for service, and left to perish in the woods, or expire on a dunghill.
>
> My master was several times offered by different gentlemen one hundred guineas for me; but he always told them he would not sell me, to my great joy: and I used to double my diligence and care for fear of getting into the hands of those men who did not allow a valuable slave the common support of life. Many of them even used to find fault with my master for feeding his slaves so well as he did; although I often went hungry, and an Englishman might think my fare very indifferent; but he used to tell them he would always do it,

because the slaves thereby looked better and did more work (I. pp.204–5).

In this instance, Equiano's seeming pragmatism appears deeply imbued with irony. The argument for the good treatment of slaves contains the backhander against his 'generous' master, firstly that 'an Englishman might think my fare very indifferent'; then the benevolent treatment of slaves is justified not on humanitarian grounds, but in the final phrase, on those of appearance and profitability – 'they looked better and did more work'. But as the chapter proceeds, the weight of the argument is directed against the ill-treatment of slaves rather than against the institution of slavery itself. Equiano denounces the barbarous conduct of the overseers, then appears to condemn the estate owners only for their absenteeism: 'unfortunately, many humane gentlemen, by not residing on their estates, are obliged to leave the management of [their slaves] in the hands of these human butchers' (I. p.207).

If this appears to let the 'humane gentlemen' slave-owners off the hook, the reader should bear in mind that slavery was still legal in much of Europe and that Equiano had no reason to think in 1789 that much more than amelioration could be hoped for. A commentator of 1815, looking back on the spirit of amelioration amongst abolitionists of the 1790s writes: 'They looked, in short, to an emancipation, of which, not the slaves, but the masters should be the willing instruments.'[20] However, in the words of Iain McCalman, 'it is important to realise that abolitionist and liberal enlightenment ideas of the kind introduced to London Jacobins by Equiano in the 1790's had been largely crushed during Pitt's suppression of the democratic political societies'[21] [e.g *The Seditious Meetings Acts of 1799*]. To return to Equiano's benevolist argument complaining of the neglect by the 'humane gentlemen' of their slave estates, he continues:

> This neglect certainly conspires with many others to cause a decrease in the births as well as in the lives of the grown negroes. I can quote many instances of gentlemen who reside on their estates in the West Indies, and then the scene is quite changed; the negroes are treated with lenity and proper care, by which their lives are prolonged and their masters are profited (I. p.208).

Again, it seems, the ironic sting might lie in the tail. The benevolist case for profitability, noted above in Adam Smith, if understood as ironic, would appear to carry more than a touch of Swift's *Modest Proposal*. The problem is that such a reading of the text as ironic sits uneasily with Equiano's next words: 'To the honour of humanity, I know several gentlemen who managed their estates in this manner; and they found that benevolence was their true interest', followed shortly after by 'I, myself, as shall appear in the sequel, managed an estate, where, by those attentions, the negroes were uncommonly cheerful and healthy, and did more work by half than by the common mode of work they usually do' (I. p.210). The sequel referred to appears in the penultimate chapter of the *Narrative* when Equiano, now a free man, is employed by a Dr Irving to purchase slaves. 'Our vessel being ready to sail to the Musquito shore, I went with the Doctor aboard a Guinea-man, to purchase some slaves to carry with us, and cultivate a plantation; and I chose them all my own countrymen' (II. p.178). The apparent contradiction between such pragmatic benevolence, and the vivid and appalling accounts of cruelty practised in the trade itself leaves something of the kind of 'gap' referred to by Andrews, which cannot be glossed over simply by reference to strategic irony.

At another stage in the argument of this chapter, Equiano, as one might expect, adopts a wholly unambiguous stance against slavery on principle: 'But is not the slave trade entirely a war with the heart of man?' (I. p.220) followed immediately by what appears to be the most patent and bitter irony in the chapter: 'I have often seen slaves, particularly those who were meagre, in different islands, put into scales and weighed; and then sold from three pence to six pence a pound. My master [Mr. King], however, whose humanity was shocked at this mode, used to sell such by the lump' (I. p.220). At this point we appear to be back with the spirit of Swift. Yet Equiano's experience as slave to Mr King is, he acknowledges, a principal factor in reconciling him to his condition: 'During the time I served Mr. King, in going about the different estates on the island, I had all the opportunity I could to see the dreadful usage of the poor men; usage that reconciled me to my situation, and made me bless God for the hands into which I had fallen' (I. pp.202–3).

I think there is something more than pious optimism here. The sense of a special destiny in his life, leading him on to fortune, is closely related I believe to Equiano's early years in Igbo. First, his name, Olaudah, he had earlier told the reader, means 'Vicissitude, or fortune also, one favoured . . .' (I. p.31); several times he italicises references to this happy destiny: 'When I compare my lot with that of most of my countrymen, I regard myself as *a particular favourite of Heaven*, and acknowledge the mercies of Providence in every occurrence of my life' (I. p.3). The latter is later confirmed by his statement that 'I was from my earliest years a predestinarian' (I. p.243) and can be related to the discarding of his initial baptism into the Church of England, and his embracing of Calvinism when later in life he is received into fellowship at the Congregationalist

Westminster Chapel. However, what appears to be Christian Providentialism, suggesting his assimilation of English values, is equally likely to indicate the reverse, the survival of the Igbo concept of *chi*, the personal spirit of destiny, and its associated providentialism – 'I was *from my earliest years* a predestinarian'.[22] As he tells us emphatically, his Igbo childhood was never forgotten, and his values lay deeply embedded in it: 'They had been implanted in me with great care and made an impression on my mind which time could not erase, and which all the adversity and variety of fortune I have since experienced served only to rivet and record' (I. pp.45–6).

If there is any ambivalence between Equiano's disgust at the treatment of slaves, and his tendency to benevolism or meliorism with regard to it as an institution, the reason again might be found in memories of Igbo childhood.[23] He tells us that his much admired father 'besides many slaves, had a numerous family' (I. p.46), and what follows indicates that he saw family and slaves as co-extensive. He writes in some detail contrasting African and American slavery, his love of Igbo and happy memories of childhood perhaps softening his recall:

> but how different was their condition from that of the slaves in the West Indies? With us they do no more work than other members of the community, even their masters; their food, clothing and lodging were nearly the same as theirs (except that they were not permitted to eat with those who were free-born); and there was scarce any other difference between them, than a superior degree of importance which the head of a family possesses in our state, and that authority which, as such he exercises over every part of his household. Some of these slaves have even slaves under them as their own property, and for their own use (I. p.27).

So I would argue that while Equiano employs an often fierce irony to contrast Christian principles with un-Christian practice in his account of the cruel treatment of slaves in the Americas, his attitude to the institution of slavery itself is characterized by what might be seen as at very least an ambivalent response. In Chapter 5, Equiano's last words to the planters are these: 'By changing your conduct, and treating your slaves as men, every cause of fear would be banished' (I. p.226). Such an explicit acceptance of the *status quo* of slavery can hardly be interpreted as ironic strategy.

Nevertheless, such strategies do occur, for instance the recurrent ironic use of the word 'Christian' which we also saw in Sancho; but often too at a more subtle and complex level. To establish the difference between such strategic irony, and the ambivalence I have claimed for

Equiano's attitude to slave ownership, I should now like to look at some of these ironies in detail to illustrate the skill with which he is capable of deploying them. Equiano was a devoted Christian, though as I have suggested his Christianity is more deeply rooted in the Igbo beliefs of his upbringing than has been recognized. When he sees a preacher sweating with pious exertions, he cannot resist the impulse to make an ironic point, contrasting the sufferings of the slave with the soft life and lack or moral purpose of many of the clergy:

> When I got into church and saw this pious man exhorting the people with the greatest fervour and earnestness, and sweating as much as ever I did while in slavery on Monserrat beach . . . I thought it strange I had never seen divines exert themselves in this manner before, and I was no longer at a loss to account for the thin congregations they preached to (II. pp.5–6).

The tone here is comparatively humorous and relaxed, without the Swiftian bitterness we have seen elsewhere, and it seems that his fiercest ironies are directed against what might be called inhuman cruelty and greed (even though we know it to be all too human), and he adopts a more genial manner with follies and absurdities, at times disarmingly directing his ironies against himself, one of the factors which conveys the engaging quality of candour and cool self-awareness characterizing the book. There are many examples of this, sometimes in terms of self-deflation, sometimes of comic self-inflation, such as the touch of vanity he allows the reader to catch a glimpse of as he plays the peacock after gaining his freedom: 'at the dances I gave, my Georgia superfine blue clothes made no indiffernt appearance as I thought. Some of the sable females, who formerly stood aloof, now began to relax and appear less coy . . .' (II. p.19). The phrase 'as I thought' neatly establishes the ironic distancing of critical self-observation. His eye for the 'sable females' points to another irony directed against himself. He tells us elsewhere that he managed to keep eight of the ten commandments: 'I found none among my acquaintance that kept wholly the ten commandments. So righteous was I in my own eyes, that I was convinced I excelled many of them on that point, by keeping eight out of ten' (II. p.118). With his veiled confession of fondness for female company in mind, we might feel able to make a confident guess at one of the two Commandments he failed to keep. And like the words 'as I thought' in the first of the two quotations above, the phrase 'so righteous was I in my own eyes' nicely established the ironic tone of what might otherwise have been a mere piece of self-satisfied piety.

Then there is the episode with the Indians when the drunken Indian governor steals the chief's hat, and Equiano intimidates the governor's party by threatening then with his Christian God (a trick remembered from an incident in the life of the arch-adventurer and empire-builder Columbus) and restores order by declaring;

> if they did not leave off and go quietly, I would take the book (pointing to the Bible), read, and *tell* God to make them dead. This was something like magic. The clamour immediately ceased and I gave them some rum and a few other things; after which they went away peaceably; and the Governor afterwards gave our neighbour, who was called Captain Plasmyah, his hat again (II. p.187).

While all this had been going on, Equiano's employer, Dr Irving, had run for cover and was keeping his head down: 'fearing that he might get into trouble, [he had] left the house and made the best of his way to the nearest wood'. When the crisis is over, the hat safely back with its owner, and the Doctor back home again, 'he was exceedingly glad at my success in getting rid of our troublesome guests'. Like the Doctor's retreat into the bush, Equiano's characteristic touch of self-congratualtion becomes itself part of the comedy of a situation which he appears to acknowledge to be unheroic, absurd, and bordering on burlesque.

But the most striking comic-ironic episode, in which Equiano openly deflates both his own vigorous commercial instincts and his high moral tone, is that of the dying passenger. Those 'superfine blue clothes' make another appearance, and Equiano directs his perceptive ironic eye upon the depths of his own 'respectable' Christian acquisitive instincts and ambitions, satirizing the 'holier-than-thou' moral stance which at times in the narrative he himself is guilty of, and on this occasion sharing the jest of human vanity with his readers. This passenger promises to give all his money to Captain Farmer when he dies, in return for care on shipboard: 'I used also to go with the Captain at his own desire to attend him [the dying passenger], especially when we saw there was no appearance of his recovery.' The Captain promises Equiano ten pounds on the man's death, and Equiano, saving every penny to purchase his freedom, as well as those superfine clothes with which he plans to impress the 'sable females' is delighted at the prospect of easy money, and 'paid out above eight pounds for a suit of superfine clothes to dance with at my freedom'. In due course, he tells the reader 'away we both went and saw the man as dead as we could wish. The Captain said he would give him a grand burial in gratitude for the promised treasure', but the man's trunks through which they search get smaller and smaller, yet contain nothing of value.

At last when we came to the smallest, and had opened it, we saw it was full of papers, which we supposed to be notes; at the sight of which our hearts leapt for joy; and that instant the Captain, clapping his hands, cried out 'Thank God, here it is'. But when we took up the trunk and began to examine the supposed treasure and long looked-for bounty (alas! alas! how uncertain and deceitful are all human affairs!), what had we found! While we thought we were embracing a substance we grasped an empty nothing. The whole amount that was in the nest of trunks amounted to one dollar and a half; and all that the man possessed would not pay for his coffin. Our sudden and exquisite joy was now succeeded by as sudden and exquisite pain: and my Captain and I exhibited for some time the most ridiculous figures – pictures of chagrin and disappointment! We went away greatly mortified, and left the deceased to do as well as he could for himself, as we had taken such good care of him for nothing (II. pp.8–11).

It is this kind of ironic self-awareness which constitutes an important element of the book's truth. The pious rhetorical agonizings which parody the tones of pious lamentation here, juxtaposed with the explicit acknowledgement of the very human but far from pious, indeed predatory eagerness to lay hands on the money, establish an ironic contrast between Equiano the Christian sufferer on one hand, and on the other the hard-nosed moneylender he was to become in London in the 1790s, and the economic survivor he had learned to be during much of his life as a slave.[24] Thus by the process of self-mockery, he is able more subtly to direct his satire against the pious hypocrisies of his day, as well as the greed of bare commercial instinct unleavened by morality or charity. Quite deliberately, he makes a 'Holy Willie' of himself, in cool mockery of the less appealing aspects of his own 'Christian' world.

In the later incidents quoted, the contradictions or inconsistencies are quite clearly consciously manipulated for ironic, even comic effect. But in the matter of Equiano's attitude to slavery the potential ironies are contextualised in such a way as to raise doubts as to whether we are witnessing simple irony, or a more complex process of truth-telling in what he reveals about himself. In such instances I am more inclined to think that, like the letter by Sancho, what some readers have taken to be irony, is itself undercut, qualified and blunted by hesitancies in his attitude to the institution of slavery.

I believe, then, that to call Equiano's attitude to slavery simply an ironic strategy is to underestimate the force of the paradox of 'unreconciled strivings', identified in his effort to come to terms with his hatred of the cruelties he had witnessed, in an uneasy relationship with his memory of the benevolent practice of slavery in his Igbo homeland and his own commercial as well as his humanitarian impulses. As an ex-slave and a leading black abolitionist voice, he was, of course, aligned with radical movements in the England in which he at last made his home. But like Sancho he was also an aspiring business man with an eye to commercial interest – indeed without such a commercial spirit he would never have earned the money to purchase his freedom. In one incident after another, Equiano dramatizes his battle to earn a few pence by trading on his own account, selling bags of fruit, tumblers, and bottles of gin, often vulnerable to the bullying tactics of dishonest white men. Even as the forty year old Equiano recorded this early stage of his life he was aware of himself as an eighteenth-century 'commercial man' like Sancho. Iain McCalman makes an interesting point about the split in English radicalism at this time. He writes of Francis Place's thoughts on the 'blackguard' or unprincipled style in late eighteenth century working-class life:

> Place believed that the majority of London's middling sort [of tradesmen] managed during the early years of the nineteenth century to throw off this essentially brutal and degrading culture in favour of a new humane and civilising code of respectability. Writing at the end of the 1820's, it appeared to him that popular manners and morals had undergone a revolution. Only the unskilled poor or professional criminal classes had clung to 'blackguard' norms and practices. Economic independence and the possession of a skilled status had formerly been enough to define an artisan as respectable, but in the 1820's he could only expect social respect if he also *behaved* respectably and acquired sober, self-improving (though non-deferential) values . . . The change was symbolised for Place by his attendance of a Jacobin reunion at the Crown and Anchor tavern on 5 November 1822. Here he met at least twenty former LCS [London Corresponding Society][25] delegates who had once been journeymen or shopmen, but were 'now all in business, all flourishing men'. In addition to himself, he was referring to men like Thomas Hardy, John Richter and Alexander Galloway, who had managed to build up prosperous businesses in their respective areas of shoemaking, engineering and sugar-refining. Hand in hand with their material advances, Place noted, went a new attachment to respectable values manifested in the cultivation of family-centred rational recreation and the provision of education for their children.

Many had adopted the moderate reformist and educational goals associated with Westminster radicalism after 1807. Place pointed by contrast to a residue of former Jacobins who had failed to improve themselves – morally, intellectually or materially – remaining fixed in the feckless, dissolute and criminal patterns of the past.[26]

It is significant that it was at the house of one of the prosperous radicals named by Place, Thomas Hardy the Shoemaker, founder of the London Corresponding Society, that Equiano was lodging in 1792, when he wrote a letter[27] to a group of abolitionist clergy at Nottingham, announcing his marriage, with an amusing glimpse of his eager eye for commerce associated with good works, 'I now mean, as it seem pleasing to my Good God! – to leave London in about 8 or 10 days more, & take me a wife (one Miss Cullen), of Soham in Cambridgeshire, and when I have given her 8 or 10 Days Comfort I mean Directly to go to Scotland and sell my 5th editions . . .', adding that he is only in London, 'this wicked town . . . to save if I can, £232 I lent to a man who [is] now dying', indicating that having established himself in the respectable and skilled occupation of valet and hairdresser in the 1770s, and become a best-selling author in 1789, he was by 1792 already involved in the moneylending business which along with the success of his book, was to supply funds which would provide comfortably for his surviving daughter Joanna after his death.[28].

Equiano's radicalism was essentially respectable, moderate, and benevolist. He died in 1797, comfortably off and respected, 'a sober honest man' Granville Sharp told his niece.[29] In this he contrasts with another Afro-British author, Robert Wedderburn,[30] who began to be active in London at the end of the eighteenth century, but was by no means so respectable. Wedderburn was the son of a wealthy Scots-Jamaican planter and one of his slaves. His father never acknowledged him as his son, and in fact sold Robert's mother when she was five months pregnant with him. He sailed as a privateer, virtually a licensed pirate, and served in the Royal Navy as main gunner and top station hand; according to McCalman it is possible that he was involved in the Nore Mutiny of 1797. After leaving the Navy, he earned a bare living in London as a jobbing tailor, but after undergoing religious and political inspiration, he took out a licence to preach as a Unitarian minister, and founded a chapel in a hayloft in Hopkins Street. Later he was to establish a sect which he called with irony characteristic of his delight in burlesque, 'Christian Diabolists, or Devil Worshippers', on the grounds that since the will of God would not, indeed *could not*, be altered by prayer, it could only be useful in our fallen world to pray to the next most powerful agent, the Devil. The spirit of his Hopkins Street sermons, from what we hear of them, was that of burlesque. He would engage in farcical theological debates with a dwarf shoemaker, Samuel Waddington. Iain McCalman describes how Wedderburn, 'the "Black Prince", and the "Black Dwarf"(as Waddington was nicknamed) functioned as a comic team convulsing their audiences with a type of mock worship . . . [which] could switch quickly from the burlesque to the melodramatic'.[31] His talent in fact was not so much literary as oral in the popular theatrical 'trickster' tradition.

He was tried and jailed for blasphemy in 1820, and the last thing we know of him is that, at the age of sixty-eight, he was sentenced to two years hard labour for brawling in the street, outside a brothel of which he was the owner, which he claimed in an outrageous defence to be a refuge for destitute women. He also claimed in his defence that a member of the very court which was trying him enjoyed the services of one of his resident women, called 'Carroty Eliza'. Wedderburn lived on the fringes of criminality, and troubled the authorities with his fiery preaching that it was the Christian duty of his flock to do all in their power to bring down a cruel, hypocritical and tyrannical establishment.

Wedderburn's writings have been even less visible than Equiano's, but happily, Iain McCalman is making them available once more, and not only that, confirming the importance of Wedderburn in the history of early-nineteenth century English radicalism as a forerunner of the Chartists of the mid-century, and of the labour movement of its close. He was a vigorous pamphleteer, author of such challenging titles as *The Axe Laid to the Root,* and *Cast-Iron Parsons* and in 1824 he published *The Horrors of Slavery*, a short autobiographical account of his slave mother and his African-born grandmother, a smuggler's agent by the name of Talkee Amy. As well as bitter denunciations of slavery and the slave trade, it consists largely of diatribes against his half-brother, a 'respectable' citizen of London, and against his deeply detested father, the Scottish doctor turned planter and slave-owner, whose ill-treatment of his mother and grandmother is a major theme of Wedderburn's book:

> To this present hour, while I think of the treatment of my mother, my blood boils in my veins; and, had I not some connections for which I was bound to live, I should long ago have taken ample vengeance of my father. But it is as well as it is; and I will not leave the world without some testimony to the injustice and inhumanity of my father.
>
> From the time my mother became the property of my father, she assumed the direction and management of his house: for which no woman was better qualified. But her station there was very disgusting. My father's house was full of female slaves, all objects of his

lusts; amongst whom he strutted like Solomon in his grand seraglio, or like a bantam cock upon his own dunghill. My good father's slaves did increase and multiply, like Jacob's kine: and he cultivated those talents well which God had granted so amply. My poor mother, from being the housekeeper, was the object of their envy, which was increased by her superiority of education over the common herd of female slaves.

I never saw my dear father but once in the island of Jamaica, when I went with my grandmother to know if he meant to do any-thing for me, his son. [He] giving her some abusive language, my grandmother called him a mean Scotch rascal, thus to desert his own flesh and blood. This was the parental treatment I experienced from the Scotch West-India planter and slave-dealer.[32]

Wedderburn was no man for Christian forbearance – the charge of blasphemy laid against him was for calling Jesus 'a bloody fool' for turning the other cheek. His fierce, often farcical ironies are more explicit than Equiano's, though like Equiano, he plays the fool as a strategy, not in the self-defensive 'blackface' tradition,[33] but aggressively and designed all the more effectively to strike his targets. He was assuredly a man of style and presence, and a master of the oral tradition. McCalman gives this account of his subversive political rhetoric and his blasphemous chapel:

At the same time there was a lighter side to Hopkins Street blasphemy . . . debates functioned as a form of theatre intended to ridicule authority and entertain listeners. Parts of the chapel's notoriety derived from the reputation of its leading speakers as performers. Wedderburn believed that many had come to see and hear him because 'his name had gone abroad as a strange and curious sort of fellow'. He had, in Richard Carlile's words, 'developed a powerful eccentricity of manner'. His coarse and profane language: his colour and physique (often described as stout): and the spectacular events of his life – the slave background, rejection by his wealthy family, experiences as a fighting sailor, criminal pauper were to say the least, arresting. He displayed the traits of many populist leaders – physical bulk, roguery, flamboy-ance, bombast, emotional religiosity and a thirst for martyrdom.[34]

If we compare the 'respectable' radicalism of Equiano with the spectacular swaggering bravado of Wedderburn, we can see, perhaps, why for all Equiano's literary skill and persuasive oratory, as he travelled throughout the British Isles selling his book and speaking against the slave trade, equally important for his success as a leader in the black community was his adoption of the radical respectability recognised by Francis Place, and the flexibility with which he adapted himself (whilst holding to the principles implanted in him during his African childhood), to the often paradoxical, or plainly hypocritical commercial and religious values of English society, particularly in defence of the slave trade.

Wedderburn, on the other hand displays a Dionysiac charisma which is wholly unlike the spirit of Equiano. Equiano is a reformer, Wedderburn a rebel, and rather than argue about preference for one or the other, we might look on them with the eye of their contemporary Blake, who in many ways resembled Wedderburn, and allow that 'Opposition is true friendship', not that Equiano and Wedderburn are exactly opposed. They are more like what Blake called *contraries*, complementing each other in their differences ('without contraries is no progression') and we should not try to reconcile their differences ('He who seeks to reconcile them seeks to destroy existence').[35] Wedderburn's stance is confrontational, showing nothing of Equiano's pragmatic adaptability. In view of the wide audience Equiano reached, as a result of the success of his book, and the prominence given to his letters to the press and elsewhere (one of them to Lord Hawkesbury was printed with the evidence of the 1789 Parliamentary Report on the Slave Trade).[36] Equiano must be recognised as an important voice guiding respectable opinion towards legislation for the abolition of the slave trade, the 'principle instrument in bringing about the motion for the repeal of the slave-act' that the Northern Irish abolitionist, Thomas Digges, claimed him to be.[37] Wedderburn must also now be recognised as a significant contributor to British radicalism, another of whose principal activists and spokesmen was a Black British voice, the Chartist, William Cuffay.[38] And as McCalman points out in the introduction to his new edition of Wedderburn's writings,[39] by the time of his death in obscurity, there was to be a resurgence of mass radicalism through such organizations as the National Union of Working Classes, and its militant successor the London Democratic Association led by Wedderburn's younger associates, and at the root of the growing working-class political movement in Britain. Wedderburn is characterized by a more consistent tone of explicit outrage against the establishment, and his more bizarre satiric spirit makes no concession to a 'respectable' audience. As a radical militant, he displays nothing of the ambivalence towards mercantilism displayed by Equiano. At the same time it might be argued that whilst recognizing the presence of skilfully deployed ironic strategies in Equiano, the less confrontational posture he adopts towards the establishment was one of the reasons for his success in the abolitionist movement with the audience of his day, though it involved him in what appear to be conciliatory attitudes towards the economics of slavery which are sufficiently discomforting to the modern reader to be glossed over or justified on the grounds of ironic strategies which might more properly be seen as moral ambivalence.

NOTES

1. Olaudah Equiano, *The Interesting Narrative of Olaudah Equiano, or Gustavus Vassa the African, written by himself* 2 vols. (London, 1789), Reprinted in facsimile with an introduction by Paul Edwards (London, 1969). Quotations below and in the text refer to this facsimile edition unless otherwise stated.
2. Quoted in the 1789 edition, see facsimile, pp.xv–xvii.
3. Angelo Costanzo, *Surprizing Narrative: Olaudah Equiano and the Beginnings of Black Autobiography* (New York, 1987), p.6.
4. Keith A. Sandiford, Measuring the Moment: Strategies of Protest in Eighteenth-Century Afro-English Writing (London, 1988).
5. William L. Andrews, *To Tell a Free Story: The First Century of Afro-American Auto-biography, 1760–1865* (Urbana, Il, 1986), p.3.
6. Andrews, *To Tell a Free Story*, p.8.
7. Andrews, *To Tell a Free Story*, p.9.
8. Stephen Gill (ed.), *William Wordsworth* (Oxford, 1984), p.593.
9. Andrews, *To Tell a Free Story*, p.24.
10. W.E.B. Du Bois, *The Souls of Black Folk* (1903; New York, 1961), p.16.
11. Andrews, *To Tell a Free Story*, p.3.
12. *Letters of the late Ignatius Sancho*, with an Introduction by Paul Edwards (facsimile of the 5th edition of 1803; London, 1968).
13. Lloyd W. Brown, review of *Letters of Sancho* in *Eighteenth Century Studies*, Vol.3, No.3 (1970), pp.414–19.
14. Adam Smith, *The Wealth of Nations* (IV.7, Part II) ed. Edwin Cannan (1776; London 1961), p.100.
15. Anthony Benezet, *Some Historical Account of Guinea* (London, 1771); for proposals relating to African trade which closely resemble Equiano's, see Appendix by Malachy Postlethwait in the edition of 1788, and for Equiano's acknowledgement of Benezet as a source see Equiano 1789 I.7n. For Ramsey and Tobin, see Equiano in *The Public Advertiser*, 26 Jan. 1788; reprinted in Folarin Shyllon, *Black People in Britain, 1555–1833* (London, 1977), pp.249–51.
16. Anon., *Reflections . . . on what is commonly called The Negroe–Cause, by a Planter* (London, 1772).
17. Roger Anstey, *The Atlantic Slave Trade and British Abolition* (London, 1965), pp.313–14.
18. *An Appeal to the Religion, Justice, and Humanity of the Inhabitations of the British Empire on Behalf of the Negro Slaves in the West Indies, by Wm. Wilberforce, Esq., M.P.* (London, 1823), p.71.
19. *North American Review*, LXVII (Oct. 1853), p.489, quoted by Charles H. Nicholas 'Who Read the Slave Narratives?', *Phylon*, 20 (1959), p.154.
20. Quoted in J.R. Ward, *British West Indian Slavery, 1750–1834)* (Oxford, 1988), p.3.
21. Ian McCalman (ed.), *The Horrors of Slavery and Other Writings by Robert Wedderburn* (Edinburgh, 1991), p.13.
22. Paul Edwards and Rosalind Shaw, 'The Invisible *Chi* in Equiano's *Narrative*', *Journal of Religion in Africa*, Vol.XIX, No.6, (1989), pp.146–50.
23. Paul Edwards, '"Master" and "Father" in Equiano's *Interesting Narrtive*', *Slavery and Abolition*, Vol.11, No.3 (1990), pp.217–27.
24. For Equiano's business affairs, see Paul Edwards, 'A Descriptive List of the Manu-

scripts in the Cambridgeshire Public Record Office Relating to the Will of Gustavus Vassa (Olaudah Equiano)', *Research in African Literature*, Vol.20, No.1, (Fall 1989), pp.471–80. For an essay on the comic elements which draw extensively on the present argument, see my article 'Humour in a Slave Narrative', in *Inter Arts*, *10* (Edinburgh 1990).

25. The Corresponding Societies were formed as radical units for working class self-improvement and political debate, often assembling in taverns. For an invaluable study, see Iain McCalman's *Radical Underworld: Prophets, Revolutionaries and Pornographers in London, 1795–1840* (Cambridge, 1988); also *The Memoirs of Thomas Hardy* (London, 1832); and Henry Collins, 'The London Corresponding Society', in John Saville (ed.), *Democracy and the Labour Movement* (London, 1954), pp.103–34. Equiano also wrote to Hardy from Scotland – see note 27.

26. McCalman, *Radical Underworld*, pp.28–9.

27. This letter was first printed, and discussed in Paul Edwards, '". . . written by himself"; A Manuscript Letter of Olaudah Equiano', *Notes and Queries*, Vol.XV, No.6, (NS) (June 1968), pp.222–5. It is reprinted in an appendix to the second edition of Paul Edwards (ed.), *Equiano's Travels*, (London, 1969), and is also included in the letters of Equiano, in Appendix I to Folarin Shyllon, *Black People in Britain, 1555–1833* (Oxford, 1977), pp.262–3. Another manuscript letter survives, written by Equiano to Hardy from Scotland. It is printed in Peter Fryer, *Staying Power: The History of Black People in Britain* (London, 1984), Appendix A, pp.403–4. In it, Equiano tells Hardy that he has written letters to the press whilst attending the Assembly of the Church of Scotland. One such letter was published in the *Edinburgh Evening Courant* of Saturday 6 May 1792. Since it has never been reprinted, I include it here:

> To the GENERAL ASSEMBLY of the CHURCH OF SCOTLAND now convened.
>   Gentlemen,
>
> Permit me, one of the oppressed natives of Africa, to offer you the warmest thanks of a heart glowing with gratitude on the unanimous decision of your debate of this day – it filled me with love towards you. It is no doubt the indispensable duty of every man, who is a friend to religion and humanity, to give his testimony against that iniquitous branch of commerce the slave trade. It does not often fall to the lot of individuals to contribute to so important moral and religious duty, as that of putting an end to a practice which may, without exaggeration, be stiled one of the greatest evils now existing on the earth – The Wise Man saith 'Righteousness exalteth a nation, but sin is a reproach to any people'. Prov.14.34.
>   Gentlemen, permit me, on behalf of myself and my much oppressed countrymen, to offer you the warmest effusions of a heart overflowing with hope for your pious efforts. It is my constant prayer that these endeavours may prove successful – And with best wishes for your health, happiness temporal and spiritual, I am, Gentlemen,
>   Your most respectful humble servant, &c. &c
>   GUSTAVUS VASSA the African.
>
> At Mr McLaren's, turner, second stair above Chalmers's Close, High Street – where my Narrative is to be had.
>   *Edinburgh, May 24. 1792.*

It is interesting that even in this expression of public piety there gleams Equiano's eye for a sale, as he advertises his book, and tells the people of Edinburgh where it can be purchased.

28. Edwards, 'A Descriptive List of the Manuscripts in the Cambridgeshire Record Office etc., pp.476–8, see note 20.

29. The letter is in the Granville Sharp Papers, earlier housed at Hardwicke Court,

Gloucestershire, now removed to the Gloucester County Record Office, in the course of which the letter seems to have gone missing. Fortunately, the letter had been copied by Christopher Fyfe. It is dated 22 February, 1811, and addressed to Sharp's niece, Jemima, who had enquired about Equiano.

30. Accounts of Wedderburn are to be found in Peter Fryer, Staying Power, pp.220–22 (see note 23); and McCalman, *Radical Underworld*, pp.50–53 (see note 22).
31. McCalman (ed.), Introduction to *The Horrors of Slavery etc.* (note 21). See also *Radical Underworld*, p.149.
32. Robert Wedderburn, *The Horrors of Slavery* (London, 1824), p.10.
33. See Robert Brake, 'The Lion Act is Over: Passive/Aggressive Patterns of Communication in American Negro Humour', *The Journal of Popular Culture*, Vol.IX, No.3 (Winter 1975), p.549. There is some discussion of this in Paul Edwards, *The Early African Presence in the British Isles*, Occasional Papers No.26, Centre of African Studies (Edinburgh University, 1990), pp.16–17.
34. McCalman, Radical Underworld, pp.148–9.
35. Quotations are from William Blake, *The Marriage of Heaven and Hell*.
36. *Report of the Lords of the Committee of the Privy Council . . . concerning the present State of the Trade of Africa, and particularly the Trade in Slaves* (1789), Part 1, No.14. The letter is dated 13 March 1788, and its argument is expressed in words almost identical to those of the *Narrative*. The text of this letter is given in the 1969 facsimile Reprint of Equiano, introduction, pp.lix–lxi, and in the appendix of Shyllon's *Black People in Britain*.
37. For Digges' letter see Equiano, 1969 facsimile of 1789 edition, Appendix B, p.xii.
38. For William Cuffay, see Fryer, *Staying Power*, pp.237–45.
39. McCalman, *The Horrors of Slavery*.

Skilled Workers or Marginalized Poor? The African Population of the United Kingdom, 1812–52

IAN DUFFIELD

The basic data for the study are derived from sources in Australian convict records on just over 200 cases of identifiable Afro-Blacks who were transported to Australia from the United Kingdom between 1812 and 1852. Occupational skill structure and literacy are used as proxies for social circumstances and compared with data on transported convicts and the general population of Britain. Arguments are also advanced as to why such a sample can be used to generalize about the Afro-Black population of the period. It is made clear that Afro-Blacks did not 'disappear' from Britain after the ending of slavery, as has been supposed. In the process, the existing historical literature is challenged and modified.

I. The Consensus on The Presence and Social Condition of Africans in Britain

In the historical literature on the history of Africans[1] in Britain, a consensus exists on Africans' lowly and oppressed place within the country's social formation, in the period of African slavery in Britain, which ended formally on 1 August 1834 (as in Britain's Caribbean colonies). However, a limitation for present purposes is that this literature is distinctly thin on the period from the 1830s to the 1850s.[2] Indeed, James Walvin's *Black and White* (1973) goes so far as to assert that this was a period of 'disintegration' of the African community in Britain.[3] The same view is still implicitly there in a later major work, Peter Fryer's *Staying Power* (1984). This proceeds from 'The Everyday Struggle, 1787–1833', packed with qualitative social information, to a sequence of short biographies of William Cuffay, Mary Seacole and Ira Aldridge plus some information on early Pan-Africanist visitors to Britain, as its portrayal of the next few decades.[4] As a consequence, the unwary reader might suppose that by early to mid-Victorian times, though some elite African individuals dwelt in Britain, there was little left worth mentioning in the way of plebeian African communities. Folarin Shyllon's two important books in the field (1974 and 1977)[5] both conclude with the formal end of African slavery in Britain following implementation of the 1833 Emancipation Act.

A rare exception to the consensus (whether explicit or implied) that plebeian African communities were residual or even more or less non-existent in Britain from the 1830s through to the mid-nineteenth century, occurs in Douglas Lorimer's *Colour, Class and the Victorians* (1978). Although empirical data on the presence and social condition of Africans in mid-nineteenth century Britian are peripheral to Lorimer's analysis of the genesis of mid-nineteenth century English racist ideology, later authors would have done well to note and build on the information that he gives in a short but detailed passage.[6] Since Lorimer's book has probably been read by every serious historian of Africans in Britain, it is odd that the hint has not hitherto been taken. Perhaps this is because historians of the African presence in the United Kingdom in the much-studied later seventeenth to early nineteenth century period, followed the broad research strategy that emerged in the early 1970s with Walvin's *Black and White*. Walvin concentrated his research on the extensive archival and printed sources on slavery in Britain and the subsequent struggle of African people and white abolitionists against it. Subsequent authors, including some such as Shyllon and Fryer who were less than charitable about his pioneering efforts, were happy enough to follow in his footsteps in this respect.[7] However, the tried and trusted Walvin research method, though it has been most fruitful even for his critics, cannot for self-evident reasons work effectively beyond 1833–34. Indeed, an important article by Lorimer, which argues convincingly that to a great extent by the 1790s slaves in Britain had *de facto* liberated themselves and made British metropolitan slavery moribund, by implication puts back the optimum period of utility of Walvin's approach by 40 years; that is, unless it is crudely assumed that the decline of African slavery was the death-knell for African communities in Britain.[8]

However, Lorimer's two works seem to suggest continuity rather than otherwise from the later eighteenth to the mid-nineteenth centuries in respect of a key question which must be asked about Africans in the first half of the nineteenth century, if their position within British society is to be better understood. The question is, what was their occupational and skill structure? Were they largely corralled into occupations and obstructed from access to potentially more secure, relatively higher status and better paid skilled and semi-skilled trades? Fryer makes much of a 1731 proclamation by the Lord Mayor of London, excluding Africans from apprenticeships in the City guilds.[9] He fails to note that the Lord Mayor only had jurisdiction over the limited area of the City, not the entire and rapidly growing metropolitan area, let alone the rest of Great Britain and Ireland. No evidence is offered that this triggered copycat policies elsewhere. Nor does Fryer demonstrate that this proclamation was effectively enforced and if so for how long.[10] The unwary reader, however, is left with the impression that from 1731 onwards there was a system of 'whites only' skilled work reservation operating at least in the greater London area, perhaps indicating a national trend. Whatever may have been the case in the City area of London in the 1730s, the evidence offered in this article suggests that in the first half of the nineteenth century the proportion of Africans in skilled and semi-skilled occupations was far from minimal, though substantially less than that in the population of England as a whole. Compared with the workforce resident in Ireland, they stand out as having a significantly higher proportion of skilled and semi-skilled manual workers than the Irish and an enormously smaller proportion of unskilled labourers.[11]

On occupations of Africans, Lorimer's *Colour, Class and the Victorians* offers the following mix. It suggests (as have other works) that in the mid-nineteenth century, as in the later eighteenth and early nineteenth centuries, there was a scattering of Africans in respectable occupations or even occasionally quite eminent positions. In the former category comes Linda Brent, a nurse and in the latter a major missionary figure, the Methodist Thomas Birch Freeman, born to an African father and a white mother near Winchester.[12] Next, African domestic servants, a strong feature of eighteenth-century Britain,[13] were still common enough in the mid-nineteenth century, though apparently becoming rare by the 1870s.[14] Thirdly (another *continuum* from the eighteenth century), African seamen are identified as a sizeable element in the crews of the Royal Navy and the British and some foreign merchant navies and as such common (if often transient) in British port cities.[15] Finally, Africans were to be observed begging on the streets of mid-Victorian cities (here Mayhew is cited among other sources), an indication that immiserisation was the lot of some of the total African population.[16] It is likely that this element would somewhat overlap the preceding two at times when the labour market was depressed. Mayhew's opinion was that 'negroes seldom, if ever, shirk work' and that though 'in the east end of London negro beggars are to be met with' they were 'seldom beggars by profession'.[17] Since Mayhew certainly strongly shared the hostility of the mid-nineteenth century British bourgeoisie to any hint of professional mendicancy and was generally thorough in his collection of information, this would seem to be good evidence of an element of immiseration. What is lacking (as in almost all the literature on the preceding period) is any basis for quantification.[18] The British censuses of 1841 and 1851 (let alone earlier, more problematic censuses) are useless for identifying Africans, for while they give place of birth, they give neither physical descriptions nor remarks

such as 'Negro', 'woman of colour', 'a black', 'mulatto', etc. Such remarks
were central in racist discourse but they have their utility for all that.
Lacking them, it is impossible to distinguish 'white' from 'black' colonially
or foreign-born persons, such as West Indians and United States' citizens,
while Africans born in Britain disappear entirely from view.

II. Archive Origins and Value of the Database of African Convicts

The database for this article is derived from the convict records in the
Archives Offices of New South Wales and Tasmania. From 1812 onwards,
the New South Wales *Indents of Convict Ships* (compiled as each convict
ship arrived at Sydney), give physical descriptions of all incoming convicts.
These were recorded for police purposes, to facilitate apprehension of
absconders. They enable clear identification of African convicts. To give
an example, James Godfrey, who arrived at Sydney aboard the ship
Norfolk on 12 February 1837, is described under the standard headings
'complexion', 'hair' and 'eyes' as having a copper coloured and pock-
pitted complexion, black and woolly hair and dark chestnut eyes.
Additionally, as often happened with entries for African convicts, to
make matters absolutely clear there was an additional remark under the
heading 'particular marks and scars; remarks'; here, the words 'half-cast'
occur.[19] George William Handy, who arrived at Sydney aboard the ship
Atlas on 19 October 1819, merely has the word 'Negro' written under the
heading 'complexion'. The compiling clerk saw no need to add details
about his hair and eyes.[20] In this instance, 'Negro', not a physical description at all but a social construct with implied attributes of physical
appearance, indicates this man was an African. To give another common
variant, Thomas Jones, who arrived in Sydney aboard the *Batavia* on
5 April 1818, has 'man of colour' (another social construct) for complexion, but black for hair and eyes.[21] In many instances the word 'black'
is recorded under all three headings of 'complexion', 'hair', and 'eyes', as
in the case of Samuel Munday.[22] All the New South Wales *Indents* in the
period under survey give information on convicts' occupation, place of
trial and 'native place' (that is, birthplace), as well as details of their
offences and sentences. Female convicts were recorded in exactly the
same way. Thus, Marian Mitchell is described as having a black complexion, black and woolly hair and black eyes, and we are further told that
she had a 'broad' nose, 'thick' lips and was a 'woman of colour'.[23] After
1826, the New South Wales *Indents* add a further range of information,
from which the item selected for use in this article is literacy, recorded in
terms of whether an individual could read and write, read only, or could
neither read nor write. It will be noted that the clerks' descriptions of

these African convicts picked on what was stereotypical in the white image of African people's appearance. It is not suggested that these are adequate or accurate descriptions in the fullest sense of human beings' physical appearances but they are adequate for constructing the database used in this article. All it takes to log incoming New South Wales African convicts transported from the United Kingdom is the time and stamina to read through tens of thousands of *Indent* entries, an arduous but not a difficult task.[24]

In the case of convicts who were transported to Van Diemen's Land (Tasmania), the research task is more difficult. The Van Diemen's Land *Indents*, though a rich source on convicts generally, do not contain physical descriptions and therefore cannot be used to identify Africans. Additionally, not all these *Indents* have survived and the extant ones are not all located in one place.[25] However, other classes of Van Diemen's Land convict records can be pieced together which do provide the necessary starting point of physical descriptions, plus the other categories of data used in the article. These are: Con 18, *Description Lists of Male Convicts, 1825–53*; Con 19, *Description Lists of Female Convicts 1841–53*; Con 23, *Alphabetical Registers of Male Convicts 1803–1849*; Cons 31–34, *Conduct Registers of Male Convicts*; and Cons 40–41, *Conduct Registers of Female Convicts*. From this mosaic of sources not only can identifying descriptions be located but also the other categories of data from the New South Wales *Indents* utilized in this contribution.

These sources yielded 193 African males convicted in the United Kingdom (other Africans were transported from the West Indian Colonies, Mauritius and the Cape of Good Hope plus a scattering from other colonies, but these are not directly relevant to the present purpose).[27] Two other males were added, both Africans born in England but who had freely emigrated to the southern hemisphere. One, Joseph Williams was a cook and butler, born in Bath but convicted at Auckland Supreme Court, New Zealand, on 1 December 1847 and again on 2 December 1847, of stealing from a dwelling house and receiving stolen property respectively. He was sentenced to ten and seven years transportation to run consecutively.[28] Charles Hall, a sailmaker, ploughman and labourer born in Newport, Isle of Wight, was convicted of burglary at Adelaide in the free colony of South Australia on 15 November 1842. He was sentenced to transportation for life.[29] This article provides abundant evidence of Africans migrating into the UK during the period 1812–52. These two cases show that others were also voluntarily emigrating from the UK.[30] Since these two men were United Kingdom-born Africans, it seemed appropriate to include them, despite their colonial convictions.

But what of African women? In fact, only six were identified, all from the 1830s NSW *Indents*. 195 males is just about sufficient from which to draw some tentative quantitative conclusions. But there is no point in quantifying the data on six individuals, so the evidence on them will be dealt with purely qualitatively. Only around one-seventh of all the convicts transported to Australia were women. But here we have a ratio of 32.67 men for every woman! This is surely a striking confirmation of the general supposition that in the United Kingdom, African males strongly outnumbered African females, a feature reinforcing the generally low proportion of all females to all males transported, to produce this mere handful of instances;[31] fortunately, the information from United Kingdom legal and semi-legal records[32] on most of these women is quite rich. Norma Myers, in her study of the 'Black Presence' in London through criminal records, 1780–1830, found 96 indictments of black males but only 11 of black females.[33] Although this is not so overwhelming a ratio of males to females as in the present instance, it too supports the view that even allowing for the fact that most crimes were commited by males (Myers states over 80 per cent in the eighteenth century),[34] with a consequent under-representation of females in criminal records, the African population of the United Kingdom was very predominantly male. This is said, bearing in mind the propensity of some historians (especially those whom, like the author, are males) to go curiously blind when confronted with evidence of women in history.

Certain categories of people have been carefully excluded from the database. These include all instances where the physical descriptions in the sources are equivocal. Very large numbers of convicts transported from the United Kingdom are listed as having dark or even black eyes, black hair and dark or swarthy skins, but one would need to be an adherent of the Joel Rogers school of Black History to suppose that this normally or necessarily indicates proximate African ancestry. In between 20 and 30 cases where the physical descriptions were conclusive enough, the other data were missing and so these individuals have been excluded; like other bureaucratic compilations, Australian convict records are not tailor-made for the perfect convenience of subsequent historians. Persons of South Asian and Polynesian origin have also been excluded, since the remit of this volume is specifically the *African* presence in the United Kingdom. However, 'African' has been taken to include Africans of the Diaspora, who in fact are the large majority of the 201 individuals whose brushes with the criminal law had the unintended effect of offering evidence over the first half of the nineteenth century on Africans in the United Kingdom. 201 cases may seem little enough. They certainly cannot tell us the whole truth about the African presence in Britain in their period. But, in extenuation, it can be pointed out that scholars have written books on the entire African presence in Britain on the basis of a no larger African cast.

In itself, the database of 195 male convicts plus the six females is obviously useful. But it is much the more so inasmuch as historians of Australia have analysed very large samples of the general body of trans- ported convicts, thus permitting comparisons which can reveal crucial differences in matters of literacy and occupational skill structure between these African males and the general body of male convicts transported from the United Kingdom to eastern Australia. From interrogating these comparisons it is possible to pose answers to the question addressed by the study. If the evidence suggests that Africans were overwhelmingly restricted to low skill (and therefore insecure and low-pay) occupations and had very low levels of literacy, then it may be presumed that immiserisation was the common if not universal lot. Contrary findings would at least suggest that Britain's African residents were an enter- prising lot, capable of finding strategies around institutional and social barriers placed in their path. More controversially, they might suggest that such barriers were not always formidable, possibly not always present.

III. The Debate Over Transported Convicts and Its Relevance

There is an obvious objection to proceeding along these lines. Put at its simplest, can African *convicts* transported from the United Kingdom to eastern Australia stand as a proxy for the unquantifiable but certainly vastly larger numbers of plebeian Africans living in Britain who never fell foul of the courts?[35] Fortunately, we are exempt from constructing a debate *ab origine* on this crucial question. It has already been done for us, in principle, by two categories of historians. These are social historians of United Kingdom crime; and social historians of the convicts transported to Australia. These are two overlapping fields of enquiry which possess rich literatures. It is likely that what holds good for the totality of people transported from the United Kingdom to eastern Australia – and here we are talking about at least 150,000 people – will also broadly hold good for these 201 Africans; or at least for the 195 males among them, if it is countered that the six females are too few to generalize from.

Historians of both crime within the United Kingdom and transportation to Australia can be divided into conservative and radical wings. George Rudé and David Philips, for example, have undermined the conservative view that nineteenth-century British crime was typically commited by members of a distinct and indeed hereditary 'criminal class'.[36] Instead, their evidence strongly suggests that criminal offenders were *typically* (no-one is suggesting in every instance) ordinary men and women of the lower classes for whom crime was not an exclusive way of life but who sometimes resorted to theft in order to supplement their meagre incomes. However, the literature on Australia's transported convicts was until much more recently dominated by the work of Australian scholars, such as Lloyd Robson, A.G.L. Shaw and Manning Clark, who clung fast to the view that at least predominantly the convicts were a determined set of hereditary social deviants who, in only too many cases, had led lives of systematic crime, idleness and dissipation prior to transportation, especially in the case of the females.[37] Lloyd Robson ends his major study of transportation with the conclusion that the convicts were neither simply 'village Hampdens' nor merely 'ne'er-do-wells from the city slums', but that weighed in the scales, the balance tips towards the latter. Robson's continuing vigorous influence is shown in some very recent works.[38] However, one recent study, *Convict Workers*, written by a team of scholars from the University of New South Wales, rudely challenges head-on this weight of opinion.[39]

The first major quantitative work on Australian convicts since Robson's in 1965, its acerbic tone towards almost every other scholar who had written in the field, especially in the very extensive contributions of its editor, Stephen Nicholas, earned it some pretty dusty reviews.[40] But it is not so easily dismissed for all that.[41] Unlike those it attacked, the book had absorbed some vital lessons from the radical revisionaries of the social history of British crime and is extremely well versed in the up-to-date social history of the British and Irish working classes, as well as deploying vital comparative elements from the rich literature on slave societies. Here are *Convict Workers'* findings on three key points, as summarised in its introduction:

> The convicts transported to New South Wales were ordinary British and Irish working class men and women. They were not professional and habitual criminals, recruited from a distinct class and trained to crime from the cradle.[42]

> The proportion of convicts in the skilled, semi-skilled and unskilled occupational categories was roughly the same as the percentages of each skill class for the English workforce in 1841. Our statistical tests confirmed that the convicts came from the same occupational population as the free workers of England.[43]

> Three-quarters of the English convicts who arrived in New South Wales could read and/or write, a significantly higher percentage than the average for all English workers (58 per cent) who could sign the marriage registers.[44]

These conclusions were partly based on an extensive series of statistical tests, partly on a reinterpretation of the evidence used by previous scholars, including those they were attacking, especially Lloyd Robson. The reliability of occupational data in the New South Wales *Indents* (which provided the database for the book in the form of a sample of 19,711 convicts arriving in New South Wales between 1817 and 1840, of whom 2,210 were women arriving between 1825 and 1840) was assessed by 'cross testing the male convicts' county of trial with regional occupation skills'. The results suggested anything but a random geographical distribution of the convicts in the UK in relation to their recorded occupations; on the contrary, a close fit emerges. Further, a high proportion of their crimes were work related.[45] This can be interpreted as evidence of a strategy by which workers, operating a subordinate class moral economy in opposition to that of their class superiors and the state, supplemented their legal wages through depredations on their employers' goods and money. Such practices are common enough in any wage labour society, including modern ones. Indeed, they are sometimes indulged in wholesale by owners and managers too, although in these instances the social meaning of the predations must be somewhat different. *Convict Workers* also compares occupations given in the New South Wales *Indents* for male convicts arriving 1817 to 1828 with the record of how they were employed in Australia as recorded in the *Census of New South Wales November 1828*.[46] It was found that in the case of those convicts who had arrived with skills in demand in the colonial labour market, there was a strong match; for instance 70 per cent in the case of skilled urban workers.[47] In comparing male convict occuptions from the New South Wales *Indents* with those represented in the United Kingdom's 1841 census, a generally good match was also found.[48] It is true that Robson, for one, was sceptical about convicts' occupations as listed in the New South Wales and Van Diemen's Land *Indents*, although he himself carefully collected such data.[49] However, if one employs his index, in nearly every instance the page references to 'occupations' lead the reader to discussions of the convicts' *offences*, which rather begs the question as to whether they typically supplemented legitimate earnings by crime, or were 'professional criminals' living off the proceeds of crime.

I am persuaded that *Convict Workers* has, on balance, the better of this argument and that the same is the case when the book discusses how reliable the *Indent* information is on the convicts' literacy.[50] The high literacy rates they found are only incredible if it is assumed that the convicts – whether male or female[51] – were largely members of a criminal class who could be relied on to proffer false information under any circumstances and who in their pre-transportation lives were utterly different from virtuous plebeians. This study accepts that *Convict Workers* demonstrates that the convicts transported to New South Wales were a rough cross-section of the lower classes of the United Kingdom. It is unlikely that the convicts transported to Van Diemen's Land were radically different in this respect. The old belief that those sent there were the worst of a bad lot rests largely on sensational but untypical stories, such as that of Pearce, the cannibal absconder from the Sarah Island penal station.[52] Following from the argument conducted so far in this section, it is suggested that the 195 African male convicts can stand as a rough proxy for their far more numerous unconvicted fellows who remained in the United Kingdom. The females are too few for quantitative purposes, but as will be seen, treated as qualitative cases they seem much like other lower class African women in the United Kingdom as represented in the existing literature and indeed much like their white female convict sisters as presented in *Convict Workers*.[53]

IV. The Question of Occupations and Skills

Analysis of the occupations and skills of the African males produces both upset and confirmation of some of the suppositions within the existing literature on the African presence in Britain. Their occupations were ranked according to the skill classification devised by Stephen Nicholas and Peter Shergold,[54] enabling the following comparisons to be made with the *Convict Workers*' male sample and the occupational data from the 1841 English census:

TABLE 1

SKILLS OF AFRICAN MALE CONVICTS, ENGLISH CONVICTS AND
ENGLISH MALE WORKFORCE (PERCENTAGES) (a)

Nicholas-Shergold Skill Class	1841 English Census	*Convict Workers* English Convicts	African Convicts (b)
1. Unskilled urban	8.2	21.6	8.2
2. Unskilled rural	20.3	4.9	1.0
3. Skilled building	7.9	8.1	4.1
4. Skilled urban	32.4	39.2	16.9
5. Skilled rural	6.9	7.0	1.0
6. Dealers	5.2	2.6	—
7. Public service (c)	5.7	4.0	36.4
8. Professional	2.9	1.5	2.0
9. Domestic service	4.6	11.2	30.3
10. Other	5.9	—	—

(a)   Table adapted from *Convict Workers*, p.72;
(b)   sources in column four as detailed in section II of this study;
(c)   includes merchant seamen as well as members of the armed forces (officers and other ranks) and excisemen.

What is most striking here is the very different distribution, in many respects, of occupations and skills among the Africans to either the distribution in the 1841 census or the *Convict Workers* sample. That only one per cent of the Africans were unskilled rural workers and another one per cent skilled rural workers strongly confirms all impressions that this was an element of the British population that was overwhelmingly urban in location right up to the mid-nineteenth century. Nor does it appear that Africans were more likely to be unskilled urban workers than the 1841 population of England was; indeed, these Africans were less so than the English convicts. In skills four and five, skilled building and skilled urban (both include semi-skilled occupations), their representation, though far from derisory, is only roughly half that in the preceding two columns. Nevertheless, any notion that it was almost impossible for Africans to enter into and practice skilled and semi-skilled trades is contradicted. Further positive evidence would be needed to establish without serious doubt whether African under-representation in skilled trades was primarily a consequence of institutionalized barriers against them, or emanated from some other circumstances. However, a more likely explanation than 'institutionalized barriers' is that so many of them were seafarers, an occupation group many of whose skills were of little demand in employment ashore, or domestic servants, neither of which could redeploy easily into artisanal trades. Among dealers – shopkeepers, merchants, salesmen, etc. – they are totally unrepresented. We may conclude that African businessmen, even petty shopkeepers, were a rarity.[55] But among seafarers and domestic servants they are hugely over-represented, these two skills accounting for two-thirds of the total.

One of the vagaries of skill classifications is that unless they are unhelpfully proliferated into an impossibly unwieldy number of skill categories, they are bound at times to lump like with not-so-like. Thus the Nicholas–Shergold skill 7, 'public service', includes army and navy officers and excisemen as well as common seafarers (naval and merchant) and soldiers of non-commissioned officer rank and below. It is important to note that the Africans in skill 7 include no military or naval officers or excisemen. They are overwhelmingly common seafarers, variously listed in the indents as seaman (42), mariner (4) sailor (14), ship's cook (2) ship's servant/steward (2), cabin boy (1), boy sailor (1), able seaman (2). Additionally there are three soliders.[56] Even without the soldiers, the seafarers alone considerably outnumber the 58 men in the database who were various kinds of domestic servant. Additionally, momentarily crossing the Nicholas–Shergold skill classification lines, there are a number of others who have a waterfront smell to their occupations. Among the skilled urban workers are three sailmakers, a caulker, three watermen and two boatmen. Adding these to the seafarers, as many as 39.5 per cent of the data base are accounted for. This is an astonishing concentration in a structurally related set of occupations. Robson's occupation table for male convicts has ten per cent as transport and communications workers (a much broader category than seafarers since it includes such land transport occupations as carter, drayman and waggoner) and three per cent for service personnel (which would include soldiers and marines as well as Royal Navy personnel).[57] By contrast, seafarers alone account for 35 per cent of the African male convicts, certainly several times the disguised percentage of seafarers in Robson's data.

This provides powerful evidence for marginalization as a strong feature of the African population, not so much because of the self-evident hardships of life at sea and its meagre rewards for rank-and-file seafarers, as because of the intermittent nature of employment and the likelihood of periods on shore without adequate means of support. As early as the mid-eighteenth century, seamen in the British merchant service had become largely proletarianized, with meagre promotion prospects and difficulty in finding work ashore other than casual waterfront labouring.[58] It is unlikely that this trend was reversed over the following hundred years, a period when British captialism was progressively emerging and with it (by definition) an intensifying proletarianization of labour was occurring. Because of their poor prospects ashore, seafarers were very vulnerable to times of rapidly falling demand for their labour, such as the end of the Napoleonic Wars.

In 1815, many naval ships were paid off and a glut of demobilized men were seeking employment on merchant ships.[59] Demobilization in 1815 was followed by a depression in the trading economy and therefore in shipping, which was at its most intense from 1816 to around 1819/1820. Thus, this was no mere short-term crisis for unemployed seamen in British ports. In the light of this, it is of particular significance that 37 individuals, or 54.5 per cent of the 68 African seafarers transported, were tried in the period 1812–19.[60] It is hard to escape the conclusion that this was a bad time to be a demobilized African seafarer in Britain. Of course, white seafarers were no doubt also suffering hardship and being pushed by hardship into crime during this period. However, they were, it would seem, a much smaller fraction of the total white than of the total African workforce. Any serious downturn in employment for African seamen would be likely to hit disporportionately hard the bigger African communities in port cities where they were concentrated. Some naval seamen received significant earnings in pay and prize money at the time they were demobilized, but that would not necessarily afford even short-term security. One hazard was the sharks waiting ashore to relieve them of their cash. When Joseph Uxbridge, an African sailor, was paid off from *H.M.S. L'Aigle* at Woolwich on 17 August 1815, he received the then substantial sum of a little over £84. But he was picked up even before coming ashore by another African, Jacob Morris, who promised to show Uxbridge and some of his shipmates a good time and invited Uxbridge to lodge with him. Perhaps Morris, a 57-year-old cook and seaman, had fallen on hard times too, although this is not clear from the evidence. In the event, after much drinking and a search for women (Morris acting the pimp), Morris knocked Uxbridge down in a dark alley and stole £60 off him. On conviction, Morris received a capital sentenced, but the sentenced was commuted to transportation for life.[61]

The 30.3 per cent of male African convicts in domestic service, compared with only 4.6 per cent of the male population of England in the 1841 census or even the 11.2 per cent among the English convicts in the *Convict Workers* database[62] strongly suggests that throughout the first half of the nineteenth century this remained one of the most common occupations for male Africans in Britain, a continuity from the period when slavery was the usual status of the resident African population. Domestic service was, of course, a highly stratified occupation; there was all the difference in the world between specialized upper servants, such as gentlemen's servants (valets), skilled cooks (as opposed to mere plain cooks) and butlers, as employed in wealthy aristocratic households and mere general indoor and/or outdoor servants in middle class ones.

Thirty-four of the 59 African males in domestic service (59.3 per cent), were variously recorded in the Australian convict records as house servants, servants or indoor servants. To these at the lower end of the domestic service skill range, and we may assume terms of employment, may be added one pot boy and five grooms making 67.8 per cent in the lowest categories of service. However, stated the other way round, 32.2 per cent were upper servants, which it is hard to imagine was not at least comparable to – perhaps higher than – the proportion of upper servants among all domestics, although general data are lacking.[63] Ten were cooks, one a pastry cook[64] (a highly specialist skill), five were gentlemen's servants, one each a footman and a steward. Clearly, there was a substantial element among the African servants in Britain in the first half of the nineteenth century who as upper servants had comparatively advantageous terms of employment and cannot be regarded as marginalized poor. Yet, they faced a serious problem for all that. In precisely the period that this study discusses, according to Theresa McBride, domestic service in England was being restructured. The eclipsing of aristocratic employment by the demand from the new middle class, which strongly preferred female domestics to males, diminished the relative (and perhaps absolute?) demand for male servants.[65] Only 4.6 per cent of English males were in domestic employment in 1841 (see Table 1 above) but a striking 14.5 per cent of the combined female and male workforce were so employed.[66] The two-thirds of African male domestics who were lower servants were presumably particularly vulnerable to this process of feminization of domestic service. It could be the case that as the number of African lower servants declined absolutely, that of African upper servants declined less slowly, so inflating their relative numbers, and disguising the real secular decline.

The indication that almost one-in-three African males were in domestic service marks them off, as much as the high proportion of seafarers, from the general population and throws light on under-representation in some other skill groups. Equally, it seems likely that the restructuring of domestic service described above was inexorably undercutting employment opportunities for male Africans in an area in which traditionally a high proportion of them had been employed. Whether displaced African servants were able to find other types of employment, and thus mitigate or overcome the effect of dwindling employment opportunities in domestic service, remains an important question which cannot as yet be answered. However, given that apprenticeships into artisanal trades normally commenced in early adolescence and entailed several years on-the-job training with little more than a maintenance wage, the prospects for adult male unemployed servants moving in that direction rather than into the pool of general labourers cannot have been promising. Quite probably, many could not find secure alternative employment, with immiserization and marginalization as the consequences.

By contrast, in the Nicholas–Shergold skill 8, professional (a rather varied category which in fact includes such occupations as clerk, entertainer and sportsmen), two per cent of male Africans compared with 2.9 per cent of English males in the 1841 census and 1.5 per cent in the *Convict Workers* male sample, might suggest that in these occupations, proportionately Africans were as well established as the general population of England. But, as in the case of the other skill categories in which very few Africans appear, the very paucity of the numbers concerned – four in skill 8 – dictates that the data must be interpreted with extreme caution. Of the four men who were 'professionals', William Dines[67] and Robert Williams[68] were both musicians; George Barrow[69] was an advocate (and as such certainly at the top of the ladder of all the Africans, male or female, in skill); and William Thompson[70] was a clerk and letter sorter. We can conclude the existence of African 'professionals' (using the term to include the range of occupations in this Nicholas–Shergold skill category) but it cannot be said with confidence that they were statistically proportionate to this element in the general population, although this remains a possibility.

If a comparison is made between the African males and the population of Ireland, then a very different picture emerges, of an African minority which, if in some though not all respects lower down the skill scale than English males, was very much higher up it than the Irish in their native country. Of course, the structure of the Irish economy dictated a different occupational mix in the Irish population to that in Britain. Nevertheless, to compare Africans in Britain with the Irish in Ireland does reveal that in the United Kingdom as a whole, they were not at the bottom of the occupational ladder.

TABLE 2

SKILLS OF IRISH MALE CONVICTS AND IRISH MALE WORKFORCE
(PERCENTAGES)[a]

Skill Class	1841 Irish Census	*Convict Workers* Irish Convicts
Labourer	55.4	77.1
Textile worker	7.1	5.9
Farmer	20.7	1.9
Other artisan	10.5	16.0
White collar workers	4.9	2.6
Other	1.5	3.2

(a)   *Source:* Nicholas, *Convict Workers*, p.73.

It is immediately apparent that the Irish were very much more likely to be labourers than the African convicts in the database.[71] None of the Africans were in fact textile workers by their first listed trade in the Australian convict sources (one was a silk-weaver according to his second listed trade). African skilled building and skilled urban workers combined amounted to 21 per cent of the database, which compares very favourably with 10.5 per cent in the 1841 Irish census and 16 per cent of Irish convicts enumerated as 'other artisan' in Table 2. The very small percentages opposite 'other' in Table 2 indicate how few Irish males were seafarers or domestic servants, compared to the percentages in the African convict database. Since a high proportion of Irish farmers were small peasant tenant farmers, even in non-famine times often living hard lives, this element, quite absent among the Africans, hardly redresses the balance in favour of the Irish.[72] It is hard to escape the conclusion that whatever relative disadvantage was suffered by African males in the United Kingdom in the first half of the nineteenth century, that suffered by the Irish in Ireland by comparison was substantially greater.

In other respects the African males stand in marked contrast to the

comparative data on occupation on both convicts in general and the
United Kingdom workforce in general. In the *Convict Workers'* sample
there were 341 occupations and as many as 1,024 in the 1841 census.[73] As
Table 3 below shows, among the African males there were only 53
occupations in all among first listed trades, while second and third listed
trades[74] add only a further nine occupations. Two factors largely account
for this. The major one is that almost two-thirds of the African males in
the database were either seafarers or domestic servants of one kind or
another. But the small size of the database would also tend to under-
represent the range of occupations among the African population.

Missing from Table 3 are the skills of an industrializing Britain.
Engineering workers such as boilermakers, or factory operatives and
miners are not represented. Neither are the natives who built the railways
of the 1830s and 1840s. The occupation mix (other than seafarers)
essentially relates to the receding eighteenth-century world, not the
emerging mid-nineteenth century one. In the longer term, Africans in
traditional skilled and semi-skilled urban occupations may have been
faced with de-skilling and marginalization by the technological changes of
the industrial revolution. Since there is no reason to believe that they
'died out' as an element of the British population after the early 1850s, we
may perhaps even project this marginalization into the second half of
the nineteenth century, although positive evidence would be needed to
test this.

V. Skills in Relation to Place of Residence and Place of Origin

There is little point in scrutinizing the smaller occupational skill elements
among the African males in relation to location, since random factors are
only too likely to produce misleading information. But the picture that
emerges from looking at skills 1, 3 and 4 (which have been combined in
this section), 7 and 9, in relation to place of trial, confirms not only the
high degree of urbanization of Africans in Britain but also that at the
times of their trials they were generally residing in places consistent with
their trades.

No less than 13 of the unskilled urban labourers out of 16 were tried in
named cities or towns, nine in the London area. 37 of the building workers
and skilled urban workers out of 41 were tried in named towns, 20 of them
in the London area. 47 of the seafarers out of 68 were tried in named ports
(here Chester and Exeter have been excluded but their location adjacent
to estuaries will be noted). Proximity to the coast seems to operate almost
as strongly among the domestic servants as the seafarers. Forty-eight of
them, at least, had residence in coastal or estuarine towns, no less than 32

TABLE 3

SKILLS OF BLACK MALE CONVICTS ACCORDING TO NICHOLAS–SHERGOLD
SKILL CLASSIFICATION (SAMPLE OF 195)[a]

Skill Category	Total (No./ % of total database)	1st Trades (No. of incidences)	2nd Trade (No. of incidences)	3rd Trade (No. of incidences)
1. Unskilled urban	16 / 8.2	Errand Boy 2 Labourer 11 Slop boy 1 Sweep 2	-	-
2. Unskilled rural	2 / 1.0	Farm labourer 2	-	-
3. Skilled building	8 / 4.1	Bricklayer 1 Brickmaker 1 Carpenter 2 Mason 1 Plasterer 1 Stone cutter 2	Cane worker 1	-
4. Skilled urban	33 / 16.9	Barber 5 Blacksmith 1 Boatman 3 Cabinetmaker 1 Caulker 1 Compositor 1 Cooper 1 Cutler 1 Harnessmaker 1 Nailor 1 Ropemaker 2 Saw maker 1 Tailor 4 Turner 1 Sailmaker 3 Shoemaker 2 Umbrella maker 1 Waterman 2 Wire coverer 1	Ploughman 1 Servant 1 Silk weaver 1	Labourer 2
5. Skilled rural	2 / 1.0	Cow boy 1 Ploughman 1	Reaper 1	-
6. Dealers	-	-	-	-
7. Public service (b)	71 / 36.4 (seafarers, 68 / 34.9)	Able seaman 2 Boy sailor 1 Cabin boy 1 Mariner 5 Sailor 14 Seaman 41 Ship servant 1 Sea cook 2 Ship steward 1 Soldier 3	Barber 1 Cook 5 Drummer 1 Officer's servt. 1 Seaman 1 Servant 1	Cook 1 -
8. Professionals	4 / 2.1	Advocate 1 Clerk 1 Musician 2	Letter sorter 1 Servant 1	-
9. Domestic service	59 / 30.3	Cook 11 Footman 1 Gent's servant 5 Groom 5 Pastry Cook 1 Pot boy 1 Servant 34 Steward 1	Baker 1 Butler 1 Carpenter 1 Carter 1 Cook 1 Groom 1 Labourer 1 Seaman 1 Servant 3 Waiter 1	Steward 1
10. Other	-	-	-	-

(a) *Source:* as listed in section II;
(b) the database contains seafarers and soldiers only. First, second and third occupations
     are listed in the sequence given in the sources.

TABLE 4

AFRICAN MALE CONVICTS' OCCUPATION IN RELATION TO PLACE OF TRIAL[a]

Nicholas-Shergold Skill Class	Place of Trial (numbers.)
1. Unskilled urban	Cork 1; Kent 1; London/Middlesex 9; Liverpool 2; Northampton 1; Surrey 2; total 16
3 & 4, Skilled building & skilled urban	Adelaide 1; Bristol 3; Derby 1; Edinburgh 2; Kent 3; Lancaster 1; Liverpool 2; London/Middlesex 20; Manchester 1; Perth 1; Plymouth 3; Southampton 1; Surrey 1; York 1; total 41
7. Public service (seafarers only)	Aberdeen 1; Bristol 4; Chester 3; Dublin 1; Durham 1; Essex 3; Exeter 1; Flint 1; Glasgow 1; Kent 6; London/Middlesex 28; Lancaster 2; Liverpool 6; Newcastle-on-Tyne 1; Nottingham 1; Shrewsbury 1; Southampton 3; Surrey 3; Winchester 1; total 68
9. Domestic service	Auckland NZ 1; Buckingham 1; Chester 1; Cork 3; Edinburgh 1; Dublin 2; Essex 2; Kirton Lincs. 1; Lancaster 4; Limerick 1; Liverpool 2; London/Middlesex 32; Preston 1; Southampton 1; Stafford 1; Surrey 4; Sussex 1; total 59

(a)   Sources as listed in section II.

in the London area, undoubtedly the city with the greatest market for domestic servants' labour. All of this is highly consistent with their occupations as recorded in Australian convict records. Indeed, if one takes the entire 195 men in the database, no less than 94, or 48.2 per cent lived in the London–Middlesex area, in contrast with the 17 per cent in Robson's one-in-twenty sample of all male convicts.[75] Even if allowance is made for the fact that people resident in this area are over-represented among the convicts as a whole in comparison to the proportion of the population living in it, it appears that up to the 1830s the capital and its immediate environs had a disproportionate amount of the total African population of the United Kingdom.

The London–Middlesex share of the African male database does diminish in the last 12 years of transportation to eastern Australia; 20 out of the 41 tried between 1830 and 1839 but only six out of 21 tried between 1840 and 1852. However, caution should be exercised here. This apparent 'decline' partly reflects the secular decline in the total proportion of London area convictions for transportable offences, compared with those in, for instance, the industrializing areas of the United Kingdom. Bearing this in mind, London apparently remained the metropolis of the African presence in Britain throughout the period under scrutiny. In the period 1840–52 Liverpool provided only two African convicts, nowhere else outside London more than one. Although this is not to say that African communities may not have survived elsewhere in Britain, this is a good indicative evidence that in London Africans remained present, probably in sufficient numbers to have formed communities, in the mid-nineteenth century.

TABLE 5

BIRTHPLACE OF ALL AFRICAN MALE CONVICTS BY REGION
NUMBERS/PERCENT)[a]

England	Ireland	Scotland	Africa	North America	West Indies	Other
38/19.5	3/1.5	3/1.5	15/7.7	65/33.3	60/30.8	11/5.6

(a)   Sources as listed in section II.

TABLE 6

AFRICAN MALE CONVICTS' OCCUPATIONS IN RELATION TO BIRTHPLACE[a]

Nicholas-Shergold Skill Class	Birthplace (numbers.)
1. Unskilled urban	*England:* Kent 1; Liverpool 1; London 4; total 6 *Scotland:* Stirling 1; total 1 *North America:* America 1; Halifax NS 1; Boston 1; St Johns NB 1; total 4 *West Indies:* Antigua 1; Demerara 1; Guadeloupe 2; St Vincent 1; total 5
3 & 4. Skilled building/urban	*England:* Bristol 1; Hull 1; Isle of Wight 1; Kent 1; London/Middlesex 10; Liverpool 1; total 15 *Scotland:* Dundee 1; Edinburgh 1; total 2 *Africa:* Africa 1; total 1 *North America:* America 3; Philadelphia 1; total 4 *West Indies:* Barbados 2; Bermuda 1; Jamaica 4; Martinique 1; St Domingo 1; St Kitts 2; Tobago 1; West Indies 3; total 15 *Other:* Isle of Man 1; Portugal 1; St Helena 1; unknown 1; total 4
7 Public service (seafarers/soldiers only)	*England:* Bristol 1; Isle of Wight 1; London 2; Liverpool 2; total 5 *Ireland:* Dublin 1; total 1 *Africa:* Africa 5; total 5 *North America:* America 11; Annapolis Va. 1; Baltimore 3; Boston 1; New York 4; New Brunswick 2; Nova Scotia 6; Philadelphia 5; Maine 1; total 34 *West Indies:* Barbados 3; Jamaica 6; Martinique 2; St Croix 1; St Domingo 1; St Lucia 1; St Thomas 1; Tobago 2; West Indies 1; total 18 *Other:* Germany 1; Lima Peru 1; Mauritius 3; Portugal 1; unknown 1; total 7
9. Domestic service	*England:* Bath 1; Birmingham 1; Brighton 1; Bristol 1; Buckinghamshire 1; London 3; Ludlow 1; Somerset 1; Wanstead 1; total 11 *Ireland::* Dublin 1; Kerry 1; total 2 *Africa:* Africa 4; Benin (Nigeria) 1; Gorée 1; Sierra Leone 3; total 9 *North America:* America 6; Maryland 1; New Brunswick 1; New Orleans 3; New York 4; Nova Scotia 1; Pennsylvania 2; Philadelphia 2; total 20 *West Indies:* Antigua 1; Barbados 2; Bermuda 2; Cuba 1; Dominica 1; Jamaica 4; Martinique 1; Nevis 1; St Kitts 1; St Thomas 1; West Indies 2; total 17

(a)   Sources as listed in section II.

Tables 5 and 6 reveal a most important though not surprising aspect of the African males; they were very much a migrant community, even without taking into account migration within the United Kingdom. Those born in the United Kingdom are strongly represented among the urban workers, both skilled and unskilled, but among the seafarers and domestic servants they are heavily outnumbered by those born elsewhere. Given that those born in England, Ireland and Scotland form 22.5 per cent of the total database but 41.5 per cent of those in building and urban skilled trades, this would suggest such Africans had a distinct advantage over African immigrants. On the other hand United Kingdom-born Africans also form 43.8 per cent of the urban unskilled workers, though this finding is somewhat limited in utility by the fact that such workers were one of the smaller though not smallest fractions of the entire database. Clearly domestic service and seafaring were dominated by African-North Americans and African-West Indians. Indeed, they jointly provide two-thirds of the *entire* African male database. In the case of the seafarers their migration to the United Kingdom was, of course, occupational. In the case of the servants, it was migration to what an earlier era had seen established as a stereotypical African occupation.

But what induced these people to migrate to the United Kingdom, beyond the will of New World masters moving to Britain with an African servant in some pre-1833 cases and the imperatives of their occupation in the case of seafarers? Lorimer suggests one motivation; Britain was a magnet for Africans from parts of the New World, especially the United States, which retained slavery longer than the United Kingdom.[76] It is also likely that many West Indian and North American slaves were aware well before 1833 that property rights in slaves had become, *de facto*, difficult to maintain in the United Kingdom.[77] The main sources used for this article do not provide quantifiable data on motives for such migration. However, in the case of one man in the database, Thomas Day, a West Indian seaman convicted in Kent on 24 July 1820,[78] there is good qualitative evidence that he fled to Britain to escape from slavery. He was encountered at Sarah Island penal station, Macquarie Harbour, Van Diemen's Land, on 11 June 1832 by the Quakers James Backhouse and George Washington Walker, who were engaged in investigating the Australian penal colonies. They reported (with evident pleasure):

The prisoner whom [Rev.] J.A. Manton has assigned to him is considered the most valuable domestic on the island. His name is Thomas Day. His parents were slaves in Spanish Town in Jamaica, and he is of sable complexion though of intelligent countenance [*sic*]. His owner wanting to dispose of him brought him to Bermuda, where he succeeded in getting on board a ship with a hope of a passage to England. The captain would not receive him however without a certificate of his freedom. Not foiled by this disappointment he bribed a soldier to befriend him by forging the necessary document which he himself dictated. To his great joy the artifice was not detected, and he succeeded in reaching British shores.[79]

Day's motives for migration to Britain are clear enough. It is hardly likely that others in the West Indies in the early nineteenth century did not escape to Britain for the same reason. In Britain, he worked as a seaman, and even for a time as a gentleman's servant.[80] The latter marked a major step up the occupational ladder, and presumably assisted him in obtaining 'cushy' work on Sarah Island, a place where many other convicts were engaged in felling, carrying and rafting timber in the harsh wilderness of western Tasmania, which has one of the world's most unpleasantly cold, wet and stormy climates.[81]

VI. Literacy

Assessing the African males' literacy is handicapped by the fact that literacy details are not included in the sources for convicts arriving before 1827 in the New South Wales *Indents*, and in only some of the Van Diemen's Land sources used. This yields only 63 cases on which literacy information is available. With caution, this gives some indication of absolute and relative male literacy levels.

TABLE 7

LITERACY OF AFRICAN MALE CONVICTS BY NICHOLAS–SHERGOLD SKILL CLASSIFICATION[a]

Skill Category	Read & write (No./%)	Read only (No./%)	Read & write + read (No./%)	Neither read nor write (No./%)
1. Unskilled urban	4/44.4	3/33.3	7/77.8	2/22.2
2. Unskilled rural	-	-	-	-
3. Skilled building	3/75.0	-	3/75.0	
4. Skilled urban	5/38.5	2/15.4	7/53.8	6/46.2
5. Skilled rural	1/50.0	1/50.0	2/100.0	-
6. Dealers	-	-	-	-
7. Public service (seafarers & soldiers)	5/41.7	2/16.7	7/58.3	5/41.7
8. Professional	2/100.0	-	2/100.0	-
9. Domestic service	10/47.6	2/9.5	12/57.14	9/42.9
10. Totals	30/47.6	10/15.9	40/63.5	23/36.5

(a)   Sources as given in section II.

Obviously, it would be very unwise to assume that all skilled rural African male workers in Britain could either read and write, or at least read, or that 75 per cent of African building workers could read and write. Likewise, the very high level of literacy indicated for unskilled urban workers must be suspect. At the very least, however, Table 7 is suggestive that significant levels of literacy were probably widespread through all occupation skills of African males in Britain. This was certainly not the case among Africans transported to Australia from the Caribbean colonies, from Mauritius, or from the Cape Colony.[82] In this respect, it may be suspected that to be an African born in Britain offered a distinct advantage over being foreign or colonial-born. Literacy may be assumed to have constituted a partial hedge against immiserization and marginalization. Whatever misgivings there might be about the accuracy of the data on literacy derived from Australian convict sources, or indeed its meaning (how fluently could the literate write and/or read?), yet *Convict Workers* at least enables a comparison of like with like. Its findings are that 75 per cent of English male convicts could either read and write, or read; while the Irish 1841 census indicated 62 per cent of the Irish at home shared the same characteristics. In Scotland, as many as 65 per cent of male convicts could both read and write.[83] Thus the level of literacy among the African database was at least comparable to that of the Irish in 1841 and was not derisory by any standards.[84] Indeed, it was well above the 40 per cent that nowadays 'seems the threshold level for economic development'.[85]

Living in Great Britain, a country whose population was generally more literate than its African component appears to have been, the illiterate Africans were clearly at some real disadvantage, especially in entering artisan trades. The literacy data are, however, far from suggesting general marginalization. It has not been thought sensible to fractionalize the African skill categories by place of origin and degree of literacy, as this would produce endless micro-categories. However, 21 of those for whom there are literacy data were born in the UK. Of these, 15 could read and write, one could read only and five could neither read nor write. Thus 71.4 per cent of these men could read and write, 76.2 per cent could read or read and write. This is not an adequate basis on which to base hard-and-fast conclusions, but it remains a possibility that Africans born in Britain were as literate as the general population. If that were the case, then we are witnessing a remarkable historical achievement by these Africans, who had apparently succeeded in distancing themselves from the low levels of literacy of Africans in British colonies.[86] In this respect, this fraction of the Africans was certainly not marginalized and indeed possessed a powerful tool against employment opportunity marginalization. On the other hand, the correspondingly lower literacy rates among the Africans born in the colonies and foreign countries has contrary implications. Among the 20 Africans born in the West Indies on whom there are literacy data, five could read and write, five could read only, and ten were totally illiterate. Yet even this is certainly a far higher literacy rate than that of African-Caribbeans transported to Australia direct from the West Indian colonies.[87] Two possible interpretations offer themselves here; either African-Caribbean migrants to Britain (voluntary or involuntary) were from the more literate sections of the African-Caribbean population, or residence in Britain gave these migrants a greater opportunity to acquire literacy. Of course it is quite possible too that both these factors were operating simultaneously.

VII. The African Women[88]

The African women are dealt with in this short section towards the end of the article, not because they were in actuality a mere appendage of secondary importance to the men, but because the research method adopted only permits them to be glimpsed, a limitation which is candidly admitted. Even the confirmation in this article of the existing supposition that among Africans in Britain there was a strong gender imbalance of males over females cannot minimalize the importance of the females. To suppose so would be to practise a vulgar quantitative history which would impede rather than aid historical understanding. Without a wider understanding of the historical experience of African women in the United Kingdom, the historical literature in the field will remain gravely limited and handicapped. In that present state of the historical literature, every small parcel of information on African women may assist future scholars to construct something better than can be offered here. In this spirit, the following information and observations are offered.

All six of the transported African females were domestic workers; a skilled needlewoman, a plain cook, a servant, a laundress, a housemaid and a laundry maid. Three were illiterate and only one could read and write, the others being able to read but not write. One was born in Mauritius, one in Martinique, one in London, one in Bristol, one in Dublin and one in Leith. Their places of trial were London (three), and one each in Bristol, Dublin and Edinburgh. All were tried and transported in the period 1832–38. These bald pieces of information can, however, be brought to life by reference to qualitative sources.

Marian Mitchell from Martinique, an illiterate married woman of 25 with a son, who was sentenced to transportation for ten years at the Central Criminal Court, London, in 1838, is unlikely to have made other than poor earnings as a laundress.[89] It appears that she supplemented her earnings by prostitution. Her heavy sentence was for stealing 7s 3½d (£0.36) from the person of Patrick Brown in Holborn. Brown's evidence was that Mitchell invited him to her lodgings. When he would not agree to this, she put her hand in his breeches and took the money.[90] Elizabeth Jones was a 24-year-old illiterate. She was also the unmarried parent of a daughter. A cook by occupation, she was born in Mauritius.[91] Her offence, committed together with a man and two other women, was the theft of one Lucy Jackson's clothes, other effects and money to the value of £2 13s 6d (£2.68) from the lodging house they both inhabited in Clerkenwell. It is clear from the evidence that the organizer of the theft was the male defendant, Henry Austin. The victim, Jackson, was an unwary young white woman who had recently arrived in London from the country.[92] We may guess that poverty and poor prospects tempted Elizabeth Jones to play a part in a crime the proceeds of which, if split four ways, would have brought her little enough reward.

Amelia Moss, a 20-year-old housemaid was convicted of man robbery (that is, robbery from the person) at Bristol Quarter Sessions on 31 December 1832.[93] This was an offence that quite commonly landed women engaged in prostitution in serious trouble with the criminal law, for the customary payment for the services of a prostitute from the poorer classes was so meagre that such women were often tempted to supplement their earnings from prostitution by theft from their clients. Thus, Charlotte Clayton, a 25-year-old needlewoman born in London, and an unmarried single parent of a daughter, stole £6 11s (£6.55, riches to a woman in her situation) from Peter Elisha in Bethnal Green, London. The circumstances make it clear that she had led Elisha to believe that she was a prostitute. She was sentenced to transportation for seven years at the Central Criminal Court on 3 April 1837.[94] Christian Sanderson or Sanders,[95] a 43-year-old widow and mother of a daughter, was a laundry maid. With a much younger white woman, Bell Sutherland, she committed robbery with violence on an elderly and drunken watch and clock-maker, William Gordon, who had been lured into an Edinburgh Old Town tenement by their confederate, young Grace Thomson. It is clear that Gordon expected, and was intended to expect, sexual services from Thomson. The sum taken was only 16s 6d (£0.83). Sanderson was sentenced by Edinburgh Court of Justiciary on 15 July 1833 to be transported for seven years.[96]

This is a grim array of evidence that urban African women in Britain in the period under review (and they were presumably as urbanized as their male counterparts) were driven to resorting to prostitution in order to make ends meet. As Deborah Oxley has pointed out, women in Britain then had a 'particularly precarious' niche in the labour market. The intensifying sexual division of labour in industrializing Britain (this was less marked in pre-industrial Britain) marginalized women in the labour market, resulting in intermittent as well as ill-paid employment, while responsibilities to family dependants remained continuous and long term. Oxley's conclusion is 'not surprisingly some women probably cushioned the impact of economic fluctuations by turning to prostitution'.[97] It is possible, though cannot be proved definitively from such a small array of cases as displayed here, that plebeian African women were particularly vulnerable to these processes and their pressures. Certainly they would in most cases have lacked the kinship support network that would have been available to their sisters in Africa itself or in the well established creole slave communities of North America and the West Indies. This difficulty was not, however, unique to African women. Lack of kinship support was commonly the lot of white women who had migrated to the big cities from rural areas of the United Kingdom.[98] Such were also prone to resort to prostitution and petty theft.[99] Plebeian African women and many plebeian white women alike lived in a much harsher world to that of élite African women, such as Mary Seacole and Linda Brent, even if their lives, too, were not always a bed of roses.

It also seems likely that the lived experience of plebeian African women in the labour market was not strongly differentiated from that of white plebeian women. True, the progressive masculinization of agricultural work from the mid-eighteenth century[100] can hardly have directly affected African women as a group, since there is no suggestion that they were any less urbanized than African men. However, the fact that in the early to mid-nineteenth century women's labour in Britain was becoming 'ghettoized' in a narrow range of occupations[101] would have had the same restricting effect on the opportunities and terms of employment of African women as any others. The individual cases briefly discussed above all fit comfortably within K.D.N. Snell's view that from the early nineteenth century, the female labour market (at least in the south and east of England) was becoming concentrated in the occupations of domestic service, dress-making, millinery, shop tailoring and prostitution.[102] A hypothesis emerges here that the forms of immiserization and marginalization suffered by plebeian African women in the period addressed may have been more influenced by changing gender roles in British society than the legacy of African slavery. Certainly, with the present limited state of empirical information about them,[103] they seem to be in clear contrast to the African males whose occupation structure was so very different from that of the male population of either Great Britain or Ireland.

Conclusions

Quantification of historical data will always raise objections as an historical method. The objections fall into two broad categories. On the one
hand, the quantitative historian can expect to be challenged 'in house', as
it were, as to whether the appropriate statistical techniques have been
adopted and properly implemented and the computed results correctly
interpreted. In the present instance, only the most simple statistical
computations have been attempted by the author, conscious that his data
are too scanty and his objectives too limited for it to be sensible to venture
into the realm of such techniques as logit analysis. The second pattern of
objection is more fundamental. The demographic generalizations conveyed by quantitative historical method are abstractions that may be
confused with actual lived experience through the blunder of reification.
As R. Evans and W. Thorpe put it in their recent critique of *Convict
Workers*: 'While we valorise statistics with a reputation of infallibility,
people objectified by them (such as convicts), "are not considered worthy
of status; they have no dignity, no power".'[104] Substitute '(such as Africans
in Britain)' for '(such as convicts)' in this quote, and we reach the heart of
how that kind of objection can be applied to a study such as this. For
some, this will be a gut reaction. Others will turn to Michel Foucault, as
Evans and Thorpe have done in their critique of *Convict Workers*. Such
critics may assert that the sources from which the basic data for this article
are derived, are an oppressive '"power/knowledge" discourse, constituted in definite institutions and organisations',[105] specifically constituted
in the legal and penal systems and their systematic records in Britain and
Australia in the first half of the nineteenth century.

To escape such strictures, the quantitative historian cannot simply
retreat further into the arcana of quantitative method and imagine her or
himself to be safe there from the howls of the mob outside the quantitative
Bastille. However, my own reading of Foucault's *Power/Knowledge* does
not lead me to believe that this text thunders an anathema on utilizing the
kind of sources deployed in this study. Instead, it warns that we should
not be captive to the epistemology and world-view encoded in such
sources. At this point, non-Eltonian qualitative historians can begin to
hold hands again with their quantitative colleagues. Both, properly,
ought to consider *all* historical sources, quantitative or qualitative, as
requiring rigorous interrogation and deconstruction, for meaning to be
extracted from them. Ultimately, like all great truths, this becomes
commonplace. What sensible ancient historian would now regard
Suetonius' *Duodecem Caesares* as an accurate and unbiased account of the
political history of Rome under the first 12 emperors? What sensible

ancient historian would on that account regard *Duodecem Caesares* as prohibited reading? The historical records of classical Greece and Rome, used in the recent past to assert the global hegemonic superiority of western culture over all others can be read in a manner supportive of the great debt of the classical cultures to Africa and Asia, as has been demonstrated by Martin Bernal.[106]

Although this study is predominantly quantitative, care has been taken to indicate (not least in the section on African females), that the Australian sources used can also lead us to valuable qualitative biographical and social data. Considerations of space have limited the depth in which this has been done in the present instance. However, in a number of previous publications the author has been able to show how the method of starting with identifications in transportation records can yield significant or even very substantial biographical information.[107] This could certainly be replicated in the vast majority of cases of Africans transported to Australia from the United Kingdom; if anyone doubts this, then reference to Mollie Gillen's splendid work on the First Fleet convicts should convince them.[108] Indeed, she was facing a more difficult research task than would anyone working from such sources on plebeian biography (African or otherwise) once transportation to Australia had become systematic in its record keeping.

The conclusions of this study must be cautious and tentative; had there been 500 each of males and females, with such data available on them as has been utilized here, it would have been possible to be more assertive, within the limitations discussed above. Additionally, quantitative information on the vital question of the labour participation rate of the African population of the United Kingdom in the first half of the nineteenth century cannot be extracted from the sources utilized.

As things stand, the very clearest indications of poverty and marginalization are among the women, but this may reflect the limited number of cases. However, it seems likely that plebeian African women's limited and insecure employment prospects were common to those suffered by urban plebeian women in Britain generally, rather than being specific to themselves. For the men, the evidence suggests something more complex; very high literacy levels among those who were born in Britain, much lower ones among those who were colonial or foreign born. The African men were no more likely to be in the lowest unskilled category than whites, and very much less likely to be in rural work of any skill level. Their range of occupations was rather narrow, though spread across all but one skill category (dealers); and has the extraordinary feature that two-thirds of them were concentrated into work as either seafarers or domestic servants. Domestic service probably provided the almost one-third in this occupation who were upper servants with relatively well-rewarded and high status employment; in the plebeian world, a 'gentleman's gentleman' was above the common herd. But to be an African servant of any sort was to be in an occupation which had become stereotypically African under slavery, a factor which such servants cannot but have been aware, and which may have caused some real unease. However, the most serious problem facing the male domestic servants was that their occupation was undergoing feminization. Seafarers were not highly regarded or in great demand on land. An African population with such a high proportion of seafarers was particularly vulnerable to any recession in shipping, and the fact that so many of the seafarers were convicted around the end of the Napoleonic Wars seems to be concrete evidence of this.

In skilled building and other urban work, Africans were under-represented though not negligibly represented; however, they seem to have been engaged in traditional trades, potentially under threat from the new technologies of the industrial revolution. The evidence does not suggest that African males were almost exclusively 'marginalized poor', for a significant minority were literate skilled workers, a few in clerical and professional occupations. But there were clearly areas of insecurity in their overall occupational structure over and beyond that experienced by the white male population of Britain. However, compared with the population of Ireland, they seem to have had some distinct advantages in skills and equality in literacy. They were present in small numbers in professional occupations (as understood by the Nicholas–Shergold skill classification), but the database was not large enough to take seriously the apparent finding that proportionately, they were present in such occupations on about the same scale as the white English population. If institutionalized and customary restrictions on African employment operated, this was in steering an undue proportion towards seafaring and domestic service (from both of which it was difficult to restructure into other secure occupations), rather than by creating any impassable barrier to employment in skilled building and urban occupations.

It needs to be recognized that Africans showed considerable enterprise in acquiring literacy and establishing themselves in considerable numbers in skilled occupations (albeit rather old-fashioned ones), despite the continuing preponderance of the 'traditional' occupations of seafaring and domestic service. This feature suggests that self-improvement can be added to self-liberation from slavery as one of the historic achievements of the African people of the United Kingdom. It also suggests – to make the point very cautiously – that the United Kingdom in the first half of the nineteenth century did not provide an environment so utterly hostile to

Africans in the workforce and to African acquisition of literacy as to prevent self-advancement from occurring. The worst case that can be made against the treatment of Africans in the United Kingdom labour market in this period, therefore, would be that under optimum conditions, African self-advancement would have been more rapid, more extensive and more secure.[109]

NOTES

1. The term 'African' has been adopted in this study as generic for the people it addresses: African-North Americans; African-West Indians; African-British; African-Continental Europeans; African-Mauritians, etc. (as defined by place of birth) as well as persons born in Africa itself.
2. A book by Norma Myers, currently under consideration for publication by Leicester University Press, covers the field in the period from the later eighteenth to the mid-nineteenth centuries, and so promises to remedy this situation. Since an earlier article by Myers (see note 18 below) adopts a quantitative approach to this subject using data from late eighteenth and early nineteenth century London Gaol Books, one awaits her full-length study with considerable anticipation.
3. Ch.12, 'Disintegration: Black Society in the Nineteenth Century', in James Walvin, *Black and White: The Negro and English Society, 1554–1945* (London, 1973), pp.189–201. It is only fair to point out that Walvin no longer holds this view. However, Walvin's later work, *England, Slaves and Freedom, 1776–1833* (London, 1986), Ch.3, pp.46–68, 'Black Society in England', remains within the chronological period hitherto most intensively studied by both Walvin himself and other scholars.
4. Peter Fryer, *Staying Power: The History of Black People in Britain* (London, 1984), pp.227–36, 237–56 and 272–7. For further information on Pan-Africanist visitors to mid-nineteenth century Britain, Imanuel Geiss, *The Pan-African Movement* (London, 1974), Ch.9, remains useful. Josephine Wright, 'Early African Musicians in Britain', in Rainer Lotz and Ian Pegg, *Under the Imperial Carpet: Essays in Black History in Britain* (Crawley, 1986), pp.14–24 and Christopher Fyfe, 'Sierra Leoneans in English Schools in the Nineteenth Century, *ibid.*, pp.25–31, both extend our knowledge of the African Presence in Britain in the first half of the nineteenth century. Mary Seacole (edited and introduced by Ziggi Alexander and Audrey Dewjee), *The Wonderful Adventures of Mrs Seacole in Many Lands* (1st edn. James Blackwood, London, 1859; repr. Bristol, 1984), gives valuable insight into the life of an elite 'high achieving' African-Caribbean woman of the mid-nineteenth century. However, none of these works addresses the continued existence of plebeian Africans in Britain after slavery.
5. Folarin O. Shyllon, *Black Slaves in Britain* (London, 1974) and *Black People in Britain 1555–1833* (London, 1977).
6. Douglas O. Lorimer, *Colour, Class and the Victorians: English Attitudes to the Negro in the Mid-Nineteenth Century* (Leicester, 1978), pp.35–44.
7. In date of publication, the first book-length treatment of the History of Africans in Britain was not Walvin's *Black and White*, but Edward Scobie, *Black Britannia: A History of Blacks in Britain* (Chicago, IL, 1972); to my best knowledge, neither Scobie nor Walvin knew about each other's work when writing their respective books. Thus, without detracting from Scobie's achievement, Walvin can none the less be regarded as a genuine pioneer. In his 'Note on Sources', in *Black Slavery in Britain* (1974), p.241, Shyllon makes a short, largely neutral reference to *Black and White*, though allowing its chapter on the Somerset Case to be good. However, by 1977, Shyllon was devoting most of the section of *Black People in Britain* on 'Secondary Sources' (pp.277–9) to a hostile critique of both *Black and White* and Walvin's *The Black*

Presence: A Documentary History of the Negro in England, 1550–1860 (London, 1971), Fryer, *Staying Power*, 'Suggestions for Further Reading', p.598, lumps *Black and White* with *Black Britannia* as 'stimulating, though both should be used with caution', rather as if the work of the two pioneers of book-length treatments of the field should be regarded as on a par with illicit drugs. Shyllon does identify some errors in *Black and White*, a legitimate and useful task of scholarly criticism, but to see no value in a work he had originally found acceptable enough seems a little odd. His condemnation of Walvin as a 'liberal' who shows a 'lack of ordinary human sensibilities towards blacks' (p.277) is regrettable. However, Professor Shyllon's important contributions to the field tower above these matters.

8. Douglas O. Lorimer, 'Black Slaves and English Liberty; A Re-Examination of Racial Slavery in England', *Immigrants & Minorities*, Vol.3, No.2 (1984), pp.121–50. The question of slave emancipation in Britain has been re-examined more recently from a different perspective by Seymour Drescher, 'Manumission in a Society Without Slave Law: Eighteenth Century England', *Slavery & Abolition*, Vol.10, No.3 (1989), pp.85–101.

9. Fryer, *Staying Power*, pp.74–5.

10. We are baldly told that the proclamation 'seems to have been effective' but no evidence is offered in support of this conclusion; Fryer, *Staying Power*, p.75.

11. The evidence is presented and discussed in this study in the section entitled 'The Question of Occupations and Skills'.

12. Lorimer, *Colour, Class and the Victorians*, pp.36–7.

13. Nor was Britain unique in this respect; for a brief indication of African domestic servants in eighteenth-century France, see Sarah C. Maza, *Servants and Masters in Eighteenth-Century France* (Princeton, NJ, 1983), pp.206–8.

14. Lorimer, *Colour, Class and the Victorians*, p.38.

15. Lorimer, *Colour, Class and the Victorians*, pp.38–41.

16. Lorimer, *Colour, Class and the Victorians*, pp.41–3.

17. Henry Mayhew, *London, Labour and the London Poor*, Vol.IV (London, 1862), p.245, quoted in Lorimer, *Colour, Class and the Victorians*, pp.41–2.

18. Somewhat of an exception is Norma Myers, 'The Black Presence Through Criminal Records', *Immigrants & Minorities*, Vol.7, No.3 (1988), pp.292–307. Myers' article addresses questions of criminality and penal policy more than occupations and skills, and is restricted in its geographical scope to the London area. It deserves mention as probably the first publication in the historical literature on the history of Africans in Britain prior to the twentieth century to utilize quantification. It should be said that Myers' sample includes Asians as well as Africans.

19. Archives Office of New South Wales (hence AONSW), *Printed Indents of Convict Ships* (hence *PICS*), 1837, pp.41–2, entry for James Godfrey, arrived Sydney from England per *Norfolk*, 12 Feb. 1837.

20. AONSW, COD/146, *Indents of Convict Ships* (hence *ICS*), June–Dec. 1819, p.399, entry for George William Handy, per *Atlas*, arrived Sydney from England, 19 Oct. 1819.

21. AONSW, COD/144, *ICS*, 1818, p.9, entry for Thomas Jones, arrived Sydney from England per *Batavia*, 5 April 1818.

22. AONSW, COD/143, *ICS*, 1817, n.p., entry for Samuel Munday, arrived Sydney from England per *Almorah*, 31 Aug. 1818.

23. AONSW, *PICS*, 1839, pp.154–5, entry for Marian Mitchell, arrived Sydney from England per *Planter*, 13 March 1839.

24. For the information of those outside Australia who might wish to use this source, the Archives Office of New South Wales can provide the indents on microfiches.

25. Earlier this century, when most respectable Australians were ashamed of their country's convict past, large slices of the VDL *Indents of Convict Ships* (and some other VDL convict records) mysteriously passed into the hands of private collectors. Some in due course surfaced again as donations to the special collections of the Mitchell and Dixson Libraries, State Library of New South Wales, Sydney.

26. Archives Office of Tasmania (hence AOT), Con 18 and Con 19, do not give convicts' native place, or place and date of trial or any penal information). Therefore, Africans first identified in these records had to be cross-checked with entries in one of the other classes of records mentioned in this section of the main text. A further problem is that in the *Alphabetical Registers of Male Convicts*, AOT Con 23, all entries for persons whose family names begin with the letters G–O are missing.

27. For blacks transported from the Cape of Good Hope and the West Indies, see Leslie C. Duly, '"Hottentots to Hobart and Sydney": The Cape Supreme Court's Use of Transportation 1828–38', *Australian Journal of Politics and History*, Vol.XXV, No.1 (1979), pp.39–20; V.C. Malherbe, 'Khoikhoi and the Question of Convict Transportation from the Cape Colony, 1820–1842', *South African Historical Journal*, Vol.17 (1985), pp.19–39; Ian Duffield, 'From Slave Colonies to Penal Colonies: The West Indian Convict Transportees to Australia', *Slavery & Abolition*, Vol.7, No.1 (1986), pp.25–45.

28. AOT, Con 37/7, entry for No.1133 Joseph Williams, arrived Hobart from New Zealand per *Julia*, 23 April 1848.

29. AOT, Con 37/1, entry for No.134 Charles Hall, arrived Hobart from Adelaide per *Dorset*, 5 Dec. 1842.

30. One way that plebeian Africans voluntarily entered Australia in the nineteenth century was by deserting ships of which they were crew members. Jim Melton, *Ship's Deserters 1852–1900 Including Stragglers, Strays and Absentees from H.M. Ships* (Sydney, 1986), p.535, summarizes the data on ship's deserters in New South Wales as including 24 seamen described in his sources as of black complexion and 77 of coloured complexion. These include Asians and Pacific Islanders as well as Africans. We can assume earlier desertions and desertions in Australian ports outside NSW.

31. L.L. Robson, *The Convict Settlers of Australia: An Enquiry Into the Origin and Character of the Convicts Transported to Australia, 1788–1852* (Melbourne, 1965), pp.170–71, Tables 2(a) and 2(b), concludes from his sample that 67,980 males and 12,460 females were transported to New South Wales, 54,640 males and 12,500 females to Van Diemen's Land. A.G.L. Shaw, *Convicts and the Colonies: A Study of Penal Transportation from Great Britain and Ireland to Australia and Other Parts of the British Empire* (London, 1966), p.74, states 'The total number of female convicts sent to New South Wales and Van Diemen's Land was 24,960, which is 15 per cent of the total number of prisoners. 'It should be noted that there is no absolute set of figures, and that these two works, as also Charles Bateson, *The Convict Ships, 1787–1868* (Glasgow, 1959), only enumerate convicts landed from ships embarking from United Kingdom ports. 'Minor' convict ships regularly arrived at Sydney or Hobart from India, Mauritius, New Zealand and the free colonies of South Australia and Western Australia, with small contingents of convicts sentenced in those places. Thus we may conclude that the totals in all these works are underestimates.

32. For example, the precognitions in the case of Christian Sanderson in Scottish Records Office, SRO/AD14/35/501; or as an example of semi-legal records the case of Charlotte Clayton, *Old Bailey Sessions Papers* (hence *OBSP*), 6th Session 1837, case 1043, p.984.

33. Myers, 'The Black Presence', pp.292–307, esp. pp.294–5.

34. Myers, 'The Black Presence', p.295.

35. Myers, 'The Black Presence', p.305, observes that there is no evidence that blacks were more involved in crime than whites. I agree with this. As for the total African population, we have nothing better than later eighteenth-century 'guesstimates', which vary from 1,400 (certainly too low) to 40,000; see Drescher, 'Manumission in a Society Without Slave Law', p.88 and note 15, p.99, which give a good summary of both eighteenth-century views and those of modern authors. It appears that as the debate over the abolition of slavery in Britain fizzled out with the *de facto* self-liberation by the 1790s of many slaves, so the game of guessing their numbers lost its appeal, leaving us bereft of even guesswork on numbers in the first half of the nineteenth century.

36. See George Rudé, *Criminal and Victim: Crime and Society in Early Nineteenth Century Britain* (Oxford, 1985); David Philips, *Crime and Authority in Victorian England: The Black Country, 1835–1860* (London, 1977). For the eighteenth century, D. Hay, 'War, Dearth and Theft in Eighteenth-Century England', *Past and Present*, 95 (1982), pp.117–60 and J.M. Beattie, *Crime and the Courts in England, 1660–1800* (Oxford, 1986), have reached similar conclusions. Their work has eclipsed that of conservative historians, who believe that Victorian crime was caused by a 'criminal class'. Examples of scholars of this school of thought are J.J. Tobias, *Crime and Industrial Society in the Nineteenth Century* (London, 1967), and *Crime and Police in England 1700–1900* (Dublin, 1979); J.H. Langbein, 'Albion's Fatal Flaws', *Past & Present*, 98 (1983), pp.96–120; M.B. and C.B. Schedvin, 'The Nomad Tribes of Britain: A Prelude to Botany Bay', *Historical Studies* (Australia and New Zealand), Vol.18, No.71 (1978). Most scholars working in this field have been strongly influenced by D. Hay *et al*, *Albion's Fatal Tree: Crime and Society in Eighteenth Century England* (London, 1977), though in Langbein's case only in a negative sense. This book firmly took the debate about crime and society in British History out of the orbit of studies of criminal deviancy and into that of power relations and struggles between different classes within the British social formation, thus putting conservative scholars (at least among historians) on the back foot.
37. C.M.H. Clark, 'The Origins of the Convicts Transported to Eastern Australia, 1787– 1852', *Historial Studies* (Australia and New Zealand), 7 (1956), pp.121–35 and 314–27; Robson, *The Convict Settlers of Australia*; Shaw, *Convicts and the Colonies*. Robson's study is distinguished by being the first to use quantitative techniques in this field; his findings are based on a one-in-twenty 'systematic' sample of convicts transported to New South Wales and Van Diemen's Land, the colonies which received the vast majority of the over 160,000 convicts transported to Australia (including Western Australia). An example of the many subsequent works which have uncritically followed these scholars on the ingrained criminality of the convicts is J.B. Hirst, *Convict Society and its Enemies; A History of Early New South Wales* (North Sydney, 1983).
38. Mollie Gillen's valuable book, *The Founders of Australia: A Biographical Dictionary of the First Fleet* (Sydney, 1988) rubs in, in its introduction, the disorderliness, squalor and dissipation of late eighteenth-century English lower class life, though does concede that more criminals were opportunist than professional (see p.xviii); a work of major revisionary challenge, Portia Robinson, *The Women of Botany Bay; A Reinterpretation of the Role of Women in the Origins of Australian Society* (Sydney, 1988) also adheres to a quasi-Robsonian opinion of the convict women as they were in their British origins, although she does allow that female migrants to London were often 'unable to find employment of any means of subsistence, apart from begging or crime' (p.14). Robert Hughes, *The Fatal Shore; A History of the Transportation of Convicts to Australia, 1787–1868* (London, 1987), Ch.6, pp.158–202, 'Who Were the Convicts', accepts and reproduces the Clark–Robson–Shaw line emphatically and without question. This is unfortunate, since Hughes' book was an international best-seller receiving uncritical acclaim from reviewers outside Australia, whose knowledge of the issues seems, in many cases, to have been restricted to the book itself.
39. Stephen Nicholas (ed.), *Convict Workers: Reinterpreting Australia's Past* (Cambridge, 1988). It may be relevant that by chance, only one member of the *Convict Workers* team, Dr Barrie Dyster, is a native-born Australian (although all the others have resided in Australia for many years). Possibly such a group felt less natural reverence for the objects of their attack, the Grand Old Men of Australian History by whom they had not been supervised as postgraduate students.
40. Among the most hostile reviews are: A. Davidson, 'A Review of *Convict Workers*', *Australian Historical Studies*, 24 (Oct. 1989), pp.480–81; J.B. Hirst, 'Convicts and Crime', *Overland*, 113 (1988) and 'Convict Past Divides Historians', *The Age*, Melbourne, 21 Feb. 1989, p.18; S. Macintyre, review article in *London Review of Books*, Vol.11, No.18 (Sept. 1989); P. Robinson, 'Getting a Nation's Record Straight', *The Age, Arts and Books*, Melbourne, 21 Jan. 1989, p.14; L.L. Robson, 'Review of

Convict Workers', *First Edition* radio broadcast, Australian Broadcasting Corporation (Dec. 1988); A.G.L. Shaw, 'Review of *Convict Workers*', *Victorian Historical Magazine*, 61 (March 1990), pp.77–8; R. Shlomowitz, '*Convict Workers*: A Review Article', *Australian Economic History Review*, Vol.XXX, No.2 (Sept. 1990), pp.67–88 and 'Convict Transportees: Casual or Professional Criminals', *Australian Economic History Review*, XXXI, 2 (Sept. 1991), pp.106–8; F.B. Smith 'Beyond the Uninviting Shore', *Times Literary Supplement* (9–15 March 1990), pp.261–2. It will be noted that some of these hostile reviewers were exercising the legitimate right of self-defence. But it is interesting to note that a distinguished United States reviewer, S.L. Engerman, who is of course not *parti pris*, sees the book in a more balanced light; see Engerman's review in *Journal of Economic History*, Vol.50, No.3 (1990), pp.745–6.

41. Significantly, the latest Australian publication to confront *Convict Workers* does so with respect; see R. Evans and W. Thorpe, 'Power, Punishment and Penal Labour: *Convict Workers* and Moreton Bay', *Australian Historical Studies*, Vol.25, No.98 (April 1992), pp.90–111. Despite taking issue with *Convict Workers* on some important epistemological and methodological points as well as on questions of punishment and other matters concerning the management of convicts in Australia, Evans and Thorpe regard the book as 'arguably the most important book on convictism to emerge in recent times' (p.91) and as providing 'a convincing riposte to the notion that [the transported convicts] were members of a criminal class' (p.92). Stephen Nicholas himself has been assiduous in engaging with the most hostile of his critics; see Nicholas, 'Understanding Convict Workers', *Australian Economic History Review*, Vol.XXXI, No.2 (Sept. 1991), pp.95–105, 'Matters of Fact: Convict Transportees Were Not Members of a Criminal Class', *Australian Economic History Review*, Vol.XXXI, No.2 (Sept. 1991), p.109 and 'Reinterpreting the Convict Labour Market', *Australian Economic History Review*, Vol.XXX, No.2 (Sept. 1990), pp.50–66. Barrie Dyster, 'Transported Workers: The Case of Mayhew Versus Mayhew', *Labour History: A Journal of Labour and Social History*, 60 (May 1991), pp.84–92, offers an able defence of *Convict Workers* by one of its co-authors, which sensibly avoids the pugilistic tone that has entered into some of the debate. The sheer volume of response, attack and counter-attack attested in this and the previous footnote is a tribute, at least, to the importance of the issues raised by *Convict Workers*. Nor is the debate exhausted; the author has information that scholars from the northern hemisphere are now mustering their belated contributions.

42. Nicholas, *Convict Workers*, p.7.

43. Nicholas, *Convict Workers*, p.9.

44. Nicholas, *Convict Workers*, p.9.

45. Nicholas, *Convict Workers*, pp.64–5.

46. Malcolm R. Sainty and Keith A. Johnson (eds.), *Census of New South Wales November 1828* (Sydney, 1985). African convicts who arrived in New South Wales before 1828 can be traced in this census in such a small number of instances that no general conclusion can be made as to whether they, too, were commonly allocated to work which correlated with their occupations as given in their NSW *Indent* entries.

47. Nicholas, *Convict Workers*, pp.65–6.

48. Nicholas, *Convict Workers*, pp.71–4.

49. Robson, *Convict Settlers*, pp.181–2, quotes as if clinching the point, an anecdote from the first voyage to Australia as Surgeon-Superintendent of a convict ship of P.M. Cunningham. This is to the effect that three-quarters of the convicts on Cunningham's ship, on arrival, gave the recording clerk 'thief' for their occupation and that the clerk then asked if he should, therefore, enter them as labourers. It does not occur to Robson that Cunningham might have had his own prejudices against the lower orders, let alone convicted felons, or alternatively that this might be a case of convicts indulging in a little safe authority baiting.

50. Nicholas, *Convict Workers*, pp.74–8.

51. For an analysis of the occupations, skill levels and literacy of the female sample see Deborah Oxley, 'Female Convicts', in Nicholas, *Convict Workers*, pp.91–4.

52. The tradition of generalizing from the sensational has, alas, been continued by Hughes in *The Fatal Shore*. For the author's views on this work, see I. Duffield, 'Blockbusting Transportation', *Australian Studies*, 1 (1988), pp.84–94. Hamish Maxwell-Stewart, 'The Bushrangers and the Convict System of Van Diemen's Land, 1803–1846, Ph.D. thesis, University of Edinburgh, 1990, Ch.5, pp.153–6, carefully evaluates the assertions by Lloyd Robson, Humphrey McQueen, M. Levy, Charles White and R.W. Giblin that the Van Diemen's Land convicts were of the very worst in terms of criminality and finds such assertions dubious. His opinion is influenced by Marie Fels' excellent article, 'Culture Contact in the County of Buckinghamshire, Van Diemen's Land, 1803–1811', *Tasmanian Historical Research Association Journal and Proceedings*, 29 (1982), esp. pp.61–3, in addition to his interpretation of his own research data. I would like to thank Dr Maxwell-Stewart for reading the draft of the original version of this article and making many helpful suggestions as to improvements as well as giving me some valuable references.
53. Fryer's index on black women in *Staying Power* extends for more than a full column, a good indication that they are not neglected in his study, which is a valuable resource in this respect. For female convicts in general, see Deborah Oxley, 'Female Convicts', in Nicholas, *Convict Workers*, pp.85–97; Katrina Alford, *Production or Reproduction? An Economic History of Women in Australia, 1788–1850* (Melbourne, 1984); Robinson, *Women of Botany Bay*, takes a markedly different line to Oxley and Alford, stressing the achievements of convict women in Australia rather than their ultra-victimization.
54. Nicholas, *Convict Workers*, pp.223–4. This gives a more sophisticated nine skill banding (or ten, including 'other') than the four bands of the more generally used Armstrong skill classification. It has the further advantage that it mitigates the tendency of the latter to rank occupations according to social status.
55. Such people certainly had existed, however. Olaudah Equiano's *The Interesting Narrative of the Life of Olaudah Equiano, or Gustavus Vassa, the African Written by Himself* (2 vols., London 1789; facsimile of 1789 edition edn. with intro. by Paul Edwards (London 1969), bears plenty of witness to his entrepreneurial spirit. The eighteenth-century boxer Bill Richmond was a skilled cabinet maker and eventually became an innkeeper; see Paul Edwards and James Walvin, 'Africans in Britain, 1500–1800', in Martin L. Kilson and Robert I. Rotberg (eds.), *The African Diaspora; Interpretive Essays* (Cambridge, MA, 1976), p.194.
56. These men were all convicted shortly after the Napoleonic Wars. They are: Andrew Colbert, tried at the Old Bailey in Sept. 1819, see AOT, Con 23/1, No.270C and *Old Bailey Sessions Papers*, 7th Session 1819, case 1288, p.454; Du Cuffe, tried at Surrey Assizes, 15 Aug. 1816, see AONSW, COD/142, *ICS*, July 1814–January 1816, per *Morley*, arrived Sydney from England 10 April 1817; and Joseph Marson, tried Middlesex April 1818, see AONSW, COD/145, *ICS*, 1818–1819, arrived Sydney from England per *General Stuart*, 31 Dec. 1818. To these may be added a fourth, William Green, tried Edinburgh 1 June 1818, whose first trade is given as cabinet maker in AOT, Con 34/1, p.58, No.119. But the precognitions of his case in SRO/AD14/18/30 reveal that he was a soldier and officer's servant in the 70th Regiment of Foot at the time of his offence. Green is extensively discussed in Duffield, 'Identity, Community and the Lived Experience of Black Scots from the Late Eighteenth to the Mid-Nineteenth Centuries', *Immigrants & Minorities*, Vol.11, No.2 (1992), pp.102–29.
57. Robson, *Convict Settlers*, Table 4 (f), p.181.
58. For a discussion of these points, see Marcus Rediker, *Between the Devil and the Deep Blue Sea; Merchant Seamen, Pirates, and the Anglo-American Maritime World* (Cambridge, 1987), pp.289–95. There is no recent monograph known to me, of comparable quality, on British seamen covering the period 1750–1850. Rediker's general picture is startlingly at variance with the panglossian analysis of service in the mid-eighteenth century Royal Navy in N.A.M. Rodger, *The Wooden World: An Anatomy of the Georgian Navy* (London, 1986). This minimizes brutal punishment and other negative aspects of the service and emphasizes the positive incentives, such as promo-

tion opportunities (including to commissioned rank) available to young entrants to the lower deck. *The Wooden World*, pp.159–61, discusses African seamen in the Georgian RN, conceding that the navy condoned the common practice of slave-owning officers deploying their slaves as crewmen, while also emphasizing 'the attractions [to Africans] of a world in which a man's professional skill mattered more than his colour' (p.159). Since any pay and prize-money accruing to a slave naval seaman would be the property of his master, it is hard to see that the positive incentives for such seamen were quite what Rodger would have us believe. The passages in *The Interesting Narrative of the Life of Olaudah Equiano* which relate Equiano's experiences at sea when slave to Lieutenant Pascal, RN, display a revealing example of an officer/slave owner appropriating his slave crewman's pay and prize money.

59. J.M. Beattie, 'The Pattern of Crime in England 1660–1800', *Past & Present*, 62 (1974), pp.47–95, points out that during the eigthteenth century the social and economic dislocations following major wars led to increases in the conviction rate and to perceived 'crime waves', with demobilized soldiers and seamen featuring strongly as 'criminals'.

60. Witness to the significant presence of African seamen in the Royal Navy during the Napoleonic Wars can be found in excerpts from the autobiography of a former (white English) Napoleonic Wars' seaman, John Brown, who had been 'drover's boy, shoemaker, soldier, strolling player, and man-o'-war's man'; see 'Literary Treasury', *Moreton Bay Courier*, Vol.XII, No.737 (Saturday 26 March 1859), back page, cols. 1–4. Moreton Bay is, of course, what is now Brisbane, Queensland. Brown not only mentions an African steward whom he encountered on his first day on his first RN ship, but also accurately, if with chauvinist and racist language, speaks of the wartime RN crews being recruited from 'men of all countries from the pot-bellied Hollander to the coast of Guinea "nigger"' (col.3).

61. An account of Morris's trial, rich in social detail, occurs in *Old Bailey Sessions Papers*, 7th Session 1815, case 864, pp.386, 389 and 390 (the pages in the original are misnumbered, there being no pp.387–8). Morris made a vigorous if unsuccessful defence, including cross-examining proesecution witnesses. Further information on Morris occurs in AONSW, COD/142, *ICS*, 1816, p.206, per *Mariner*, arrived London from England, 11 Oct. 1816.

62. Robson's one-in-twenty sample of all NSW and VDL convicts found only four per cent of male convicts in what he calls 'personal service'; see Robson, *Convict Settlers*, Table 4 (f), p.181.

63. It would be possible to construct a sample of white male servants transported from the UK to NSW and to determine its ratio of upper to lower domestic servants, for comparative purposes, but considerations of time precluded this. Neither Robson nor Nicholas provided ready-made comparative data on this point. No data on the ratio of upper to lower servants are cited in McBride (see note 65 below for a full reference to this work).

64. This man was Richard Simmonds, 23 years of age and born in America. Of a revolutionary disposition, he attended the radical mass-meeting at Spa Fields, London, on 2 Dec. 1816, and then led a mob in sacking a gunsmith's premises in the nearby Minories, standing his ground sword in hand, 'more bold than the rest', when a troop of Life-Guards arrived to suppress this attempt to arm the people against the state; see *OBSP*, 2nd Session 1817, case 216, pp.91–2. In Australian convict records he can be found in AONSW, COD/143, *ICS*, 1817, arrived Sydney from England per *Almorah*, 31 Aug. 1817 and in AOT Con 23/3, No.71S, arrrived Hobart from Sydney per *Pilot*, [n.d.] 1817. He is mentioned in Iain McCalman 'Anti-Slavery and Ultra Radicalism in Early Nineteenth Century England: The Case of Robert Wedderburn', *Slavery & Abolition*, Vol.7, No.2 (1986), pp.99–117.

65. Theresa M. McBride, *The Domestic Revolution: The Modernisation of Household Service in England and France* (London, 1976), p.15.

66. McBride, *The Domestic Revolution*, Table 2.2, p.36.

67. William Dines, AONSW, COD/149, *ICS*, Feb.–Dec. 1821, p.345, arrived Sydney from England per *Dick*, 12 March 1821.

68. Robert Williams, AONSW, COD/143, *ICS*, 1817, p.355, arrived Sydney from England per *Lord Eldon*, 30 Sept. 1817. He is listed in the *Census of New South Wales November 1828*, No.W1590, p.394 as a shepherd, free by servitude, in the employ of John Jones, landholder, at Bathurst in the interior. This is in line with *Convict Workers'* finding that it was generally convicts whose original occupations were in little demand in the colonial economy who ended up in an unrelated occupation in New South Wales. Since Williams' *ICS* entry informs us that he was born in Jamaica and that he was 22 years old on arrival, he is among those African convicts whose lives had taken them from a slave colony to a penal colony.

69. George Barrow, No.1153, AOT, Con 23/1, arrived Hobart from England per *Georgiana*, 13 April 1829;) also occurs as No.1153 in AOT, Con 18/8.

70. William Thompson, AONSW, *PICS*, 1833, pp.201–2, arrived Sydney from England per *Lloyds*, 18 Dec. 1833.

71. For what it is worth, one of the eight African males convicted in Ireland was an errand boy (and so in Nicholas–Shergold skill 1), convicted in Cork in 1838; see Charles Bankes, AONSW, *PICS*, 1838, pp.138–9, arrived Sydney from Ireland per *Clyde*, 10 Sept. 1838. The other seven were servants or seafarers.

72. For a discussion of Irish farming and farmers in the first half of the nineteenth century, see Cormac O'Gráda, *Ireland Before and After the Famine; Explorations in Irish Economic History, 1800–1925* (Manchester, 1988), Ch.2.

73. Nicholas, *Convict Workers*, p.69.

74. Listing of occupations in this article is in the same order as in the sources from which the data are taken.

75. Robson, *Convict Settlers*, p.178, Table 4 (d).

76. Lorimer, *Colour, Class and the Victorians*, p.40, gives an instance from Merseyside in 1857 and Ch.3 is devoted to 'Black gentlemen' in mid-Victorian England, many of whom were North Americans engaged in the anti-slavery struggle.

77. The existence of a multi-racial ultra-radical plebeian political culture, fermenting in and connecting the port cities of both sides of the Atlantic in the eighteenth century, has been argued by Marcus Rediker and Peter Linebaugh; this would strongly support the notion that Africans in North America and the West Indies were well aware of developments in Britain and *vice versa*; see Marcus Rediker, 'Good Hands, Stout Heart, and Fast Feet: The History and Culture of Working People in Early America', and Peter Linebaugh, 'All the Atlantic Mountains Shook', both in G. Eley and W. Hunt (eds.), *Reviving the English Revolution: Reflections and Elaborations on the Work of Christopher Hill* (London, 1988); Linebaugh and Rediker, 'The Many-Headed Hydra: Sailors, Slaves, and the Atlantic Working Class in the Eighteenth Century', *Journal of Historical Sociology*, Vol.3, No.3 (1990), pp.225–52; Rediker, *Between the Devil and the Deep Blue Sea*. The brilliant exploration of the career of the African-Jamaican (or, strictly, African-Scottish Jamaican!) ultra-radical, Robert Wedderburn, in McCalman, *Radical Underworld* esp. Chs.3 and 7, also reveals the flow of information and radical political ideas between the African and other plebeian communities on both sides of the Atlantic in the late eighteenth and early nineteenth centuries.

78. AONSW, Con 23/1, 208D, Thomas Day, arrived Hobart from England per *Countess of Harcourt*, 1821.

79. James Backhouse and Charles Taylor, *The Life and Labours of George Washington Walker, of Hobart Town, Tasmania* (London and York, 1862), p.64. I am particularly grateful to Dr Hamish Maxwell-Stewart of the Wellcome Research Unit, University of Glasgow, for this reference.

80. Backhouse and Taylor, *Life and Labours of George Washington Walker*, p.64.

81. South-West Tasmania remains almost entirely an uninhabited wilderness to the present, an area of storm-bound coasts with few safe harbours, backed by precipitous ranges whose valleys are clad with dense cold rain forest. The interior has not been inhabited by humans since the last ice age; see Rhys Jones, 'Hunters and History: A Case Study from Western Tasmania', in Carmel Schrire (ed.), *Past and Present in*

Hunter Gatherer Studies (Orlando, OR, 1984). As for Thomas Day, Backhouse and Walker encountered him during a brief spell of good luck. On 25 July 1827, he had received a free certificate on expiry of his original sentence; see AOT, Con 23/1, Thomas Day, No.208D, arrived Hobart from England per *Countess of Harcourt*, 1821. However, Day received a sentenced of 7 years from Hobart Town Supreme Court on 8 June 1828, and a further sentence of 7 years from the same court on 28 March 1829, following his participation in a daring escape attempt from Sarah Island. On 13 Aug. 1841, Hobart Town Supreme Court imposed two further extensions of sentence of one year each on him. He was not a free man again till 1845, 25 years after his original sentence of transportation; see AOT, Con 34/1, Thomas Day, No.208D, p.181. Thus, Thomas Day's ultimate freedom came 11 years after the 1834 emancipation of slaves in the British Empire would have granted it, had he remained in the West Indies.

82. Unpublished research data, from similar sources, in the author's possession, shows that literacy rates among these convicts was exceptionally low. Also see note 84 below.

83. Nicholas, *Convict Workers*, p.75.

84. Nicholas, *Convict Workers*, p.77, Table 5.8, gives the literacy rates of 21 less developed countries in the 1970s. The highest literacy rate was that of Egypt, with 48 per cent.

85. Nicholas, *Convict Workers*, p.770.

86. Nicholas, *Convict Workers*, Table A7, p.211, finds that of 320 males tried outside the UK, 54 per cent could neither read nor write, 8.8 per cent could read only and 37.2 per cent could both read and write. The table lists these men as 'foreign' by trial – which should, of course, be colonial in the vast number of instances. Many of these 320 are certainly Africans from Caribbean colonies, the Cape of Good Hope and Mauritius. The discrepancy between these data and those on Africans transported from the United Kingdom are very striking.

87. See note 86 above.

88. At the African Studies Association of the United Kingdom/Royal African Society Conference on the *African Presence in the United Kingdom*, The Africa Centre, London, 13–14 Dec. 1991, at which an earlier form of this article was given as a paper, it was vehemently asserted by some participants that those who gave papers had ignored African women. I would be delighted if any of these critics, or anyone else, could draw my attention to any African women transported from the United Kingdom to Australia between 1812 and 1852, whom I have overlooked in this article.

89. Marian Mitchell, AONSW, *PICS*, 1839, pp.154–5, arrived Sydney from England per *Planter*, 13 March 1839.

90. *OBSP*, 11th Session 1838, 21 Sept. 1838, case 2204, p.873.

91. Elizabeth Jones, AONSW, *PICS*, 1839, pp.152–3, arrived England from Sydney per *Planter*, 13 March 1839. She was tried at the Central Criminal Court on 20 Aug. 1838 and sentenced to transportation for ten years.

92. *OBSP*, 10th Session 1838, case 1831, pp.587–92.

93. Amelia Moss, AONSW, *PICS*, 1833, arrived England from Sydney per *Buffalo*, 5 Oct. 1833.

94. Charlotte Clayton, AONSW, I, 1837, pp.223–4, arrived Sydney from England per *Henry Wellesley*, 22 Dec. 1837; her case is reported in *OBSP*, 6th Session 1837, case 1043, p.984.

95. For a detailed discussion of Christian Sanderson, see Duffield, 'Identity, Community and the Lived Experience of Black Scots'.

96. Christian Sanderson or Sanders, AONSW, *PICS*, 1846, pp.179–80, arrived Sydney from England per *Numa*, 13 June 1834; there are fascinating details about this case in SRO, AD/14/33/501.

97. Oxley, in Nicholas, *Convict Workers*, p.79.

98. Deborah Oxley, 'Convict Maids', unpublished Ph.D. thesis, University of New South Wales, 1991, argues that female immigrants into large British cities were in general a particularly vulnerable group, highly likely to resort to petty theft and/or prostitution because their low wages, limited employment opportunities and insecurity of employment compounded their loss of such security as the rural family structure had tradition-

ally given them. I am grateful to Dr Oxley for affording me access to her thesis, and look forward to the publication by Cambridge University Press of a monograph based upon it. Current doctoral research by Kirsty Reid of the University of Edinburgh Department of History on her forthcoming doctoral thesis, 'Female Convicts, Work and Resistance in Van Diemen's Land, 1820–1842', also supports Oxley's views in this respect.

99. Kirsty Reid informs me that during research in Tasmanian archives in 1991–92 for her doctoral thesis (see note 98 above), she collected much data indicating that separation from kinship support occurred commonly among young Irish-born female transportees, convicted in the British cities to which they had migrated. Many such transported Irish women had resorted to prostitution to supplement their meagre and uncertain earnings from legitimate occupations.

100. This is discussed in M. Roberts, 'Sickles and Scythes: Women's Work and Men's Work at Harvest Time', *History Workshop*, 7 (Spring 1979), pp.3–28; and in K.D.N. Snell, 'Agricultural Seasonal Unemployment, the Standard of Living and Women's Work in the South and East, 1690–1860', *Economic History Review*, Vol.34, No.3 (1981), pp.407–37.

101. Oxley, 'Convict Maids', p.199.

102. Snell, 'Agricultural Seasonal Unemployment', pp.419–20.

103. It is an urgent task for the existing evidence on African women in eighteenth and early nineteenth-century Britain to be systematically reviewed and further empirical data to be rigorously sought out (what happened to the daughters of Christian Sanderson, Charlotte Clayton and Elizabeth Jones?) and the resultant findings published. Valuable comparative literature is available in the form of such works as Barbara Bush, *Slave Women in Caribbean Society, 1655–1838* (London, 1990); Angela Davis, *Women, Race and Class* (New York, 1981); Elizabeth Fox-Genovese, 'Strategies and Forms of Resistance: Focus on Slave Women in the U.S.', in Gary Okihiro (ed.), *In Resistance: Studies in African, Caribbean and Afro-Caribbean History* (Amherst, MA, 1986); Arlette Gautier, 'Les esclaves femmes aux Antilles françaises, 1635–1848', *Reflexions Historiques*, Vol.10, No.3 (1983), pp.409–35; Deborah Gray White, *Ar'n't I a Woman? Female Slaves in the Plantation South* (New York, 1985); Jacqueline Jones, *Labour of Love, Labour of Sorrow; Black Women, Work and Family from Slavery to the Present* (New York, 1985); to give a mere selection of an increasingly rich literature. Some hitherto overlooked cases of slave women in Scotland are mentioned in June Evans, 'African-Caribbeans and Their Historical Contact with Scotland and the Scottish People', unpublished paper presented at the *Second Scottish Conference for Geography Postgraduates* (University of Glasgow, 16–17 Sept. 1991). For those who might wish to contact Ms Evans with either queries or further information, she is a doctoral candidate in the Department of Geography, University of Edinburgh.

104. Evans and Thorpe, 'Power, Punishment and Penal Labour', p.96. The internal quotation is from Michel Foucault, *Power/Knowledge: Selected Interviews and Other Writings* (New York, 1980), p.93.

105. Foucault, *Power/Knowledge*, p.95.

106. Martin Bernal, *Black Athena: The Afroasiatic Roots of Classical Civilization*, 2 vols. (London, 1987 and 1992). An odd feature of this important work is that it is often distinctly diffusionist, as if Bernal has simply stood that typical epistemology of the nineteenth century imperialist world view on its head.

107. See Ian Duffield, 'Martin Beck and Afro-Blacks in Colonial Australia', *Journal of Australian Studies*, 16 (1985), pp.3–20; 'Billy Blue: A Legend of Early Sydney', *History Today* (Feb. 1987), pp.43–8; 'The Life and Death of "Black" John Goff: Aspects of the Black Convict Contribution to Resistance Patterns in Eastern Australia', *Australian Journal of Politics and History*, Vol.33, No.1 (1987), pp.30–44; and 'Identity, Community and the Lived Experience of Black Scots' which explores in some detail four case histories of Africans resident in Scotland who were ultimately transported to Australia.

108. Mollie Gillen, *The Founders of Australia: A Biographical Dictionary of the First Fleet*

(Sydney, 1989). This work identifies the First Fleet African convicts and seamen.
109. I wish to thank Dr John Perkins, of the Department of Economic History, University of New South Wales, for reading the penultimate version of this study and making a number of most helpful comments and suggestions. As in the case of Dr Maxwell-Stewart, Dr Perkins bears no responsibility for any remaining errors or failings; these are all my own.

Ethnic Identity, Transience and Settlement: The Kru in Liverpool Since the Late Nineteenth Century

DIANE FROST

Kru migrants in Liverpool represent in several ways a unique group of immigrant workers. First, they were 'twice migrants', having migrated from their original homeland in eastern Liberia to Sierra Leone before coming to Liverpool. Secondly, they retained a transient status because, as seafarers their constant contact with Freetown meant they retained a firm grasp on the possibility of return even after they had settled. Kru transience manifest itself through the perpetuation of a Kru ethnic identity and through their relationships with local women. Continuing commitments to both their wives and home in Freetown meant that such relationships were often short-term or common law. Those Kru who did make the shift in status from transient seamen to settlers perpetuated their Kru ethnic identity, since this served as a defence mechanism against their marginal status, and the hostility meted out by white society. Settlement in Liverpool bestowed on the Kru 'dual membership' of both British society, through the realm of work and marriage, as well as membership of a parallel African enclave through recreation and community. The perpetuation of a Kru ethnic identity in the face of apparent 'assimilation' places the Kru experience with those of other migrant groups that have settled in Britain.

Kru migrants found in Liverpool from at least the late nineteenth century onwards originated from eastern Liberia and often came to Liverpool via Freetown, Sierra Leone. The Kru constituted an ethnic group that acquired a reputation as expert seafarers. Througout the nineteenth century they were encouraged to migrate to the British colony of Free-

The author wishes to thank Mel Walker, Tony Lane, John Peel, Elizabeth Tonkin and David Killingray for constructive criticisms on earlier drafts of this study. It was drawn from her Ph.D. thesis, 'The Kru in Freetown and Liverpool: A Study of Maritime Work and Community During the 19th and 20th Centuries', undertaken in the Department of Sociology, University of Liverpool, 1992. The study is primarily based on fieldwork in the Toxteth area of Liverpool in 1988 and 1991.

town in order to supply British merchant ships with reliable and skilled seafaring labour. It was their work as seamen in the trade between West Africa and Liverpool that led to their presence and eventual settlement in Liverpool and other port cities. In Liverpool the Kru were characterized by transient work and community relations that differed in important respects from white-British seafaring communities (who although transient had a more settled community to which they could return), and from other black communities who were neither predominantly seafarers nor essentially transient. For example, Afro-Caribbeans. Yet the Kru did share a transient status in common with other non-seafaring immigrants, for example, Pakistani sojourners, who came for a limited period to earn money before returning home.[1] However, unlike Pakistani migrants, who, after eventually settling permanently, began to bring their wives and children, Kru settlers did not follow this pattern. Instead they tended to inter-marry with local women.

It will be argued that the Kru in Liverpool passed through two stages. The first transient stage was of course prescribed and defined by the nature of their work, because, as seamen, they were constantly moving between Freetown and Liverpool. The second stage through which the Kru moved was that of settlement, where individual Kru permanently settled in Liverpool for various reasons. While such stages might have assumed dominance during particular historical periods (settlement was particularly salient in the 1950s), on the whole the community throughout this period was characterized by both stages simultaneously, with some individuals settling while others remained transient. The study will first seek to examine the nature of Kru transience through an assessment of their work as seafarers, followed by the implications of this on their community in Liverpool. It will be shown how Kru transience manifests itself through (a) the perpetuation of an ethnic identity, and (b) through Kru marriage patterns in Liverpool. Secondly, it will be argued that the shift in status from transients to marginalized settlers, did not see the demise of a Kru ethnic identity and culture. On the contrary this was perpetuated in the context of Liverpool, but this time for different reasons.

Such developments place the Kru experience with those of other migrants, and as such, may be related to the ethnographic literature that emerged in the 1960s and 1970s. This in itself was a response to earlier functionalist thinking of the Chicago School that focused on the 'melting pot' theory of migrant cultures. Ethnographic studies such as those of Khan and Dahya on Pakistani immigrants,[2] and Stuart Hall and Ken Pryce on Afro-Caribbean immigrants,[3] highlighted the complexity involved in cultural adaptation that immigrants faced. This process involved neither complete assimilation nor total preservation of 'original' cultures, and many, particularly second generation immigrants, were often trapped 'between two cultures' in the words of Watson.

There continues to exist a myriad of small ethnic groups in the UK today, whose experiences have yet to be documented before they are lost. Such experiences exist on two levels; first, these stories often present fascinating and interesting material in themselves, adding to our knowledge of multi-ethnic society; secondly, the experiences of such groups contribute to a greater understanding of the complex processes involved in ethnic identity. It is hoped that this account of the Kru in Liverpool goes some way towards contributing to this wider body of knowledge.

I

West African labour employed in the British mercantile trade can be traced back at least to the eighteenth century when black sailors were used to fill shortages left by white sailors. As trade grew with Africa in the eighteenth century, increasing numbers of Africans were employed on board ship, and throughout the eighteeth and nineteenth centuries transient black seamen's settlements could be found around the dockland areas of London and Bristol.[4] The importance attached to black seamen in the British mercantile trade was reflected in an Act of 1823 that stated they were 'as much British seamen as a white man would be'.[5] Kru seamen who formed the bulk of West Africans recruited from Freetown, proved invaluable during the so-called 'legitimate trade' era (and had incidentally been an asset during the slave trade) which emerged after the abolition of the slave trade. Here Kru labour contributed to the extraction and transportation of primary products such as palm oil, timber, ground nuts, cocoa, iron ore, rubber and diamonds, that were taken from West Africa to Europe in the latter half of the nineteenth century. Palm oil which became the most lucrative item of West African trade in this period was used in various processes for the manufacture of margarine, candles, soap, and also as a lubricating agent for machinery. A captain engaged in the West African trade in the 1850s explained the importance of palm oil at this time: 'The trade which formerly flourished at all these places, was that in slaves, but for some years past that in palm-oil . . . has greatly developed itself, the quantity produced amounting annually to more than 7,000 tons, which are shipped to America, France and England.'[6] Figures for Nigeria and the Gold Coast between the period 1899–1951 illustrate the upward trend in the tonnage of such exports to Europe.

TABLE 1

EXPORTS OF SELECTED COMMODITIES FROM NIGERIA
AND THE GOLD COAST, 1899-1951

Nigeria

'000 tons	1899–1901	1919–21	1929–31	1935–37	1951
Palm Oil	14	80	129	150	150
Palm Kernals	52	192	255	346	347
Groundnuts	–	45	151	242	141
Cocoa	–	20	53	91	122
Cotton	–	4	6	11	15
Hides and Skins	–	4	6	7	14
Timber	27	29	34	44	394
	93	374	634	891	1,183

Gold Coast

Cocoa (000 tons)	1	145	218	272	230
Timber (£000's)	70	123	104	112	4,977

Whilst West Africa provided the raw materials needed by European capitalism for greater economic growth and the production of manu-factured goods, Europe found a market for these goods in Africa. West African seamen proved to be an asset in several ways during this trade. They were reputed to be hard workers and rarely complained, and it was assumed with the arrival of the steamship in the mid-nineteenth century that they could withstand the heat of the engine-room more readily than Europeans, especially in the tropics. Thus one ship's master preferred West African seamen because of their 'better discipline and greater energy, and these reasons operate still more in their favour if the voyage is in tropical areas'.[7] Moreover, by the first decade of the twentieth century, West Africans engaged at African ports were paid lower wages than British crews, and therefore provided a cheap source of labour. In addition, West Africans were seen to be less belligerent and not as militant as their British counterparts. Yet, perhaps the initial impetus behind the engagement of West Africans on ships articles was to replace white crew who had fallen sick or had died from fever. The notoriously high mortality rate of white seamen sailing to West Africa had earned it the appropiate title of the 'White Man's Grave'. So while other factors helped maintain and perpetuate the engagement of West Africans on ships' articles, the origins of this could be found in the need for replace-ment local labour to take that of white seamen.

Initially Kru recruited on Royal Navy merchant ships were mainly used to save European labour from ships work on the West African coast. Thus the Kru were recruited on an Anti-Slavery Royal Navy vessel in the 1820s for this very reason: 'We hired 30 Africans called Kroomen who are always ready to serve as seamen on board of a man-of-war, or any other vessel, so long as they continue on that coast . . . they are employed on any service which would expose Europeans too much to the climate, such as wooding, watering, pulling in boats . . .'[8] Soon Kru were increasingly being used on trips back to Europe and America when labour shortages occurred.[9] Since ships' officers and shipowners believed that African labour could put up with the heat of the engine-rooms better than Europeans, they began to employ them on the trips to Liverpool as firemen and coal trimmers. African seamen, and Kru in particular, gradually began to replace white engine-room ratings during the first decade of the twentieth century. Their employment was encouraged by the fact that they were cheaper to employ and, it was alleged, they were less partial to drink.[10]

Later Kru came to occupy positions as ordinary and able-bodied seamen on deck, in addition to their engine-room work. There is little evidence to suggest that significant numbers of African ratings ever succeeded in rising to officer status before the Second World War. Instead Kru and other West Africans were confined to those positions that might be labelled unsuitable for European crews, for example the heavy manual work of firemen, trimmers and stokers in soaring temperatures, or the more menial jobs on deck. Firemen and trimmers became exclusively West African jobs on the trips between the UK and West Africa, and it seems the Kru ethnic group dominated here, or at least dominated the crews recruited at Freetown.[11] During and after the Second World War increasingly non-ethnic Kru (particularly Creoles, Mende, and Temne) began to occupy a larger share of the seamen recruited from Freetown.

It was because of their work as seafarers then, that Kru came and spent time in and around the ports of the UK while they were between ships. This was particularly so in the case of Liverpool. The transience of the Kru was underlined by the use of seamen's hostels in Liverpool. Thus in the 1920s Elder Dempster and Company had an 'African Hostel' on Upper Stanhope Street, where unemployed Kru seamen were housed at a rate of 6p per night for board and lodgings. This was deducted from their wages when they signed up for work.[12] The transient status of Kru seamen was also apparent with the introduction of the Aliens Acts in 1920 and 1925. These aimed to restrict further immigration of black colonials because of the slump in world trade generally and shipping in particular. Those classed as 'Aliens', that is, those who could not prove British nationality as colonial subjects, could be deported and had to register with the police. This legislation was particularly harsh in Cardiff where it was used to classify *all* blacks as aliens in spite of proof of British nationality.[13]

By 1926 the Home Office stated that almost all West African seamen found in Britian had come here on Elder Dempster ships and were not required to register under the 1925 Special Restriction (Coloured Alien Seamen) Order. However, they were asked to register under a separate arrangement kept by Elder Dempster for West Africans serving on their ships.[14] This had been in existence for some time in Liverpool and Hull. The objective of this separate agreement was to ensure that employees of Elder Dempster remained in their service while in the UK, and did not drift into more permanent employment, for example on shore where their presence would cause resentment and even 'racial disturbances' as it had in 1919.[15] This would also guard against the claiming of unemployment insurance by West Africans. Not only did these measures enable the immigration authorities in Liverpool to have greater control over black crews, and worked to eliminate what was seen as competition for jobs between black and white workers, but it also ensured that West African seafarers found it more difficult to settle in Britain. Thus transience was not necessarily something that was chosen by the Kru; often it was imposed on them.

The aftermath of the Second World War saw new opportunities for colonial subjects generally in the realm of shore work with the desperate labour shortage. Shore jobs previously out of bounds to blacks opened up, including the newly emerging service economy and light manufacturing. The simultaneous decline in the old staple industries, particularly shipping, saw Kru seamen resident in Liverpool or between ships from Freetown, taking up shore employment in the late 1940s and 1950s. They worked in various industries such as Vauxhall Motors, Imperial Chemical Industries, the Gas Board, and as boilermen in hospitals.[16] It seemed that the transience of the pre-Second World War era was being broken down as the needs of the British economy expanded employment opportunities. Active recruitment for labour in the colonies, especially the Caribbean, meant that it was now more acceptable for blacks generally to work on shore, and this of course opened up opportunities for the Kru at a time when shipping was in decline. Some took advantage of this development, especially those who had grown tired of going to sea and wished to work in more settled employment. Shore employment may also have paid more than seafaring, particularly for those who were engaged on articles in Freetown which paid a lower rate than those domiciled and signed on in Liverpool.

While some intended to settle in Britain by applying for domicile, or had even stowed away, others had no intention of settling and were in Liverpool simply to make a modest amount of money to take home on their return. The Kru had much in common with other migrants in this respect, except that a real possibility of going home was retained because of their seafaring work. Thus the shift into shore employment in the late 1940s and 1950s was temporary for some Kru until shipping picked up against in the 1960s.

II

A study of four randomly chosen Kru families in Liverpool during doctoral research attempted to yield data concerning residence, marital relations, offspring, and linkages with the wider black community. The construction of family genealogies (see Appendix) while not representative of Kru do highlight the experience of a particular section of that community. In particular they illustrate the linkages these Kru men have made with white-British society as represented by their marriage to predominantly white women. They also show the extent to which their offspring have remained wedded to the black community through marriage. Unstructured interviews have revealed the marriage patterns of these families. The families used here in no way claim to be a representative sample of the Kru in Liverpool. Rather they are case studies the aim of which is to highlight the experience of a particular section of that community.

The majority of the Kru men represented in the genealogies have come from polygamous family structures whereby their fathers have had two or more wives at any one time, the one exception being where the father was a clergyman. The practice of polygamy amongst rural peasant Kru of Liberia made economic sense. Thus while the men worked along the West African coast, either on the ships that went from Freetown or in-shore work, their wives working as a labour unit farmed and 'brushed the bush' ready for planting. However, with the settlement of Kru in Freetown, which grew as an urban centre during the nineteenth century, such a large number of wives was not economically viable, though this still gave prestige. Moreover, it was in the interest of a married couple to have as many children as possible to provide for them in their old age. Often then, Kru continued to have more than one wife at any one time, though increasingly these were held in succession.

Kru who settled in Liverpool from the early twentieth century up until the 1950s had often had several wives in Freetown, whether at the same time or in succession. Serial marriage remained a feature of Liverpool Kru life, where in the case studies, three out of four of these had been married (in the broadest sense) with children, to two or more women. In addition Kru who settled in Liverpool in the 1940s and 1950s were often still married to women in Freetown. Many of the marriages that occurred between Liverpool women and Kru tended to be common law. While it could be argued that this was a cultural trait that was transported from Freetown there has to be an additional reason as to why it worked in a very different context. What is clear is that common law relationships again seemed to underline the transience of the Kru in Liverpool. One possible explanation for this phenonemon was the economic situation of the Kru. Thus as seafarers, Kru men were obliged to leave their wives in Freetown an allotment of money out of their weekly wages. If a Kru man legally married a Liverpool woman he would be obliged to also leave her an allotment. This of course was impractical and undesirable, especially in cases where the idea of permanent settlement in Liverpool was not always seriously considered. Moreover, many passed through an intermediate stage when they first began to come to Liverpool, with existing family commitments in Freetown, and also growing commitments to girlfriends in Liverpool. Common law marriage to women in Liverpool was one way of getting around this problem. It did not bind them to permanent settlement if they were undecided, nor to a relationship that involved financial support while they were still supporting a family in Freetown. Of course intentions to settle could produce the opposite. Thus the four Kru represented in the genealogies did in fact legally marry their partners and settled permanently.

It would appear, then, that marriage patterns were bound up with the Kru's attitude to settlement in Liverpool. If they intended to settle, perhaps they were more likely to make the relationship official (and of course for some, marriage might provide one way of gaining domicile here). If on the other hand they had no such intentions, common law relationships might be preferable. Common law marriage represented a perfectly satisfactory arrangement for Kru seamen who were undecided on settlement, but what did the women gain from this? After all not only did these women become involved in socially unacceptable relationships with African men, but such relationships were frowned upon because of their common law nature. In a few known cases, it fulfilled a particular need at the time. Thus in one case, a woman had split up from her husband and was unable to support herself and children. The children were taken into care. Then she began living with a Kru man who eventually managed to get the children back for her. Indeed it was not uncommon for Kru men to take on other men's children even if his partner became pregnant to another man while he himself was away at sea. The popular image of white women who associated with black men throughout the inter-war years and later in the 1950s and 1960s was one that assumed such women were or had been involved in prostitution. It is uncertain who the women in common law relationships were except to say they were white and working class on the whole and not all had been prostitutes or had necessarily had some personal crisis in their lives.

III

Of the Kru seamen who came to Liverpool some inevitably settled, either by 'jumping ship' or by becoming domiciled through the official channels. There was also an unknown, but probably very small number of Kru stowaways who settled in Liverpool. The actual number of Kru who settled at any one time was never more than a few hundred. This figure did not increase through natural growth because of the absence of Kru women, and the tendency of Kru men to have children that were black British of African descent. Settlement also saw the Kru adopting British citizenship; it witnessed their entry into shore employment particularly in the post-war period, and their marriage to British women, all of which were indicative of 'assimilation' into British society. Yet such developments did not witness the abandonment of Kru ethnic identity and culture. As with other migrant groups to Britain, the Kru adapted cultural expressions to British society, and maintained an ethnic identity, even after they had permanently settled. How then was this maintained and why?

Kru ethnic identity was kept alive among those who had settled, through their constant contact with Kru seamen over a long period of time. This operated at several levels. First there was the contribution that transient Kru seamen made, whose comings and goings between Liverpool and Freetown helped maintain important ties beween the two Kru communities. These represented a tangible link with their homes in Freetown, and in particular their families and friends, since they were often the bearers of news and gossip. These seamen also maintained close social association with the Liverpool Kru through their participation in the clubs and societies the Kru had set up. While this contact was important in reinforcing Kru cultural expressions, for example, language, food, and social activities, such men were also a consistent reminder to the Liverpool Kru, of who they were and where they had come from. Second, was the steady stream of Kru that settled over the years. These served to replenish the existing settled community by both adding to its numbers, and by providing new blood to a community which could not reproduce itself in the same way culturally. Thus at both levels, various factors served to perpetuate a Kru ethnic identity. The crucial question then is *why* this was maintained, given that various factors had worked against it, for example the apparent assimilation of Kru through work and marriage.

The maintenance of a Kru ethnic identity and cultural forms in the context of Liverpool cannot be explained in terms of cultural–religious differences. As Christians, the Kru have never adopted religiously-based cultural values that differed radically from the society where they settled, for example, Islamic values. If they had, this might have provided one possible explanation for the maintenance of distinct cultural and ethnic ties. Secondly, it has been claimed by some, such as H.R. Issacs,[17] that ethnic identity is a 'natural' part of human nature that emerges spontaneously to meet the human need for belonging. Yet this cannot explain the perpetuation of a Kru ethnic identity, since there was nothing 'natural' or inherent about Kru identity. It has constantly been modified and changed, manifesting itself in various forms and types over time and within the general Kru diaspora. Kru identity in Liverpool provided the basis of an ethnic community because there was local occasion for it. It could only be maintained and perpetuated if prevailing conditions were favourable. What then were these conditions?

This has to be explained in terms of the marginal social status that the Kru in Liverpool occupied, coupled with the racial hostility they were subjected to. Thus in Liverpool a form of 'reactive ethnicity' developed where by Kru ethnic identity was encouraged in the context of community as a defence against discrimination and hostility. Thus social and cultural institutions, for example, the setting up of a Kru Society and Club represented, amongst other things, an attempt to foster mutual support among Kru and help them cope with the hostility of white society. Indeed this was part of a much wider pattern whereby national and ethnic organizations emerged among the African and Afro-Caribbean communities between the 1940s and 1960s.[18] The two Kru Clubs were organized for and by the Kru in their community. The Kru Society in Liverpool was set up in 1948 and became the headquarters for all Kru in Britain. The society began as an informal burial club where money was collected from individual Kru. When membership reached 200 plus it was decided to register the organization officially and expand its functions. At its height in the 1950s and 1960s it had a membership of several hundred. Subscriptions varied according to whether members were in or out of work. The Society occupied various premises in the Toxteth area of Liverpool during its existence and operated as a social society with a bar, games room, as well as a mutual-aid society. An informal Kru Club replaced the Kru Society in the 1970s when the Kru community began to dwindle. Here a handful of elderly Kru males met in a member's house every other Sunday, where a small weekly subscription was collected. The money was used for Christmas celebrations and to contribute to members' funerals.[19]

The ways in which Kru ethnic identity manifest itself in Liverpool (through language, food, social activities) was an expression of the groups cultural preference or tradition, but ultimately it was the external constraints of racism that led to its continuation in the context of community. What has been said about South Asians and West Indians equally applies to the Kru in Liverpool:

> . . . it should be recognised that the external constraints such as the migrants position in the labour and housing markets, or the discrimination he faces, are ultimately prior to the internal preferences of the group . . . It is the external constraints of discrimination which set the limits within which South Asians and West Indians in Britain operate. *But the particular behaviour of different groups may only be finally explained in terms of the culturally determined choices made within these limits as well as the various ethnic strategies used to counteract, circumvent or overthrow those constraints.*[20]

Of course the Kru like most West Africans and other migrant groups also identified themselves with broader groups. Kru identified with other Sierra Leoneans and Liberians, and with other West Africans generally. A political identity also emerged in the post-war period between West Africans and other groups such as Afro-Caribbeans and black British people. This rested on two factors. First the classification of these groups by white society as all being 'the same', and secondly, the shared history of colonialism, as well as a common experience of hostility in Liverpool.

The Kru came to occupy an intermediate position in Liverpool. Thus while those that permanently settled adopted British citizenship, increasingly worked in local shore industries after the Second World War, spoke English, and married and had families that were British, they were never fully accepted as such and continued to be perceived and treated as outsiders. This then highlighted their marginality in British society since the Kru were not accepted as 'British' and they were continually reminded of their racial/ethnic differences with the host society.

Kru ethnic identity did not then merely represent a clinging on to an anachronistic way of life that was inappropriate and outmoded in the context of Liverpool. On the contrary, Kru cultural forms were modified and moulded to fit the particular conditions of Liverpool. It represented a practical attempt to come to terms with their predicament – a foot in each camp of on the one hand, white society through work and marriage, and on the other, the black community where they resided and socialised. In many ways they were 'dual members'.

IV

The marriage of Kru seafarers and local white women represented more than marital union between two peoples, it was symbolic of the historical socio-economic links that had developed between West Africa and Liverpool. International trade and the development of a world economy had direct social consequences. It has made possible the flight of labour from the underdeveloped world to the economies and enclaves of the developed. This can be seen most clearly in the flight of the Kru from their original homeland of Liberia to the British colony of Freetown, and eventually Liverpool.

It was economic forces then that brought together in the first instance working class white women, themselves sometimes from once immigrant Irish families, and Kru seafarers, many from poor peasant families that had migrated to Freetown in search of greater economic opportunities. The settlement of Kru seamen and the forging of permanent relationships with local women had consequences for both. New sets of relationships would present themselves to which both would become tied. For Kru men two types of relationships emerged. First was that with white-British society through work, marriage and family; secondly was his relationship with other immigrant Africans, particularly those of his own ethnic group. The women for their part would also be confronted with new relationships through marriage to Kru men, in addition to their long standing relationships with family and friends. Yet these relationships could be jeopardized through marriage outside of their own race. At the same time, new relationships were often formed with the husband's ethnic group, with the wider black community through residence here, and often with other women who had married black people.

Marriage itself presented the opportunity to strike up new relationships between a Kru man and his wife's friends and family. In two case studies of Kru families in Liverpool, Kru men married women who had been married before and already had children. In one case, the children were young enough to be adopted as the Kru husband's own, and he therefore assumed the role of father to his wife's children. Kru men also had their own children who, having been born in Liverpool and pre-dominantly reared by their British wives, were black British of African descent. This gave an additional dimension to the relationship Kru men had with British society and its people. In addition where contact was maintained between the women and their parental family, again this made for greater social interaction between Kru and British society, though in some cases their families ostracized women who married Africans.

Through domicile, work, and family, Kru men had followed the path toward assimilation and adaptation to their new homes. They worked alongside British workers, whether this was on the ships, in the dry dock, or in the factories and industries of Liverpool. They adopted British nationality or maintained dual nationality, and finally they had married local women and had children that were British. Yet because of their marginal status they still maintained their identity as Kru, and as West Africans in common with others. Many Kru men who settled in Liverpool then, straddled two societies. In the sphere of work and marriage, the Kru participated in British society, working alongside British workers and having British wives. In the spheres of community and leisure, Kru men created an African enclave, to correct the marginality they were subject to in wider British society. Here they became tied into another set of relationships both with other Kru and other West Africans. Such linkages were strongest in the context of community – through the neighbourhood, the clubs, and the societies and organizations that emerged here.

The initial bonds formed between Kru and other early black settlers had occurred in the sphere of work, particularly seafaring, where this continued to have some influence on the social activities that emerged in Liverpool's dockland area. Yet the demise of the shipping industry in the post-war world and the shift of black seafarers into shore work meant that the community became the medium for forging of such relationships. Centres such as Stanley House set up in 1943 provided a club for black people, including seamen and their families to socialize free of discrimination. Stanley House situated at the heart of Liverpool's black community on Upper Parliament was patronized by West Africans, West Indians and Liverpool blacks and their families, and was intended to encourage better inter-racial relations particularly between blacks and whites.[21] National and ethnic organizations already established continued, and new ones emerged with increased migration by New Commonwealth immigrants. While Kru men straddled what could be seen as two social worlds, the women who married Kru men were often placed in an ambiguous social position. Marriage to an African man often excluded these women from certain areas of mainstream society. It strongly influenced the actual district in which they would live. They were on the whole confined to the Liverpool 8 (Toxteth) area – an area of concentrated black settlement. It also included the pubs and clubs they could visit, again being mainly confined to the Liverpool 8 area. The decision of white women to live in what was designated the unofficial 'Coloured Quarter' of Liverpool was partly related to their husbands' needs as seamen, where proximity to work was important. Here Kru seamen could also be assured of finding accommodation through the help of fellow Africans who occupied 'African houses'. Yet many continued to live here even after they had retired from the sea or had found shore work. This was due to the husband's desire to stay close to his countrymen in the face of white hostility, as well as the discriminatory practices of housing agents (both private and council). Moreover, white women who married Kru men were often willing to take up residence within the black community after having been rejected by the white. In many ways these women had little choice but to become part of the black community, short of abandoning their husbands.

These women then, like their Kru husbands, also became members of two overlapping societies, though of course the nature of this differed. For these women their status as white-British was obscured by their association with blacks, and their race partially set them apart from the black community. Yet such women have been more readily accepted by the black community than they have by white-British society as a whole. It is this then that accounts for their settlement in the predominantly black area of Liverpool, and their subsequent isolation from mainstream white society during the 1950s and 1960s.

Conclusion

The transience of the Kru in Liverpool was occupationally based; it derived from the nature of seafaring. Inevitably this occupational transience penetrated the community which was built on seafaring, and depended on it for its very existence. Transient marriage patterns through the widespread practice of common law marriage reflects this transience well. While this shows that the Kru acknowledged their transient status through their adoption of a practical strategy in dealing with their circumstances, their transience was also prescribed and underlined by government legislation in the 1920s. Moreover, the maintenance of Kru ethnic identity by those who had settled permanently and participated in British society as far they were permitted, was a response to their treatment as transients, and as people were made to feel that they did not belong. So while Kru transience derived initially from the nature of their work as seamen, they continued to be perceived as transients and outsiders because of their immigrant status.

The Kru community depended on transient ship workers for its survival, for its consistent input of new blood to sustain it, since in the absence of Kru women it could not reproduce itself in the same way culturally. Thus when the factors that actually brought the community into existence no longer existed – that is shipping, which also of course dictated its transient nature, the community inevitably becomes static and settled.

However, ironically, without the transient seamen who sustained the Kru community of Liverpool, the eventual fate of that community is doomed.

NOTES

1. B. Dahya, 'Pakistanis in Britain: Transients or Settlers?', *Race*, Vol.14, No.3, (1973), p.246.
2. Dahya, 'Pakistanis in Britain', p.236; V. Khan, 'The Pakistani Mirpuri Villagers at Home and in Bradford', in J.L. Watson (ed.), *Between Two Cultures* (Oxford, 1977).
3. A.S. Hall, *et al.*, *Policing The Crisis* (London, 1978); K. Pryce, *Endless Pressure* (Harmondsworth, 1979).
4. M. Banton, *The Coloured Quarter* (London, 1955), p.23.
5. J. Walvin, *The Black Presence – A Documentary History of the Negro in England, 1555–1860* (London, 1971), pp.12–13. Also *Black and White – The Negro and English Society 1555–1945* (London, 1973), pp.51, 197.
6. *Nautical Magazine* (1855) p.414. Also see A.G. Hopkins, *An Economic History of West Africa* (London, 1973), for increases in palm oil imports.
7. Public Record Office, Kew (PRO) HO 45/11897/332187.
8. J. Holman, *Travels in Madeira, Sierra Leone, Teneriffe* (London, 1840, 2nd edn.), p.63.
9. G.E. Brooks, Jr., *The Kru Mariner in the 19th Century: A Historical Compendium* (Newark, DE, 1972), pp.23–4, 35. Also *Nautical Magazine* (1855).
10. K. Little, *Negroes in Britain. A Study of Race Relations in English Society* (London, 1948, revised edn. 1972), p.89. Kru labour was also extensively recruited from the mid-nineteenth century onwards for use throughout colonial West Africa and beyond.
11. Ships Articles of Agreement for Elder Dempster ships 1890s–1948.
12. PRO HO 45/11017/377969. Police Report, Jan. 1920.
13. P.B. Rich, Philanthropic Racism in Britain: The Liverpool University Settlement, the Anti-Slavery Society for the Issue of "Half-Caste" Children, 1919–1951, *Immigrants and Minorities*, Vol.3, No.1 (1984), p.70; A.H. Richmond, *The Colour Problem* (Harmondsworth, 1955) p.34; Little, *Negroes* p.85; R. Ramdin, *The Making of the Black Working Class in Britain* (Aldershot, 1987), pp.102, 491.
14. PRO HO 45/12314 No.476/761, Jan. 1926.
15. See P.N. Davies, *The Trade Makers* (London, 1973) on the Liverpool shipping company Elder Dempster. For accounts of the 1919 'Race Riots' see R. May and R. Cohen, 'The Interaction Between Race and Colonialism; A Study of the Liverpool Race Riots, *Race and Class*, Vol.XVI (1974); J. Jenkinson, 'The 1919 Race Riots in Britain: Their Background and Consequences', unpublished Ph.D. thesis, University of Edinburgh, 1987, also by Jenkinson, 'The 1919 Race Riots in Britain', in R. Lotz and I. Pegg (eds.), *Under the Imperial Carpet: Essays in Black History 1790–1850* (Crawley, 1986), N. Evans, 'The South Wales Race Riots of 1919', *Llafur*, Vol.3, No.4 (1983), pp.5–29.
16. Interviews Mr Doe, Mr Weetah, Mr Morris, Mr Davies, Mr Toby, Mr Johnson and Mr Dixon, Liverpool 1989 and 1991.
17. H.R. Issacs, 'Basic Group Identity', in N. Glazer and D. Moynihan (eds.), *Ethnicity: Theory and Experience* (Cambridge, MA, 1975).
18. See R. Ramdin, *The Making of the Black Working Class in Britain*, and D.R. Manley, 'The Social Structure of the Liverpool Negro Community With Special Reference to the Formation of Formal Associations, unpublished Ph.D. thesis University of Liverpool, 1959.
19. Annual Returns of 'The United Kroo National Society 1950–1962, Register of Members and their Next of Kin, (no date). Both held in private hands, Liverpool.
20. R. Ballard and C. Ballard, 'The Sikhs: The Development of South Asian Settlements in Britain', in J.L. Watson (ed.), *Between Two Cultures: Migrants and Minorities in Britain* (Oxford, 1977), p.53.
21. See *Liverpool Echo*, 22 Oct. 1943.

APPENDIX

These Kru family genealogies are unique in terms of the pattern of kinship they represent, but at the same time many features characterize these families. They show polygamous and/or serial marriage patterns when in West Africa and the marriage of Kru males with British (mainly white but also black) women in Liverpool after settlement. The latter illustrates the linkages Kru men have made with predominantly white British society through such marriage patterns. The marriage patterns of their offspring show that these have remained on the whole wedded to the black community through marriage.

FAMILY A

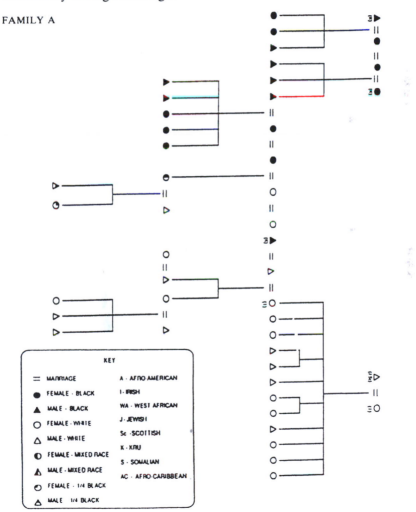

KEY

=	MARRIAGE	A -	AFRO-AMERICAN
●	FEMALE - BLACK	I -	IRISH
▲	MALE - BLACK	WA -	WEST AFRICAN
○	FEMALE - WHITE	J -	JEWISH
△	MALE - WHITE	Sc -	SCOTTISH
◑	FEMALE - MIXED RACE	K -	KRU
◮	MALE - MIXED RACE	S -	SOMALIAN
◔	FEMALE - 1/4 BLACK	AC -	AFRO-CARIBBEAN
◭	MALE - 1/4 BLACK		

FAMILY B

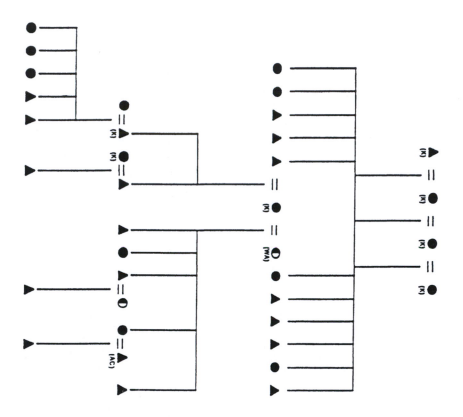

FAMILY C

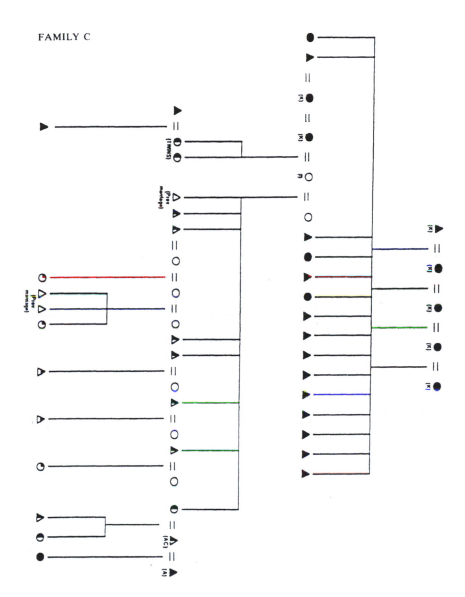

FAMILY D

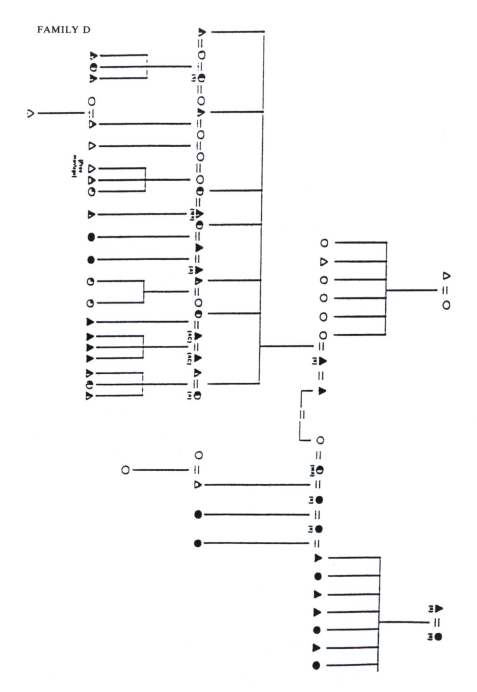

West African Students in Britain, 1900–60: The Politics of Exile

HAKIM ADI

The number of mainly West African students in Britain steadily increased in this century. After 1920 African students were increasingly influenced by pan-Africanist ideas and the nationalist movements, as well as radical politics and the experience of racial discrimination in Britain, and they formed various political organisations. The most important was the West African Students' Union which served as a nationalist pressure group and training ground for many West African student-politicians until the mid-1950s. The WASU published a journal, supported nationalist activity in Africa, lobbied the Colonial Office, and resisted attempts by that government department and humanitarian bodies to direct African student political activities in Britain.

For hundreds of years before the beginning of this century West African students have been arriving in Britain. Those that came of necessity tended to be members of the coastal elite or members of other wealthy and aristocratic families. This was not always the case however and during this century numbers of students from humbler backgrounds have also made the journey to Britain. Some came to attend boarding schools such as Queens College, Taunton, but probably the majority came for higher education, tending to prefer law and medicine. The students often favoured the London colleges but West Africans also studied at Newcastle and Durham, Oxford and Cambridge, Glasgow and Edinburgh, and at Trinity College Dublin. After 1945 more students were to be found in other colleges, pursuing a much wider range of courses than was the case before the war. In part such changes were due to the fact that colonial governments made some attempts to 'Africanize' many professional posts.

The numbers of students who came increased sharply throughout the century. In 1913 the Rev. John Harris collected the names of about 60 West Africans living in London, of whom around half were students. In 1925 the Nigerian Progress Union claimed to have 30 members throughout Britain. In 1927 the Colonial Office calculated that there were 45 West African undergraduates in Britain, and between 1930 and 1940 numbers rose from 50 to just over 70. By the early 1950s, however, it was calculated that there were over 2,000 students in Britain and over 1,000 in London alone.

In spite of this long history of student arrivals it seems that it is particularly in the last hundred years that West African students began to take part in political activities in Britain, to form organizations and campaign, not only for their own interests in Britain but also for the political, social and economic emancipation of the colonies. This study is an attempt to survey the political activities of such students during the present century.[1]

1900–12

One of the earliest organizations to include West African students was the African Association, formed by the Trinidadian Henry Sylvester Williams in London in 1897. Formed to encourage pan-African unity, especially throughout the British colonies, it had as its assistant secretary the Nigerian Moses Da Rocha, who at that time was a student at Edinburgh University.[2] It seems that a number of West African students were involved with the Association and in the work to organize the Pan-African Conference which took place in London in 1900. Students from Edinburgh University seem to have been particularly active during these early years and another, Richard Akiwande Savage, a future editor of *The Gold Coast Leader* represented the Afro-West Indian Literary Society of Edinburgh, of which he was President, at the 1900 Conference. Savage was also a member of the University Student Representative Council from 1898–1900 and a regular and well known contributor to the Scottish press.[3]

In 1902 West African medical students at Edinburgh persuaded the Dean of the Faculty of Medicine, Professor Simpson, to write in complaint at the openly discriminatory policies of the West African Medical Service, which barred from appointment those of 'non-European parentage'. A letter was also sent on behalf of all the West African students at Edinburgh. It made clear their opposition to this policy, which not only threatened their careers but was also a complete reversal of former government policy in West Africa.

Another example of student politics at Edinburgh is the appearance in 1906 of Keir Hardie's 'Zulu Letter'. The 'Zulu' in question was actually the Sierra Leonean medical student H.R. Bankole Bright, who was to become one of the founders of the National Congress of British West Africa and the West African Students' Union.[5] Bankole Bright had written to Hardie apparently approving of his criticisms of British misrule in Africa, and giving the impression that he was a Zulu student. In reply Hardie wrote a further fiery denunciation of British imperialism including the hope that 'the day will speedily come when your race will be able to defend itself against the barbarities being perpetrated against it by hypocritical whites'.[6]

Following the publication of the letter, questions were raised in parliament, while at the university Moses Da Rocha wrote a scathing criticism of Bankole Bright in a letter to *The Lagos Standard*. Da Rocha's response suggests that there were some important political differences between West African students at Edinburgh, a situation which Da Rocha himself admitted when he spoke of 'jealous Black Traitors and conspirators' in his correspondence with the Afro-American John Edward Bruce.[7] What is also clear is the high level of political activity amongst West Africans at Edinburgh, who lobbied politicians and wrote in the press both in Britain and West Africa. It was this kind of activity that was to occupy another Nigerian student from Edinburgh University, Bandele Omoniyi.

Omoniyi is best known for his book 'A Defence of the Ethiopian Movement' which was first published in 1908, but he also wrote in the Scottish and West African press and the *Labour Leader* of the Independent Labour Party, as well as writing a number of letters to members of the government and Ramsay Macdonald. Known at the university as 'a genuine enthusiast in the cause of the Negroes', most of Omoniyi's student life in Britain was spent attempting to defend the interests of Africans throughout the Empire. As a result, like many who would follow him he fell foul of the Colonial Office, a fact which may have contributed to his early death in Brazil at the age of 28.[8]

Ethiopianism in whatever form seems to have been popular at least among some West African students in Britain during this period. By 1904 there was an Ethiopian Association of Edinburgh, which included amongst its members the Nigerian medical student Ayodeji Oyejola.[9] In Liverpool in 1904, the Ethiopian Progressive Association (EPA) was founded 'by West African and West Indian natives, students at the various colleges'. The Association appears to have been short-lived but amongst its aims were: 'To create a bond of union between a) all other members of the Ethiopian race at home and abroad, b) to further the interest and raise the social status of the Ethiopian race at home and abroad; and to try to strengthen the friendly relationship of the said race and the other races of mankind.'[10] Such sentiments were precisely those of the Pan-African Conference in 1900 and show some consistency in the students' concerns.

So what were these concerns? Both individual West Africans and those organisations they joined were pan-African in scope. As the EPA expressed it they were concerned with 'matters of vital importance concerning Africa in particular and the Negro race in general'. Links were established with prominent African-Americans and their organisations, while in Britain those from West Africa and the Caribbean joined together to further their interests. Thus concerns ranged from the Natal uprising in South Africa to discrimination in the West African Medical Service, and the 'pacification' campaigns in Nigeria. The students were also concerned to raise the status of Black people in general, stressed the achievements of Blyden and Horton and extolled the virtues of a glorious African past. They were also concerned about racism and the colour bar in Britain. Omoniyi wrote that 'The treatment accorded to Africans in the Native-land and abroad by the ignorant classes of white men and those who ought to know better generally "make one's blood boil"', so strengthening friendly inter-racial relations was high on the agenda. In their appeals to the government the students exhibited a remarkable faith in the former's good offices, generally viewing government policies as simply mistaken or misapplied by 'the man on the spot'. Nevertheless their stay in Britain usually served to heighten the students' awareness of political issues, often as a result of the racism they found here, and familiarized them with a range of political opinions and organizations.[11]

An important part of student political activity was literary as can be seen from the writings of Savage, Omoniyi, Bankole Bright and Da Rocha, while the EPA had its own journal *The Ethiopian Review*. Fictional work such as the writing of J.E. Casely Hayford and Kobina Sekyi was also used to highlight the difficulties faced by West African students in Britain[12]

1912–25

Following the Universal Races Congress held in London in 1911 a number of new organizations and individuals became concerned with fostering 'inter-racial unity' of one sort or another. Commercial and humanitarian interests, represented by such organizations as the African Society and the Anti-Slavery and Aborigines Rights Protection Society (ASAPS), were alarmed at the development of racism and the colour bar in Britain, which they felt might provoke anti-British feeling amongst African students, which they would then transmit to their compatriots in Africa. These interests therefore saw the need to 'foster a more sympathetic spirit', and 'to remove certain social disabilities', as Sir Harry Johnston expressed it, in order that anti-colonial sentiments might be extinguished and the unity of the empire preserved.[13]

Various schemes such as a 'Universal Races Club' were suggested which might bring African students into contact with the 'better' side of British life. The aim of the 'well-wishers', such as the ASAPS, to shield African students from untoward or subversive influences, remained as a major goal for both government and many religious and humanitarian organizations until the 1960s. However, they pursued this aim in the face of British racism and colonialism and from these it was impossible to shield the student[14] For their part, the students also began to organize themselves, stirred by such indignities as the announcement by London University Graduates' Club in 1914, that it would operate a colour bar and therefore that Africans would be ineligible for membership. However, at the end of 1912, after consultation with the Colonial Office, the ASAPS together with the African Society began to plan for a conference for all Africans in the country, under the guidance of the ASAPS's energetic secretary Rev. John Harris.

Harris had the support of missionaries, educationalists and government officials as well as many prominent Africans resident in Britain, all of whom attended the conference held in April 1913. About 40 Africans attended, although many were businessmen rather than students. The declared aims of the conference, tackling the problem of discrimination and the colour bar, encouraging loyalty to the empire, and spreading Christian civilization, were acknowledged by all the participants, while the students cited examples of the kind of problems they faced.[15] Subsequently, however, students in Britain and opinion in West Africa turned against the idea of a student hostel or club which Harris proposed, for fear that this would lead to government control of students' lives[16] On the eve of the Great War the stage was set for the confrontations which would continue until the 1950s. The idea of the student hostel was at the heart of the matter, for who would assume control, the students, the Colonial Office or the 'well-wishers'? The Colonial Office certainly became more interested in exerting some influence over the students. In particular it wished to keep them away from anti-colonial and subversive influences, and over the years formed an uneasy alliance with the well-wishers led by John Harris and the ASAPS. For their part the students began to realize that both the conditions in Britain and in West Africa, and elsewhere, meant that they had to become more organized and begin to put more political pressure on the Colonial Office. They would also seek allies but at the same time try to preserve their independence and a spirit of self-reliance.

In 1916 the African Students' Union was formed under the presidency of the Sierra Leonean law student E.S. Beoku Betts. Mainly a social and cultural organization, it appears to have been relatively short-lived and probably folded when its president returned to West Africa in 1917.[17]

Also in 1916, following a meeting for West African students at the house of Lady Victoria Buxton, a West African Christian Union had been founded by the Nigerian Oladipo Lahanmi, but soon collapsed 'owing to the departure of some of its leading members'. It was restarted in 1917 'as a joint union of West African and West Indian students', closely connected with the Student Christian Movement (SCM) which in the same year established Student Movement House at 32 Russell Square in central London.[18]

The SCM was already in touch with Harris and equally concerned about the effects of the colour bar and racism and the fact that these gave rise to the 'seditious tendencies alleged among foreign students', and 'natural nationalist dissatisfaction with their position as subject races'. The SCM stated that the West African students were: 'the shyest and most difficult of all. Many are Christians, which appears to make them more anxious to avoid all Christian agencies. There is some rather undefined bitterness on the score of exploitation and bad government at home.'[19] Following the war important new organizations were being formed. In 1918 the African Progress Union (APU) was founded as 'an Association of Africans from various parts of Africa, the West Indies, British Guiana, Honduras and America, representing advanced African ideas in liberal education'. It declared its purpose as 'voicing African sentiments' and 'furthering African intersts'[20] Businessmen rather than students were the dominant force in the APU, but amongst its major aims was the intention to 'establish in London "a home from home", for social recreational and intellectual improvement, where movements may be promoted for the common welfare, and friends entertained'.[21] The 1919 'race riots', the part that colonial troops had played in the war and the increase in the Black population in Britain propelled the APU and another newly formed organization, the Society of Peoples of African Origin (SPAD) to become more vocal in their demands. At the same time the well-wishers were also reconsidering what kind of action they should take in these new conditions in order to maintain their influence over the students.

In 1919 the SCM, APU and the newly formed Committee for the Welfare of Africans in Europe (CWAE) held joint meetings to discuss a proposed social centre for Africans. Harris wished to open a hostel as 'the basis of a memorial to the African race for its part in the Great War'.[22] But by 1919 the APU were refusing to have anything to do with the scheme; indeed both the APU and the SPAO were at this time pursuing their own independent hostel plans, fearing 'a place run entirely by Englishmen for Africans'.[23] Harris continued with his mission to save Africans from 'those pernicious doctrines and habits' and began his lifelong role as a guardian to young African students in Britain.[24]

The APU continued with its own schemes to exercise 'benevolent guardianship' over the 'hundreds of African students who go to England each year', in rivalry with Harris and the CWAE. The CWAE clearly recognized that the students 'would be leaders of public opinion tomorrow' and stressed the importance of keeping them on the right lines. It was even suggested that the government should officially receive and train the students 'so that they could go back with ideas that should be helpful to the community out there and a safeguard for the future administrations of these colonies'.[25]

In February 1922 a further joint conference was held attended by a large number of the Africans resident in London; according to the APU there were about 300 at the time.[26] The Conference showed that differences over the hostel question even existed in the APU, and even more importantly some students claimed that the APU did not represent their interests, while they were deeply suspicious of the motives of the CWAE. The Conference almost seemed to signal the end of West African student reliance on the older leadership of the APU, and the realization that they must begin to organise themselves both at a social and political level. Such aspirations coincided with the emergence of the National Congress of British West Africa (NCBWA) and a new West African nationalism and self-reliance.

1923–30

Already in the early 1920s West African students were forming new organizations to further their interests. An Edinburgh African Union with mainly West African officers was, for example, formed in 1922.[27] However it was the Union of Students of African Descent (USAD) which became the most prominent organization of the African students during the early years of the 1920s. The Union grew out of the earlier West African and West Indian Christian Union, founded in 1917. After attracting a number of non-Christian members the name of the union was changed and grew in size from 21 members in 1921, to around 120 by 1924, including Indian and English associate members.[28] At first the Union seems to have been dominated by West Indian students, but in 1923 H.A. Hayfron-Benjamin from the Gold Coast became president and from then on the Union concerned itself more with West African concerns. Although the USAD declared itself an apolitical cultural and social organization, it soon found itself ranged against both the press and the Colonial Office, after a series of racist articles which culminated in offensive remarks concerning the West African section of the 1924 Empire Exhibition at Wembley.[29] The USAD protested to the Colonial Secretary and eventually the Governor of Nigeria intervened to prevent the publication of further derogatory articles.[30]

This successful protest marks a turning point in the activities of the students. Although protests had been made before, this one was of a much more assertive nature and it shows that the students were now prepared to organize themselves to fight against the racism they suffered from in Britain. They were certainly aided by the publication of their letters and resolutions in *West Africa,* which meant that they now had a much wider public profile. The Empire exhibition also focused attention on West African affairs and brought prominent West Africans to Britain. The students therefore had favourable conditions for all their activities. During 1924 USAD was addressed by Dr James Aggrey and by the Nigerian Legislative Council member Dr C.C. Adeniyi-Jones. Such meetings contributed to the wide ranging debate over the future of West Africa and the issues facing West African students in Britain.[31]

Also in 1924 the Nigerian Progress Union (NPU) was founded by the Nigerian law student Ladipo Solanke and Amy Ashwood Garvey, ex-wife of Marcus Garvey. According to Solanke the NPU was founded 'to solve the social, industrial, economic and commercial problem of Nigeria from the platform of Education of the masses of the Nigerian peoples'. It aimed to develop educational facilities in Nigeria in co-operation with the government and missionary bodies.[32] A major feature of the NPU, which had about 12 founder members, was its links with Nigeria; both Adeniyi-Jones and Henry Carr were patrons. The NPU also sought 'the foundation of a much needed hostel in London for all African Students.' It seems likely that Solanke and the other Nigerians were dissatisfied with the rather limited cultural activities of the USAD. Although Solanke and some others maintained their membership of both unions, the NPU marked a transition from the joint activities of African and Caribbean students in the USAD and APU to the more focused interests of the West African Students' Union (WASU).[33]

From early 1923 the Colonial Office was increasingly faced with the problem of exactly how to deal with the presence of students and other Africans in Britain. There was the colour bar and the problem of accommodation, and also the increasing number of students and others who either arrived as stowaways or who could afford a passage to Britain, but then became destitute or failed to finish their studies. The Colonial Office as well as bodies such as the CWAE favoured some sort of control and supervision over students, but feared that any move in this direction might further antagonize the students or their parents.[34]

In July 1925 Bankole-Bright a member of the Legislative Council of Sierra Leone visited London. His presence in the country and influence on the students were to lead directly to the formation of the West African Students' Union on 7 August. Bankole-Bright urged the students to forge a unity in Britain that would mirror that established by the newly formed National Congress of British West Africa.[35] Some West African members of other organizations, especially of the USAD, opposed forming a new union. However most of the students clearly saw the need for an organization which aimed 'to afford opportunity exclusively to West African students in Great Britain and Ireland to discuss matters affecting West Africa educationally, commercially, economically and politically, and to co-operate with the NCBWA'.[36] Under the leadership of Ladipo Solanke the Union established itself as the main cultural and political focus for West Africans in Britain for the next 25 years. It also served as a training ground for many future political leaders, and played an important role agitating for an end to colonial rule.

Following the formation of the WASU the union launched its own journal also called the *Wasu* in March 1926. The journal set out to explain the concerns of West Africans to the world at large, especially the need for progress and development. Over the years the *Wasu* played a major role in championing the concerns of West Africans in Britain, not least in their demands for independence from colonial rule. In the early years the journal was much concerned with the concept of West African nationhood and 'the equality of the races'. These were also the main subjects of two publications by members of the WASU, Solanke's *United West Africa at the Bar of the Family of Nations* published in 1927, and J.W. De Graft Johnson's *Towards Nationhood in West Africa*, published in 1928.[37]

In its early years the WASU revived the question of a student hostel and from 1928 appealed to West Africa for funds in order to establish some self-reliance. However the Colonial Office was also showing some interest in such a scheme, not least because of the effects of the colour bar particularly on accommodation. According to Colonial Office information, in 1927 there were about 125 African students at universities in Britain, mainly in London and Edinburgh. Most of the students had problems with accommodation and in the words of Hanns Vischer of the Colonial Office 'they feel very bitter against us as a result of their experiences in Britain'. This state of affairs was seen as regrettable because as Vischer pointed out, 'these men on their return to Africa are most likely to occupy important positions in their own community.[38] Vischer's plan was to work with the WASU, so that by encouragement the union might come under the influence of the Colonial Office which officially would remain in the background. Solanke and the WASU had their own plans which involved getting what they could from the Colonial Office but retaining their independence and that of the proposed hostel, and for this purpose Solanke travelled to West Africa on a fund-raising trip in 1929.[39]

The latter half of the 1920s therefore witnessed major developments in the organization and activities of West African students in Britain. Even after the founding of the WASU the NPU continued to function as did the USAD, which held regular weekly meetings, often with a West African focus. In 1926 the USAD and the APU unsuccessfully petitioned the Colonial Secretary over the lack of scholarships for West African students. In addition to these three unions a Gold Coast Students Association was also active and there were African associations at both Cambridge and Edinburgh Universities. The students also managed to develop a number of international links duing this period. The WASU and especially Solanke were greatly influenced by Marcus Garvey who even donated his house as the Union's meeting place. The Union also had contact in the USA, Caribbean, South Africa, the Belgian Congo and Brazil, whilst in 1926 two of its members attended the World YMCA Conference in Finland.

1930–39

The period of the Depression worsened the economic and political situation in both Britain and West Africa. In particular racism and the colour bar in Britain forced the students to take action to defend themselves, while a number of new organisations appeared such as the West African National Association and Harold Moody's League of Coloured People (LCP), which in their own ways both sought to alleviate the problems facing students and other Black people in Britain. In 1932 the President of the WASU, Oluwole Ayodele Alakija, successfully sued a London Hotel which had refused him a room because he was 'a man of colour'.[40] The case highlighted the problems facing the students, was widely reported in the British and West African press and led to a general clamour for government action. The Colonial Office was well aware that future leaders were being alienated and in May 1932 the Colonial Secretary made a speech to the Africa Society, pointing out the disastrous effects of racism. It was in these conditions that further attempts were made to establish a student hostel.

The LCP, which included several West African members, as well as the WASU and the Colonial Office were all interested in such a hostel. The Colonial Office managed to co-opt Harold Moody, the President of the LCP, on to their semi-secret committee which hoped to establish a hostel for 'all coloured people' in spite of the contrary plans of the WASU. However, as soon as Solanke returned from West Africa in 1932 it became clear that two rival schemes existed. With the money raised in

West Africa the WASU opened their hostel in Camden in March 1933, while the Colonial Office beset by financial and other problems was finally able to open their London hostel, Aggrey House, in October 1934.

The WASU immediately attacked the opening of Aggrey House as an attempt by the Colonial Office to control the activities of African students, because of the 'rousing of National consciousness among the younger elements in West Africa'.[41] Moody and all those connected with it were denounced as traitors, while the WASU issued an appeal 'to every lover of freedom to help us check this scheme of imperialism which would strangle the very thought of its subjects and control their every action and opinion'.[42]

The campaign which the WASU launched to boycott Aggrey House is important for a number of reasons. The students were clearly right about the Colonial Office's attempts to exert some influence over them, and saw this as being detrimental to their political development and to the cause of West African independence. The independence of the hostel was seen as vital if they were to campaign successfully in Britain for their rights and for colonial freedom. Indeed the Union saw attempts to curtail student activities in London as being closely connected with 'imperialist oppression in the colonies', such as the introduction of the new Sedition Laws.[43] The resulting campaign drew the students closer to the anti-colonial forces in Britain, the League Against Imperialism, the Negro Welfare Association and the National Council for Civil Liberties, those 'subversive elements' which so concerned the Colonial Office and the 'well-wishers'.

It is likely that there was also rivalry between the WASU and the LCP as to who should represent West African students in Britain. Relations between the two organizations did improve towards the end of the 1930s, but the struggle with the Colonial Office over Aggrey House as well as their other problems only served to radicalize the students during this period.

Solanke had taken the opportunity afforded by his 'mission' to West Africa to establish firmer links with prominent political figures on the coast and had created the basis for the future Youth Movements by establishing branches of WASU throughout the region. The Union and the Gold Coast Students' Association (GCSA) in Britain maintained a high level of activity directed towards West African issues throughout the 1930s, including support for the two delegations sent from the Gold Coast to petition the British government and action over the Cocoa hold-ups. As a result of the Italian invasion of Ethiopia there was an intensification of political activity among the students and many calls for a 'Black United Front' in Britain.[44] During the latter part of the 1930s the students mounted a campaign to oppose any transfer of West African colonies to Germany as was being proposed by the Rothermere press and others.[45]

It was in this climate, with the growing threat of war and the radicalization of the students that both the CWAE and the Colonial Office stepped in to provide the students with the financial assistance which allowed them to open a new hostel in 1938. The Union had been in serious financial difficulties since the mid-1930s and had been forced to accept help from Hanns Vischer and Sir John Harris. As a result, the new hostel was the subject of rival CWAE and WASU claims of ownership for many years.

Although this new arrangement might be thought to have compromised the WASU, it was precisely during this period that many students were coming under the influence of radical and Marxist politics, particularly as a result of the activities of Padmore, Wallace-Johnson and others, and of organizations such as the International African Service Bureau. At least one student, Desmond Buckle a member of the rather apolitical GCSA, eventually became closely connected with the activities of the British Communist Party, and caused some concern in the Colonial Office.[46] The Colonial Students Committee in its 1938 report suggested that the Victoria League might be able to introduce students to respectable families in Britain who could divert them away from subversive influences. In 1940 over 60 students were in touch with the Victoria League, including Desmond Buckle![47]

1939–45

The war was to have a major impact on the students. The British and other Allied governments found it necessary to call for support from the colonies and therefore emphasized that the war was being fought for freedom, democracy and self-determination. The expectations of people in West Africa and students in Britain were therefore raised as a consequence, while at the same time the Colonial Office did everything possible to work with the students. During the war for example the Union received visits from Lord Lloyd, the Colonial Secretary, and Clement Attlee the deputy Prime Minister. The WASU therefore assumed a much higher profile as a result of the war and was able to exert a much greater influence. It submitted a series of memoranda to the government and was probably the first West African organization to demand 'complete self-government within five years after the war', a demand which as a result of public opinion in both Britain and West Africa, even the government was forced to discuss and act upon during these years.[48]

The Union used its position to agitate for more political action in West Africa itself. Solanke in particular sent a constant stream of letters to his contacts, many of them ex-members of the Union. At the same time the WASU was able to act as a spokesman for farmers' organizations, trades unions and even individuals in West Africa who wished to petition the British government. This activity was taken a step further in 1942 when the West African Parliamentary Committee was formed to coordinate and increase pressure on the government. The Committee comprised five members of the Union and five Labour MPs including the future Colonial Secretary Arthur Creech Jones. The MPs were able to raise questions in Parliament which strengthened the effectiveness of the Union as a pressure group agitating for colonial freedom. The formation of the Parliamentary Committee also marked a high point in the relations between the Union and the Labour Party, which had been growing stronger since the late 1930s. The attention of Creech Jones, Sorensen, Haden Guest and others seemed to represent a great advance in the status of the Union. These and other MPs, as well as Rita Hinden of the Fabian Colonial Bureau, were extremely close to the students during the war years, and were invited to contribute to the two major conferences organized by the Union. In 1940 Sorensen had stated 'I elect myself to be one of the speakers in the House of Commons not only of your grievances but also of your aspirations'. But the post-war Labour government failed to live up to the expectations of many of the students who vigorously supported it in the 1945 General Election.[49]

As noted above, during the war years the Colonial Office was even more concerned to influence the students away from any subversive influences. It was joined in this endeavour by a new group of largely Chistian well-wishers who aimed to carry on the work of Sir John Harris following his death in 1941. The Colonial Office appointed J.L. Keith as student welfare officer in the early years of the war, while the well-wishers were represented by the Rev. Harold Grace and Canon J.M. Campbell and what became known as the Dean of Westminster's Committee.

The Committee was as concerned about the possible alienation of African students as Harris and the CWAE had been. In co-operation with the WASU they planned to raise enough money to open a larger hostel necessary to accommodate students whose numbers were expected to increase substantially after the war. The WASU was already receiving financial support from the Colonial Office and the Colonial governments, but the new agreement was accepted as the Dean of Westminster's Committee only publicly demanded that the new hostel house a chapel, and that a chaplain, approved by WASU should be appointed. It was as part of these plans that Solanke was sent to West Africa on a second fund-raising trip in 1944.[50] Eventually, in 1949, the WASU was able to open a second hostel on Chelsea Embankment.

The war years led to even greater awareness amongst the students of international issues, but did little to diminish their concern with their own treatment in Britain. As noted above the problem of colour prejudice continued to worry the Colonial Office and the well-wishers and a number of complaints about discrimination against African and Black ARP wardens, servicemen and munitions workers were made to the Colonial Office during these years. Indeed in 1942 the Minister of Information was forced to 'declare War' on the colour bar in an article in the *Sunday Express*.[51]

The experiences of the war clearly prepared many of the students for greater political activities at its end. For example, from 1941 the WASU had organized a study group which discussed topical issues and prepared briefing papers to inform students and other interested parties including the West African Parliamentary Committee. These discussions also contributed to raise expectations, especially for an end to colonial rule, but paradoxically in London the students appeared to be in some danger of becoming more and more dependent on external financial support which could only compromise their independence. In 1944 the WASU became an incorporated body with a board of directors which included Lord Listowel, Rev. Reginald Sorensen MP and Canon Harold Grace.[52]

1945–49

The post-war period was one of the most complex and politically dramatic for West African students in Britain. In 1944 an Ibo Union was formed at Cambridge, and there followed a serious split between the Yoruba and Ibo students in the WASU itself. This split reflected political rivalries in Nigeria, especially those within the Nigerian Youth Movement, but also showed the growing importance of local rather than regional West African politics. In 1945 Obafemi Awolowo formed the exclusively Yoruba Egbe Omo Oduduwa, while three years later a Yoruba Federal Union, linked to the National Council of Nigeria and the Cameroons (NCNC) was started by Kola Balogun. In the same year a separate Nigerian Union of Great Britain and Ireland was also established, all of these seeming to diminish the influence and importance of the WASU. In addition to the WASU in London, West African student organisations were also active around the universities at Oxford, Cambridge, Glasgow, Newcastle and Exeter, as well as the Association of Students of African Descent in Dublin, which had been formed in the 1930s.

Many more West Africans students were able to come to Britain after the war and the new generation were clearly strongly influenced by the growing political movements within the colonies. Parodoxically, at a time when it seemed as if the WASU was losing its influence and that regional and pan-African concerns were dying, the Union and its members stepped up their political activity. The students from the Gold Coast including Nkrumah, who was elected Vice-President of the Union in 1945, came to the fore and the WASU seemed to be at its most radical.

In 1945 the students, and Nkrumah in particular, played an important part in the Pan-African Conference in Manchester and in the various activities organised in support of the Nigerian general strike. That same year also saw the formation of the West African National Secretariat (WANS) which included amongst its aims 'to foster the spirit of unity and solidarity among the West African territories' in order to realize 'a United West African National Independence'. The WANS revived the notion that 'West Africa is one Country' just at the time when other political forces, including many students in Britain, were more concerned with local politics based on narrow national interests. Nkrumah became the secretary of this new radical organization which included amongst its leading members other students such as Kojo Botsio, Bankole Akpata and Bankole Awooner-Renner.[53]

It was also during this period that Nkrumah started The Circle among members of the WASU. The Circle was a small revolutionary cell organized like a secret society in order to form a vanguard group within WASU, which would take the lead in political activities. The long-term aim of the Circle appears to have been to prepare its members to transform West Africa into a 'Union of African Socialist Republics'. It seems that Botsio, Akpata and Awooner-Renner were members, but little is known about the group's activities.[54] In 1946 WANS and WASU organized a West African conference which included representatives from the French colonies. The main theme of the conference was the creation of a 'united and independent West Africa' and it attempted to revive the idea of a West African Congress along the line of the earlier NCBWA. The activities of the WANS, Nkrumah, and many other students showed their increasing sympathy for the Soviet Union and Communism. During this period much stronger links were established between West African students and the British Communist Party, and the WASU even sent delegates to the Party's Congress. The students also had strong links with the World Federation of Democratic Youth and the International Union of Students and representatives were sent to its Prague conference in 1950.[55]

The increasing radicalization of many students was in part prompted by their dissatisfaction with the actions of the new Labour government. This government was now ruling over the colonies and was slow in its attempts to put into practice the many promises made in the past. Creech

Jones was Colonial Secretary precisely at the time when the nationalist struggle was accelerating in West Africa. The violent suppression of the ex-servicemen's demonstration in the Gold Coast in February 1948 led to a major campaign of protest in Britain involving the WANS, the WASU, the Gold Coast Students' Union and the newly formed African Students' Union in Manchester. It was actions such as this, and the shooting of miners at Enugu in November 1949, which turned the students away from the Labour Party towards more revolutionary politics. As a result the WASU itself came under attack for promoting radical political aims.[56]

The Commmunist Threat

Since the late 1920s the WAU had been in contact with a number of left-wing organizations and individuals, both in Britain and throughout the world. The 1930s was a period when the members of the Union and other students from the colonies, increasingly came into contact with the politics of anti-imperialism, anti-fascism and socialism. The very fact of colonialism, however, and the position of colonial students in Britain, the problem of discrimination and racism in accommodation, admission to higher education and employment, meant that many of them were forced to view life and politics afresh, from a more radical standpoint, whatever their origins. For this reason they were often drawn towards the more radical and left-wing organizations and individuals, who were most likely to support them, be sympathetic to their plight, and be opposed to colonialism. At the same time organizations such as the communist-led League Against Imperialism (LAI) were eager to exert influence over the young colonials so as to encourage radical political changes in the colonies themselves. From the early part of the century it was precisely this relationship, with all its potential dangers for the Empire, which Colonial Office officials and other defenders of the Empire feared. They therefore did their best to shield colonial students from such subversive influences and from the more unpleasant aspects of life in Britain. However, this proved an impossible task. Not only were the colour bar and discrimination not eliminated, but also, because of the very nature of colonialism, events occurred in West Africa and in Britain which would continue to fuel the nationalist sentiments of West African students, and propel them towards an increasingly radical critique and solution of their problems. During the 1930s anti-imperialist organizations, such as the International Africa Service Bureau (IASB), developed within the African and Caribbean communities in Britain, while the activities of George Padmore and I.T.A. Wallace-Johnson created a new Marxist, as well as anti-imperialist milieu, which held great attraction for many West African students.

The WASU's link with the left in Britain seem to have begun as a result of Solanke's friendship with Kenyatta in the 1920s, and the latter's links with the LAI, Reginald Bridgeman, and the Indian-born Communist MP, Shapurji Saklatvala. Kenyatta was also closely linked with the Profintern's International Trade Union Committee of Negro Workers (ITUC-NW) which also established links with the WASU.[57] Throughout the 1930s the WASU established closer links with Bridgeman and the LAI and the affiliated London-based Negro Welfare Association (NWA). It was this organization, led by the Barbadian communist Arnold Ward, which the Ghanaian student Desmond Buckle first joined in the late 1930s. Yet another organization linked to the LAI was the National Council for Civil Liberties (NCCL), which assisted WASU during the Aggrey House campaign.[58] From 1937 the British Communist Party began to take a more direct interest in the colonies and until the outbreak of war produced the *Colonial Information Bulletin*, which carried news from Britain, the Caribbean and Africa. It is likely that from this period the Communist Party made efforts to recruit some West Africans such as Buckle and the Nigerian Babalola Wilkey.[59] What is clear is that the students were in close contact with pro-communist organizations and individuals, such as Paul Robeson and Nancy Cunard, who exerted some influences, even though Solanke and many others remained suspicious of communism and the Soviet Union.[60]

The war years clearly did much to raise the status of both communism and the Soviet Union. As mentioned above Nkrumah and the WANS were clearly influenced by communist thinking, as were many other WASU members. By 1948 the Colonial Office was lamenting 'the addition of so many of the young West African intelligentsia to form communist associations in the UK and the printing of communist articles in the West African native press'. Bankole Awooner-Renner, the chairman of WANS and member of the WASU, was even reported to have sent a petition to Stalin 'on behalf of the progressive people of West Africa' complaining of conditions in the colonies and asking for land for settlement in the Soviet Union!'[61] As a result of links with the Prague-based International Union of Students (IUS), many members of the WASU and other West African students looked towards the Soviet Union and Eastern Europe for their political inspiration, and by 1952 there were 11 Nigerians studying in East Germany.[62] The WASU continued to support the IUS even after the British National Union of Students (NUS) had left it, and rejected the NUS view that 'the IUS is a partisan political organisation which is little more than the student section of the Cominform'.[63]

Solanke however always remained suspicious of communism and opposed the growing influence of the ideology on the students. He reluctantly supported demands for self-government, and was totally opposed to the WASU resolution of 1947 which demanded completed British withdrawal from West Africa. However Solanke was in West Africa between 1944 and 1947 and had little influence over the students in Britain. After the opening of the new student hostel in 1949 he found himself opposed both by the younger pro-communist students such as Adenekan Ademola, Joe Appiah, and Ademola Thomas, and by Reginald Sorensen and J.M. Campbell, representatives of the Dean of Westminster's Committee who exerted increasing control over the new hostel. Solanke complained both to Sorensen and the Colonial Office about increasing communist influence in the WASU but received surprisingly little support.[64] The Colonial Office seems to have taken the view that Sorensen had some moderating influence over the students and was not sympathetic towards Solanke. On the other hand, they continued to shown concern over WASU and other student links with the IUS, as well as the critical tone, and to some, pro-communist line of student articles.[65]

During the early 1950s many students used Marxist phraseology in their statements, or were sympathetic towards the Soviet Union. The Nigerian Student Union in Britain for example, declared in 1953 'there is common ground between the colonial peoples and the communist world', yet the Colonial Office considerd that in general their views were 'surprisingly good and responsible'.[66] From 1947 the Colonial Office had formed an advisory committee to consider 'the political significance of African students in GB'. Closer links were established with the students and in November 1951 the Colonial Secretary established a Consultative Committee on the Welfare of Colonial Students in the UK. The Committee included amongst its membership Reginald Sorensen and other MPs as well as representatives from the WASU, the Nigerian and Gold Coast Unions and the Sierra Leone Students' Union. It provided a forum where matters could be discussed and resolved and meant closer contact between the Colonial Office and student militants such as Ade Thomas who represented the WASU.[67]

The attempts by the Colonial Office and various well-wishers to steer the students away from the subversive influences of communism and other radical ideologies had only limited success. By the early 1950s the British Communist Party had its own West African student branch. In part the Colonial Office's failure was because, as J.L. Keith explained: 'what drives African students into undesirable political fields is what has happened and is happening in Africa . . . African colonial government is not "democratic" until it is there will be political feelings and agitation among the students of a kind which plays into the hand of Communists and other propagandists.'[68] In addition, however, the colour bar and racial discrimination continued to radicalize the students and make them sympathetic to ideologies and countries which appeared to have no room for racism. It is of interest that it was the leading British Communist R. Palme Dutt who declared in 1958 that 'the real foundation of the colour bar and racial discrimination lies in the colonial system'. However, very often the students' radicalism vanished when they returned home. They were 'proletarians in Westminster and bourgeois in Lagos', as one ex-student put it.[69]

But the students and their organizations here did play an important part in the anti-colonial struggle. From the beginning of the century and continuing throughout the 1950s, they acted to put pressure on the Colonial Office, and to win the support of MPs and the British public. In addition to many active campaigns the students saw the importance of the written word and they published journals and wrote articles accordingly. There can be little doubt that the time the students spent in Britain and their activities whilst they were here were extremely important in their political development and often of direct importance to political advance in the colonies themselves. The political and social conditions in Britain and the conflicting views and ideologies which surrounded the students during their stay, all contributed to this development. It is in this context, that the WASU and other student organizations have been correctly seen as training grounds for the future political leaders of West Africa.[70]

NOTES

1. Details of the activities of West African students can also be found in R. Jenkins, 'Gold Coasters Overseas 1880–1919: With Specific Reference to Their Activities in Britain', *Immigrants & Minorities*, Vol.4, No.3 (1985), pp.5–52; P. Rich, 'The Black Diaspora in Britain: Afro-Caribbean Students and the Struggle for a Political Identity, 1900–1950', *Immigrants & Minorities* Vol.6, No.2 (1987), pp.151–73; P. Fryer, *Staying Power: The History of Black People in Britain* (London, 1984), pp.436–40; D.A. Lorimer, *Colour Class and the Victorians* (Leicester, 1978), pp.56–68, 217–9; F.O. Shyllon, *Black People in Britain* (Oxford, 1974), pp.45–66. Some details of student numbers can be found in J.L. Keith 'African Students in GB', *African Affairs*, Vol.45 (1946), pp.65–72; A.T. Carey, *Colonial Students: A Study of the Social Adaptation of Colonial Students in London* (London, 1956).
2. P. Esedebe, *Pan-Africanism: The Idea and Movement 1776–1963* (Washington, DC, 1982) p.47.
3. Esedebe, *Pan-Africanism*, p.49. On R.A. Savage see *The Student* (Edinburgh University, 20 Oct. 1898), p.8. See also J.A. Langley, *Pan-Africanism and Nationalism in West Africa 1900–45, A Study in Ideology and Social Classes* (Oxford, 1973), p.189.
4. Public Record Office, Kew (PRO) CO 96/403/11591.
5. See A.J.G. Wyse, *H.C. Bankole-Bright and Politics in Colonial Sierra Leone* (Cambridge, 1990), and M.C.F. Easmon, 'Sierra Leone Doctors', *Sierra Leone Studies*, n.s. 6 (1956), pp.81–96.
6. *The Scotsman*, 5 July 1906, p.7.
7. G. Shepperson, 'An Early African Graduate', in G. Donaldson (ed.), *Four Centuries,*

Edinburgh University Life 1583–1983 (Edinburgh, 1983), pp.96–7, ref.3. Other articles by Da Rocha are to be found in *The New Age*, June 1906, and *The Lagos Standard* 1 Aug. 1906.
8. See Hakim Adi 'Bandele Omoniyi – A Neglected Nigerian Nationalist', *African Affairs*, Vol.90, No.361 (1991), pp.581–605.
9. Adi, 'Bandele Omoniyi', p.585, note 11.
10. Adi, 'Bandele Omoniyi', p.583, note 9.
11. For Omoniyi's views on racism and colonial government see Adi, 'Bandele Omoniyi'.
12. Adi, 'Bandele Omoniyi', p.583, note 9. On the early writing of the Casely-Hayfords and Sekyi see Jenkins 'Gold Coasters Overseas'.
13. 'Conference for Africans', *Journal of the African Society*, Vol.XII, (1913), p.425.
14. African businessmen were also concerned about the students. See F.W. Dove to Harris, 18 April 1913. Rhodes House Library, Oxford (RHL) Mss. Brit. Emp. s.22 G431.
15. *Anti-Slavery Reporter and Aborigines' Friend* April 1913, pp.56–60.
16. *African Times and Orient Review ATOR)*, April 1914, p.98 and *The Lagos Standard*, 7 June 1914.
17. *ATOR*, Feb. 1917, p.36; Dec. 1917, p.113; March 1917, p.48; Aug. 1917, p.46; and Sept. 1917, p.61.
18. See Student Christian Movement Archives, Selly Oak College, Birmingham (SCM). Report of the General Committee of SCM 1915–16, p.38. On the SCM see also *The Student Movement*, 24/1, p.6. Also J. Green, 'A Brown Alien in a White City', in R. Lotz and I. Pegg (eds.), *Under the Imperial Carpet: Essays in Black History 1780–1950* (Crawley, 1986), pp.208–17; and Rich, 'The Black Diaspora in Britain'.
19. SCM Archives. 'Memo on present condition of work among foreign students', 1918.
20. *The African Telegraph* (London) Dec. 1918, pp.89–90.
21. *The African Telegraph*, Dec. 1918, pp.89–90.
22. RHL. Mss. Brit. Emp. s.23 H2/56, Harris to Sir Owen Phillips, 24 Feb. 1919.
23. RHL. Mss. Brit. Emp. s.23 H2.56, APU to Harris, 23 April 1919, Hercules to Harris, 23 April 1919, and Cockin to Harris, 13 May 1919.
24. RHL. Mss. Brit. Emp. s.22 H2/57 Harris to Lord Cromer, 23 June 1919; and on Harris's guardian role, Harris to Olive Temple, 21 Nov. 1919.
25. *African World*, Supplement, 30 Nov. 1921, p.viii.
26. *West Africa*, 4 March 1922, pp.167–8.
27. On the Edinburgh African Union see *West Africa*, 25 Feb. 1922, p.133.
28. *West Africa*, 25 Oct. 1924, p.1179.
29. *West Africa*, 22 March 1924, p.247 and 10 May 1924, p.445; also PRO CO 554/64/23120, USAD to Colonial Secretary, 14 May 1924.
30. See Governor Clifford's letter to the USAD in *West Africa*, 7 June 1924, p.615.
31. *West Africa*, 6 Sept. 1924, p.942.
32. *The Spokesman*, April/May 1925, p.26.
33. Solanke Papers, Gandhi Library, University of Lagos. (SOL) Box 56, file 4, 'Nigerian Progress Union'.
34. PRO CO 554/67/47017, 'Control of African Students Coming to Great Britain to Study', n.d.
35. *West Africa*, 15 Aug. 1925, p.1002, and G. Olusanya, *The West African Students Union and the Politics of Decolonisation 1925–58* (Ibadan, 1982), pp.6–9.
36. Olusanya, West African Students Union, p.9.
37. J.W. de Graft Johnson, *Towards Nationhood in West Afric, Thoughts of Young Africa Addressed to Young Britain* (London, 1928)), and L. Solanke, *United We-t Africa at the Bar of the Family of Nations* (London, 1927).
38. PRO CO 323/1025/60050. 'Native Colonial Students in the UK', 1929.
39. Solanke apparently also wished to visit West Africa to develop Garvey's United Negro Improvement Association (UNIA). See SOL.78 Solanke to Garvey, 25 Nov. 1928.
40. *West Africa*, 5 March 1932, p.209.
41. *The Truth About Aggrey House: An Exposure of the Government Plan for the Control of African Students in GB* (London, 1934).

42. *The Truth About Aggrey House*, p.6.
43. PRO CO 323/1281/31474. Resolution of WASU meeting, 1 March 1934.
44. *Wasu*, Vol.5, Nos.2/3, p.25. The split between the GCSA and the WASU is complex and dates from at least 1929 and continued until 1938. In part there was an attempt by the Gold Coast students to combat what they saw as Nigerian domination of the WASU and the splits were not directly linked to the Aggrey House dispute. Personality clashes certainly played a part, and the Gold Coast students were very critical of Solanke's alleged extravagant spending in West Africa. From 1934 the WASU made a number of attempts to encourage more unity between the Nigerian and Gold Coast students, but it was not until the opening of the WASU's new hostel, and as a result of the Cocoa Hold-up in 1938, that the majority of Gold Coast students renewed their WASU membership.
45. On the background to the German colonies question see *West Africa*, 31 March 1934, p.330; 7 April 1934, p.359; 14 April 1934, p.384; 21 April 1934, p.408.
46. See Langley, *Pan-Africanism and Nationalism*, p.343, and on Colonial Office concern, PRO CO 323/1679/5. Memo by C.G. Eastwood, 2 June 1939.
47. *Report of the Colonial Students Committee appointed by the Secretary of State for the Colonies* (HMSO, Dec. 1938).
48. Olusanya *West African Students Union*, pp.48-52. The WASU's ability to get the ear of the government during these years was largely due to its links with the Labour Party. It was also able to use the differences between the parties in the wartime coalition to its own advantage. When Attlee visited the WASU in August 1941 he was prepared to state, 'I look for an ever-increasing measure of self-government and political freedom in Africa', a statement which was soon contradicted by Churchill's well-known comments on the Atlantic Charter. The WASU, *West Africa*, and others exploited these differences throughout the war years. In addition to the many memoranda sent to the Colonial Office, from 1941 the WASU also organized a series of annual conferences, which included Labour Party speakers, to discuss the future of West Africa. Colonial Office officials spoke of the resolutions passed at the 1941 conference as 'interesting and perhaps significant', and noted that WASU and CO thinking concurred on some issues. For example, see PRO CO 554/130/7 , F.J. Pedler minute, 14 Oct. 1941; O.G.R. Williams minute, 3 Oct. 1941; A.G. Dawe minute, 1 Nove. 1941.
49. See, for example, G. Kio Amachree, 'Why Colonial Students Supported Labour at the Last Election', *Wasu*, Vol.XII, No.2 (March 1946), p.19; cf. Bankole Akpata, 'The Labour Government: Record of Unfulfilled Promises', *World News and Views*, 28/31, 7 Aug. 1948, p.330. See also *West Africa*, 29 June 1940, p.46.
50. *Report of the Anglo-African Committee of the Missionary Council of the Church of England* (London 1942).
51. *West Africa*, 26 Sept. 1942, p.931.
52. *West Africa*, 12 Feb. 1944, p.127.
53. Langley, *Pan-Africanism and Nationalism*, pp.357-68.
54. Langley, *Pan-Africanism and Nationalism*, p.365. See the article below by Marika Sherwood, 'Kwame Nkrumah: The London Years, 1945-47', pp.164-94.
55. On the IUS see *Wasu News Service*. Nov. 1952, pp.9-13 and PRO CO 876/153/11024. Memo by L.M.W. Robison, (Asst. Educ. Advsr, CO) Sept. 1950.
56. Olusanya, *West African Students Union*, pp.91-2; and PRO CO 537/2638/14322/2, 'Review of Communism in the Colonies', 8 Oct. 1948; and CO 537/7618/11246, G.E. Sinclair (Ministry of Defence) to C.Y. Carstairs (Student Welfare, CO), 21 Jan. 1952.
57. For example, see SOL 78. Solanke to Ford, 22 Feb. 1929.
58. See Bridgeman Papers. Brynmor Jones Library, University of Hull, DBN 24/21A. 'Report of the International Secretariat of LAI 1943'.
59. On Wilkey see Langley, *Pan-Africanism and Nationalism*, p.343.
60. For example, SOL 78. Solanke to the Alake of Abeokuta, 1939.
61. PRO CO 537/2638/14322/2. Memos of 8 Oct. 1948, and 13 Aug. 1948. In 1946 Awooner-Renner had written his book *West African Soviet Union*, published in London by the WANS press.

62. *Wasu News Service*, 1/4, Nov. 1952, pp.9–13. On Colonial Office concern over West Africans in Eastern Europe see PRO CO 876/153/11024/13. L.M.W. Robison, memo, 4 Sept. 1950.
63. *Wasu News Service*, 1/6 Jan. 1953, p.2.
64. Olusanya, *West African Students Union*, p.92; and SOL 45. Solanke to Sorensen, 20 Sept. 1951, and 19 Oct. 1951.
65. See PRO CO 1028/13. J.L. Keith memo, 14 Jan. 1953.
66. PRO CO 1028/14. J.R. Williams memo, 6 July 1953; and the Nigerian Union's Presidential Address 'A Preface to Policy', 8 Feb. 1953.
67. PRO CO 1028/28/139/03. Consultative Committee on the 'Welfare of Colonial Students in the UK'.
68. PRO CO 537/2573/11020/30/1. J.L. Keith memo, 3 June 1948. Information on the Communist Party's West African branch from interview with Kay Beauchamp, 1988.
69. Interview with A. Ekineh, 6 Jan. 1993. R. Palme Dutt, 'Britain's Colonies and the Colour Bar', *Labour Monthly*, Dec. 1958, pp.529–38. Student problems as a result of the colour bar and racism remained even during the 1960s; see G.K. Animashawun, 'African Students in Britain', *Race* Vol.5 (1963), pp.38–48.
70. West African politicians who passed through these training grounds include Kwame Nkrumah, Kojo Botsio, J.B. Danquah, H.O. Davies, Kola Balogun, K.A. Jones-Quartey, Ayo Ogunsheye and Milton Margai. It is noticeable that West African women students were less prominent in the WASU and other organizations. By the mid-1940s a West African Women's Association was founded in Britain by Irene Cole and by the early 1950s a Nigerian Women's League had been formed. However, I have not yet uncovered much information about these organizations or about the political activities of other West African women students in Britain.

African Students in Britain:
The Case of Aberdeen University

JOHN D. HARGREAVES

This contribution derives from a study of Aberdeen University's overseas connections, commissioned as part of its Quincentennial History Project. Aberdeen's contribution to the education of African students has always been modest; in a 1963–64 table of overseas students, it ranked fifteenth among British universities, with about 70 students from Africa. Although its experience may or may not be typical, the study suggests that it may exemplify some national trends.

I

The modern university of Aberdeen was constituted in 1860 by the union, under Act of Parliament, of King's (1495) and Marischal (1593) Colleges. The General Medical Council, established two years earlier, recognized the degrees of Scottish and Irish universities, as well as extra-mural qualifications obtained through the teaching hospitals; Aberdeen's recently re-organized Medical School thus became a centre of medical education for the whole empire. Students who passed the entrance examination, or could produce a recognized certificate obtained overseas, and could pay the fees were accepted regardless of origin. The largest number of overseas students came from Ceylon, where they made notable contributions to the development of the profession and to local medical education; but Nathaniel King graduated MB ChB in 1876 and Sylvester Cole in 1883. Both were private students from the Sierra Leonean elite, who after practising dispensing in a Freetown hospital may have been directed to Aberdeen by Governor Samuel Rowe, a graduate. King completed clinical studies at King's College, London and qualified as MRCS before completing his degree with two years in Aberdeen; Cole spent all four years of his course there. Little is known of their social experience in the city, but it seems likely that any embarrassment was caused by uninformed benevolence rather than racial malice. Both returned to Africa as loyal subjects of Queen Victoria – King to private practice and community service in Lagos, Cole to government service (including a spell as acting District Commissioner) in the Gold Coast.[2]

For over 60 years after 1883 no Black African student graduated in Aberdeen (though about 120 South Africans did so, three-quarters of them in medicine). The great expansion of the African empire did not expand opportunites for Africans to obtain higher education or employment. Well-to-do members of the West African elite continued to seek professional qualifications in the UK (or, in the inter-war years, in North America); but medical students either qualified through the teaching hospitals or tended to concentrate in the Universities of Edinburgh and Glasgow, or at Newcastle (as a by-product of Durham University's relationship with Fourah Bay).[3] Aberdeen still took a small trickle of students from Asia and the Caribbean; but despite falling numbers did not actively recruit overseas. This was not yet a subject on which universities required a 'policy'.

Nor was there any strong government policy before the war. A Director of Colonial Scholars, working from the office of the Crown Agents, made arrangements for the placement, welfare and financial support of some 150 students holding scholarships from colonial governments. From 1939 numbers were reduced, but in 1942 they began to rise again, as colonial governments prepared for post-war development and passages were (somewhat reluctantly) sanctioned for private students. Responsibility was now transferred to J.L. Keith, as head of a new Welfare Department within the Colonial Office, whose most urgent concern was to find suitable accommodation, for colonial war-workers as well as for students. In September an Advisory Committee on the Welfare of Coloured People in the UK was set up under Lord Listowel (with Harold Moody and Wellesley Cole as members and the Gambian J.L. Mahoney as Secretary). Lord Cranborne initially intended the Committee to concentrate on supervising the colonial hostels maintained in London and elsewhere, but it quickly began wider discussions of how students, those key figures in the more progressive colonial policies now emerging, might be given more positive experiences of life in the UK. There was much discussion of how good advice and hospitality might be dispensed through private bodies such as the churches and the Victoria League (whose rather patronizing efforts were largely focused on London and Edinburgh); but it soon became clear that the greatly-increased numbers of both scholarship and private students to be expected after the war could only be accommodated by tapping new centres. Residential universities were preferable; failing that, those with Halls of Residence could provide salutary contacts with British students; but eventually universities like Aberdeen would also be drawn upon.[4]

II

Aberdeen received its first approach from the Colonial Office on 2 August 1944, when the Medical Faculty accepted the department's request to provide three places annually for scholarship-holders from the West Indies. In May 1946 a broader appeal came from the Foreign Office (through the British Council and the Universities Bureau of the British Empire), that universities should (despite the pressure of ex-service applications which was now being felt) increase their intake of foreign students 'in the wider national interest'. This seems to have primarily envisaged students from Europe, America and the old Dominions, and the Colonial Office had to follow up by appealing that a generous share in any quota should go to students from colonies lacking their own universities. But at first Aberdeen received few applications. It was probably the personal interest of Principal Hamilton Fyfe which led in 1945 to the admission to the Honours course in History of two distinguished graduates from Fourah Bay, Kenneth Dike and H.E.B. John (who however rapidly transferred to Durham in the hope of finding a warmer climate). The Faculties of Medicine and Science (where undergraduate places were most in demand) were finding it difficult to satisfy home applicants. From 1947 a few Ghanaians were accepted in Science and in Arts; during the early 1950s four Sudanese graduated in Economics or History, and the Kenyan Simeon Ominde took a first in Geography in 1954. One African country was now providing applicants for post-graduate research; six Egyptians took Ph.D.s between 1947 and 1955, half of them attracted to the work on animal nutrition which John Boyd Orr had established in the Rowett Institute. But the grand total of Africans graduating in Aberdeen during the ten years after the war was only 17.[5]

The 'wider national interest' was however about to require a more active role. Colonial Office plans for more rapid economic, social and political development greatly increased the flow of African scholarship-holders and private students; it seemed essential to ensure that study in Britain would foster loyalty to the new evolving Commonwealth. In July 1947 a memorandum from the new African Studies Branch emphasized the crucial importance of 'incorporating' African students, as future leaders, in 'the social, political and economic scheme' being developed by Andrew Cohen and Arthur Creech Jones. 'It would scarcely be too much to say that the whole political future . . . is bound up with these few men, whether as the heirs to government in West Africa or leaders of the principal race in the future partnership governments of East Africa.' In the first place it was necessary 'to increase the contact between the African students and cultured Englishmen and women and to gain access for them to the best type of English homes'; the Welfare department therefore set up another advisory committee to traverse the well-travelled territory of accommodation, organized hospitality, tea-parties and film shows. But now, as the cold war intensified fears of communism, a new emphasis was placed on measures (in which the Colonial Office was anxious that its own hand should not obtrude) to counter 'extremist political propaganda' by organizing informal programmes of civic and political education.[6]

Such a strategy implied a deeper engagement of civil society with the new colonial mission. Although the foundation of the IUC in 1946 had involved a few senior academics in colonial university development, not many found time to interest themselves in the extra-curricular activities of their own students. Some discreet political initiative from above was needed; and (as with the shift in African policy two years earlier) the occasion was provided through the Fabian Colonial Bureau. Early in 1948 Arthur Creech-Jones visited a Fabian conference at Pasture Wood; the episode was described in Wodehousian language by an official who was also present. The Secretary of State apparently

> stopped a bucket of Bolshie stuff from some of the Colonials present. He was distinctly stirred up about it, and in a few sentences I had with him he was full of 'something must be done about it', etc. Vickers and I both thought it was too good an opportunity to miss of capitalizing on the opportunity of ensuring that the S. of S.'s explosion should be exploded into the transmission

– and so secure more resources for the Welfare department.[7] Rees-Williams, the Parliamentary Under-Secretary, appears to have been even more 'stirred up' by experiences with student audiences, suggesting a vigorous anti-communist campaign, and 'a word with the universities' about restricting admissions.[8]

This suggestion of restriction was vigorously resisted by the Welfare Department. Keith agreed that colonial governments might be asked to be more careful in assessing qualifications of scholarship-holders, but strongly defended the conduct and good sense of the majority. If most were ardent nationalists 'this anti-government attitude is largely due to factors in the Colonies and not to experiences in this country'. In the process of dispersing colonial students more widely Vice-Chancellors had agreed to allocate scarce places to colonial students, who now formed four per cent of the British student body, and 'it is inconceivable that we should throw away this advantage'. Keith likewise rejected a later suggestion by Cohen for special tutorial supervision; official paternalism would never remove genuine political grievances. Unsuitable accommodation remained a serious problem, but solving this would require additional resources.[9]

Since the alarming experiences of Creech-Jones and Rees-Williams were followed by genuine colonial emergencies in the Gold Coast and Malaya, they were indeed 'transmitted' into action. On 23 June the Secretary to the Cabinet set up a Committee of officials from the Foreign, Colonial and Commonwealth Offices 'to review existing arrangements for safeguarding the interests and ensuring the welfare of overseas students in the UK'. Much of its report, eventually submitted in October 1949, was devoted to reviewing problems of hostel accommodation for an overseas student body now estimated at 10,000 – 3,500 from the Colonies, 3,450 from India, some 2,000 from the old white Commonwealth. Its great merit was to see the overseas student body as a whole: to declare special colonial hostels a temporary measure until places could be found in integrated halls of residence or suitable lodgings; and implicitly to recognize that colonial officials, however well-intentioned, could not be effective in the work of civic and political education. It therefore agreed that the British Council, already an agent for the reception and welfare of many foreign and Commonwealth students, should take over similar responsibilities from the Colonial Office, and should greatly extend its facilities and staff in 19 university towns outside London, including Aberdeen.[10]

Post-war governments, far from regarding overseas students as a source of finance for the university system, were thus prepared for some modest public investment in order to improve their experiences in the UK. (The Inns of Court were repeatedly criticized for 'commercializing the whole business' by extracting fees from private students without providing extra-curricular amenities.)[11] Such policies were of course judged to be in Britain's national interest, and might thus be represented as of neo-colonial intent. Officials felt doubly inhibited in approaching universities; not only were students alert to dangers of indoctrination, but extreme sensitivity was judged necessary in advancing suggestions which might be felt to prejudice university autonomy. John Foster, secretary of the CVCP, often acted as intermediary.[12]

But the British Council, despite its close relationship with government departments, won widespread confidence by the manifest goodwill and good sense of its approach. As it told the Cabinet committee, it was:

> opposed to regarding Colonial students as a 'separate category' and thus engendering and encouraging the attitude of the Colonials that they are 'problem children' . . . Such success as the Council has

achieved is believed to be partly due to the fact that Council officers are not Government officials, but partly also because all overseas persons, white or coloured, old or young, distinguished or humble, are treated as human beings towards whom the Council's responsibility is that of ensuring that their time in the UK is profitable, as pleasant as possible, and that they return to their own countries with at least some understanding of the life and thought of this land.[13]

III

In Aberdeen the Council's base for 27 years was to be Provost Ross's House, a recently restored sixteenth century residence leased from the National Trust in 1954. This not only served as a social centre where groups like the African Students Association (and the various national societies formed from time to time) could hold their meetings and parties, but as a place of inter-action with the local community. Besides gatherings sponsored by the Council itself, students used the Centre as a place where they could invite classmates, teachers, landladies and other friends, to attend dances and receptions or simply spend an evening in the bar. In the late 1960s the Centre recorded a membership of 170 – 'rather more than one-third of the students in the area' (a calculation including many non-university students). Successive Area Officers (and their long-serving deputy, Clara Smith) arranged accommodation, social contacts and vacation activities with sensitive care. But accommodation became more difficult with the expansion of student numbers in the 1960s; the Area Officer tried with small success to persuade the university to provide for the special needs of mature African students arriving for post-graduate study with their families.

Although inevitably there were some cases of racial conflict or misunderstanding, memory suggests that most Africans found their studies in Aberdeen a positive experience. An interview with one (admittedly very successful) student in the university's oral archive recalls Aberdeen as 'a good place to be in', with warm, helpful and unprejudiced people. Reciprocally, as the size of the African community in Aberdeen grew during the 1950s and 1960s, university teachers, without any need of direction from above, began to appreciate the contributions which overseas students brought to university life. In 1949–50 fifty overseas students constituted 2.42 per cent of the full-time student body; in 1954–55 the figure was 89 (5.38 per cent); in 1959–60 208 (9.16 per cent).[14] The medical faculty, as pressure of home demand fell off, became more willing to recruit overseas students; the Nigerian tentatively admitted in 1951, Ajibayo Akinkugbe, proved more than satisfactory, and from 1952 it agreed to accept two students annually who had completed their pre-medical courses in Ibadan. Many other Africans followed. Between 1956 and 1967 46 students from Black Africa received the MB ChB degree; at least six of these later returned to take the MD.

The science faculty too proved increasingly willing to accept under-graduates from what the Robbins Report classified as 'less-developed countries'. Demand was particularly strong in applied sciences, where Aberdeen offered courses not yet available in the new African univer-sities. Between 1955 and 1965 35 Africans took the BSc in Forestry, and 25 that in Engineering, and they sometimes provided a substantial part of these classes. (But only one African graduated in Agriculture, specialized tropical courses being available at the Imperial College in Trinidad.) Students from 'less-developed countries' also contributed substantially to the growth of post-graduate study in the faculty. The Egyptian Educa-tional Bureau continued to sponsor students in Aberdeen; between 1947 and 1967 47 Egyptians took Ph.D.s in science, and others were sent for short courses in statistics. During the 1960s they began to be joined by students from Black Africa. Even more significant for the university was the overseas students' contribution to the new M.Sc. degree, which it first awarded in 1960; it seems that these new instructional courses would hardly have been viable without them. Out of 143 persons listed in University Calendars as receiving this degree between 1963 and 1969, 63 came from overseas, including 31 Africans, 18 Asians and 4 from Latin America.

In Arts-based subjects and pure sciences, numbers were smaller, since equivalent courses were available in many African universities. But a few post-graduates began to arrive in the mid-1960s. The university did not rush to commit itself to the formal exchange programmes which the IUC encouraged, but some limited departmental arrangements were made. The History department, for example exchanged graduate students with the University of Ghana; Adu Boahen acted as external examiner in 1965; Dr Fred Omu from Lagos held a Leverhulme Fellowship in 1966–67. The growth of such contacts stimulated the foundation of the African Studies Group in 1966, as an informal body to further the development of African Studies within the University.

IV

By the mid-1960s more and more individuals and departments had come to place high value on the participation of African, and other overseas, students in their work. They were therefore surprised and disturbed by a statement which Anthony Crosland, Secretary of State for Education and

Science, made on 21 December 1966 in a written reply to a 'planted' Parliamentary Question. Its effect was to raise by £50 the fees payable in the future sessions by students from outside the UK who had already begun courses in universities or further education establishments; and to set the level of university fees for such students entering in or after 1967 at £250 per year. To ensure compliance, the block grants from the UGC, which constituted 75 per cent of Aberdeen's income, were to be reduced proportionately.

Although it may now not seem unreasonable that students should be asked to pay as much as £250 for their education, this unexpected and high-handed initiative marked a turning-point in official attitudes, not only towards foreign students but towards university autonomy. Overseas students were no longer viewed as a source of strength in external relations but as financial burdens, requiring subsidy. The new policy seems to have originated in a simple search for financial economies by civil servants who did not appreciate its implications; Crosland later complained that 'The officials had either misjudged or failed to warn me of the likely reaction in the universities and the whole announcment and presentation were totally mishandled'.[15] It did nevertheless faithfully reflect a growing introversion on both sides of British politics. Crosland himself, while sincerely professing socialist internationalism, had in his best-selling *The Future of Socialism* (1956) given priority to promoting a more egalitarian society in the UK, and most of his energy at the Department of Education and Science (DES) was therefore directed towards equalizing opportunities for young people by promoting comprehensive secondary education in England and Wales. Though also committed, by Labour's endorsement of the Robbins Report, to a simultaneous expansion of higher education, Crosland was not always sympathetic to university claims; his own experience being largely confined to Oxford, he tended to assume that they had plenty of money.[16] Compelled (by Cabinet resistance to his own prescription of devaluation) to make economies, Crosland saw fees as a safe target; at around £70 a year students – from rich and poor families alike – were getting a cheap education.

Since the adoption of the Anderson Committee's report on student grants it would have been possible to raise fees all round with little hardship to home students. In Scotland this would have meant a relatively simple accounting adjustment between the University Grants Committee (UGC) and the Scottish Education Department (SED), but in England there would be political complications with local authorities. So Crosland, having established a fund to alleviate hardship for students already on course, went ahead with a ruthlessness characteristic of his generation of Labour intellectuals; nor is there any sign of scruple in the published diaries of his Cabinet colleagues, Benn, Castle and Crossman. The decision cannot have been welcome to the Foreign and Common-wealth Office; but old arguments of academic diplomacy counted for less in the straitened circumstances of the 1960s. The burden of protest thus fell primarily on the universities themselves.

Although students in Aberdeen responded less militantly than their colleagues elsewhere, the Senate, at its meeting of 25 January 1967, was unanimous in deploring the government's decision. Academics were reluctant to accept the new doctrine that cheap education represented a subsidy to overseas students. In the view of departments anxious to strengthen their research capacity by developing postgraduate courses, or (like Forestry in Aberdeen) to maintain undergraduate courses of value to the local economy, the marginal costs of additional students were out-weighed by benefits they could bring to academic life. Critics might inter-pret some protests as attempts to defend growing departmental empires – an attitude which may have found some echo in new African universities, unhappy about the brain drain of some of their best potential students. But in the Aberdeen case this view has limited validity, since most African students were in subjects like engineering, soil science or medicine, where the capacity of national universities built up more slowly than in arts or pure science; many such students transferred after taking their basic science courses locally. As the professor of Forestry pointed out, a more likely effect of increased fees would be to divert students to Germany or the USA, to the prejudice of British cultural and political influence in the world.

A deeper fear (voiced in Parliament on that same Burns' Day by Donald Dewar, MP for South Aberdeen) was that the government's failure to consult reflected contempt for university autonomy. It seems that the UGC may have been informed of the change, but there was not even perfunctory consultation of the Vice-Chancellors' Committee. Some universities claimed that this government *diktat* infringed liberties guaranteed by their Charters; others were simply outraged at being obliged to discriminate between their own students. But equality of treat-ment for persons of equivalent status within the academic community was an aspect of egalitarianism which had not occurred to Crosland, nor was it an argument powerful enough to persuade his hard-pressed colleagues to reverse the decision.

So universities belatedly faced the fact that by accepting increased public finance for their great post-war expansion they placed their own historic autonomy in jeopardy. A few principled persons suggested ignor-ing the government directive and facing the loss of income from the UGC; but the price of this seemed too high. Aberdeen, like other universities, did supplement from its own resources the funds which the government had provided to alleviate personal hardship; and the Vice-Principal and Rector's Assessor devoted much time and care to disbursing these. But the principle of differential fees was conceded, with consequences which even the critics had not fully foreseen.

In an expanding university, the expected fall in numbers was more pronounced in relative than in absolute terms. The statistical return of 1968–69 shows 216 overseas students, compared to 236 the previous year (with some move to part-time rather than full-time study); but this represented a drop from 5.4 per cent to 3.8 per cent. Numbers and proportions remained at about this level till 1973–74. But by that time the deterrent effect of the £250 fee had been offset by lower living costs due to the depreciation of sterling; and, more important, rising oil-prices had provided increased resources which producing countries were willing to devote to education. By 1977–78 the proportion of overseas students in Aberdeen University had doubled, to 7.6 per cent, while that in British universities as a whole rose from 9.1 per cent (1972–73) to 12.8 per cent.[17] National figures show overseas undergraduates increasing more rapidly than postgraduates, with the great majority coming from richer countries: Europe, America, industrializing countries in eastern Asia, and notably oil-producers. In Africa this meant above all Nigeria, which by 1978–79 supplied 6,336 out of 82,774 overseas students (at all levels) in the UK. Conversely, the financial constraints on African countries without oil grew increasingly severe; while the number of students from OPEC countries rose by 36 per cent between 1975–76 and 1977–78, that from least developed countries fell by 23 per cent.[18]

The Aberdeen data, however, though incomplete and not always directly comparable with earlier figures, suggest some deviation from these national trends. While the largest increases were shown in students from Malaysia and the USA, numbers from Africa also grew slightly during the later 1970s. They also represented a wider spread of countries; there was no spectacular increase in Nigerians. This may suggest that certain Aberdeen departments were supported by sponsors; development agencies favouring courses in applied natural sciences, while some churches provided scholarships to Andrew Walls' department of Religious Studies.

The Callaghan government, seeking to reconcile egalitarian principles and international objectives with growing financial stringency, apparently appointed a cabinet sub-committee to seek a coherent policy on overseas students; but no conclusions were announced before the 1979 election, and meanwhile policy was made from hand to mouth. In 1975–76 fees for all students, home and overseas, were increased by a flat £70; subsequent increases were larger, with new differentials against overseas students. In

January 1977 the government, having undertaken to reduce expenditure as a condition of a loan from the International Monetary Fund, began asking institutions to reduce their overseas intakes; but it did not indicate how this should be done, and in Aberdeen as elsewhere total numbers continued to increase. On 24 November 1978 the UGC warned universities that their grants were based on the 1975–76 figures of 14,000 under-graduates and 17,000 postgraduates; and in February decreed an actual reduction to 29,000 in all by 1981–82. Aberdeen was told to reduce its numbers by a drastic 44 per cent to 239.

The Aberdeen Senate, like academics everywhere, was deeply worried by this new encroachment on its autonomy, and also by 'the apparent lack of consistency in the Government's attitude'. The lines along which the Cabinet was seeking consistency are indicated in a speech which Shirley Williams (a minister who clearly found measures she was required to implement particularly distasteful) made to a World University Service conference in December 1978. Accepting the calculation of an annual subsidy of £100,000,000 (based on average costs) she postulated that this should be kept constant in real terms; that this would be better done by restricting admissions than by the market principle of increasing costs; and that the government should intervene by redistributing the 'subsidy' in accordance with its own priorities. Some of these would clearly be political; Mrs Williams did not refer, as members of Senate did, to the recent agreement by the Foreign Office, to receive 1,000 Chinese, or to the imminent need to make special provision for Zimbabwe. She did mention the inescapable claims of students from the European Com-munity, shortly to be evaded by the reciprocal arrangements under which EC students are treated as 'home-based'. For the rest, students of out-standing ability could be attracted by offering generous scholarships; students engaged on courses of demonstrable value to developing countries, and also refugees, would be assisted from specifically earmarked funds. These desirable innovations were to be financed by redistributing future savings on the higher education budget, and would presumably restrict the residum of places which universities could freely offer to students in other categories.[19]

The policies adumbrated by Mrs Williams, and still in process of implementation at the time of the general election, were unpopular in universities, for reasons of self-interest as well as of principle. Since the DES had greatly overestimated home demand in the 1970s, overseas students were frequently filling university places which would otherwise have remained vacant; and their fees, which in many cases greatly exceeded the marginal costs of their education, were a welcome source of revenue. The concept of subsidy made sense only if it were assumed that the true cost of a student's education was determined by crude calculations, relating the total number of students to total university expenditures. But since the universities had failed to find ways of reconciling academic principle with financial dependence on the state, the new government of Margaret Thatcher decided to apply the principles of the market, using the continuing growth in overseas numbers to justify imposing a cultural revolution on the universities. Shortly after its election the new government decreed a 20 per cent increase in overseas student fees; and on 1 November 1979, on the occasion of its White Paper on public expenditure, it announced that overseas students commencing courses in 1980–81 would be expected to pay a fee covering the full cost of tuition, as defined by the UGC on the financial advice of the DES. By applying market principles, the financial interests of universities and Treasury were brought to coincide; both would benefit from an increased flow of overseas students, provided that these were rich enough. In February 1983 the Foreign and Commonwealth Office, after discussions with the Overseas Students Trust, secured recognition that national interests justified selective increases in direct subsidy to specific categories of overseas students; but the specific proposals of this 'Pym package' reflected diplomatic priorities, and only a few of its provisions were of potential value to Africa.

V

I have not attempted a systematic study of this latest phase of Aberdeen University's history, and the concluding section of this study consists of broad impressions and general reflections. Under the new financial regime the fortunes not only of the university as a whole but of individual departments, and even the jobs of individual teachers, depend quite heavily on recruiting large numbers of overseas students who are able to pay fees which in 1990–91 ranged from £5,100 for arts-based courses to £12,650 for the three years of clinical medicine. Nevertheless, the university has been quite successful in overseas recruitment, with almost a thousand overseas students in 1990–91 (not all liable to overseas fees). This included 96 Africans. The bulk of these appear to be sponsored by developmental or aid agencies, many from southern Africa or Ethiopia; only Kenya offers much scope for recruiting private students.[20]

There is competition among universities, which is no doubt basically healthy, to recruit gifted students who have been able to win competitive awards from the UK government, the charitable foundations or – which for most Africans must be increasingly rare – from their own governments. It is difficult to say how the experience of such students in Aberdeen compares with that of their predecessors, or of their contemporaries in other institutions. In most cases they must expect rather less tutorial teaching or personal supervision; the new university culture places high premiums on productivity, which can most easily be improved by devoting less time and resources to individual students. But they still find good laboratory and library facilities, if somewhat more crowded at times. As far as welfare and social life is concerned, the centre in Provost Ross's House has been closed since 1981, but a reduced British Council establishment still does much for the welfare of its own sponsored students. And the university itself has somewhat extended its responsibility for finding accommodation for families, though this is sometimes in the less desirable Council estates. It is difficult to generalize about social attitudes; both cross-cultural under-standing and racialist thinking are probably stronger in Aberdeen than 50 years ago, though violently overt racial prejudice has been rarer than in larger conurbations. Private hospitality is probably offered less frequently; but in the past such contacts were often stilted and formal, and many Africans still make good friends in Aberdeen, through the churches or elsewhere.

But the University no longer confines itself to accepting applications from those who have identified Aberdeen as a good place to study; members of staff are now designated as part-time recruiting officers. The great fiefdoms are of course in the richer countries of America, Asia and the Middle East. Africa is rightly expected to provide few students who have the means as well as the desire to study overseas; the university invests few resources in a continent which it treats as an appendage of the Middle East. The relevant recruiter is a distinguished and experienced Africanist, sensitive to the problems of Africans studying overseas. There are, however, certain tensions inherent in the relationship between the university and the overseas student; none of these is new, but all appear to have been heightened by the new academic environment of the 1980s. It would be improper for a retired academic to attempt any general assess-ment, but certain nagging questions persist.

(1) How easy is it now to maintain a just and common standard in the matter of *Admissions*? At undergraduate level the Scottish universities attempt to apply a common policy through SUCE, their joint Council on Entrance. Though they have always admitted the possibility of waivers for able candidates lacking the right certificates, in the past admissions officers were usually cautious in granting these without a convincing inter-view. For postgraduates it was easier to supplement exam results with referees' reports when assessing academic potential; but whereas in the past caution often seemed in the applicant's best interests, there are now financial incentives to err on the side of liberality. The specific difficulty of assessing competence in the English language is however less serious for

Africans than in some other cases, and if necessary improved remedial teaching is now available (at a price). In sum, it appears that, while for the majority of Africans study in the UK has become almost impossible financially, for those with funding academic barriers are now more easily surmounted.

(2) Is it always possible to maintain standards of *Academic Supervision* commensurate with the new fees? Formerly many academics took pride and pleasure in meeting the special needs of African postgraduates, sometimes devoting a disproportionate effort to guiding their studies. In the new order this is counter-productive, since the simplest way for universities to improve what is cynically called their 'efficiency' is to reduce the time devoted to individual students. Similarly the overseas undergraduate, in common with his British fellows, must expect a smaller ration of tutorial time. If additional guidance is needed, for example in writing-up, it seems that this may sometimes be delegated to other persons, perhaps at additional expense to the student. Though more is paid in tuition fees, less is to be expected in return. In practice, help is often offered as freely and generously as before; but this is by individuals not fully adjusted to the new university culture.

(3) How will the new free market in postgraduates be affected by the new concern to control standards of *Examination*? Academics have long felt a tension between their obligations to persons and their obligation to maintain academic quality by reference to established standards. In subjects with a high cultural content, 'standards' for those of different cultural background can rarely be precisely defined. Examiners have always varied in their readiness to allow for this in what is inevitably in part a subjective assessment; but many must now find it particularly difficult to maintain extreme rigour with candidates whose family savings have been heavily invested in a university degree. (And, to put the matter in the language of the market-place, a record of academic failure is likely to depress future demand.) Now that universities are so concerned to monitor their standards of assessment, perhaps the market will eventually find its own level; but this may be at some human cost.

To conclude, those who see it as their mission to bring about a complete change in university culture seem to have found in overseas students a field in which it has been relatively easy to move towards the new model of the market-place. In Aberdeen as elsewhere the cultural revolution is not complete; unreconstructed elements of the old regime of academic community still hold their isolated outposts. Whether they can ever mount a counter-offensive, and what long-term effects the new order will have on the university's international relations, remain to be seen. This historian is not optimistic.

NOTES

1. Appendix V, *Commonwealth Universities Yearbook*, 1965. Colleges of the University of Wales are counted separately, London University as one.
2. See J.D. Hargreaves, *Aberdeen to Africa* (Aberdeen, 1981), pp.81–3. For their two Oxford contemporaries see R. Simmonds, *Oxford and Empire: The Last Lost Cause?* (London, 1986), pp.170–71.
3. M.C.F. Easmon, 'Sierra Leone Doctors', *Sierra Leone Studies*, n.s. 6, 1956, pp.81–96 (which however omits King and assigns Cole to St Andrews).
4. For the work of this committee, see Public Record Office, Kew (PRO) CO 876/16, 17, 18, 19 and 69.
5. Details of Aberdeen students are drawn from the University Archives; fuller reference will be given in my forthcoming volume for the Quincentennial History project.
6. PRO CO 537/2592, 'The Political Significance of African Students in Great Britain', Memo by G.B. Cartland, July 1947. For the context of general policy, see, for example, J.D. Hargreaves, *Decolonization in Africa* (London, 1988), pp.95–107. See F. Borsali, *Colonial Scholarship Policies, and British Policy Towards Colonial Students 1939–1950: The West African Case* (Algiers, 1985), pp.26ff.
7. PRO CO 537/2574, H.P. Elliott to Keith, Pte, 13 Feb. 1948.
8. PRO CO 537/5274, Minutes by Rees-Williams, 13, 16, 20 and 22 Feb. 1948.
9. PRO CO 537/2573, J.L. Keith, 'Colonial Students in UK and Eire', 25 Feb. 1948. Meeting in Minister of State's Room, 76 May, Minute by Keith, 3 June 1948.
10. PRO CAB 130/38; *ad hoc* meeting, 23 June 1948; CAB 134/604, Official Committee on Welfare of Overseas Students, Report, 7 Oct. 1949.
11. PRO CO 537/2574, Minute by Rees Williams, 20 Feb. 1948.
12. PRO CO 537/5206, Draft minute of 23 March 1950.
13. PRO CAB 134/604, Memo. by British Council, 13 Aug. 1948.
14. Overall figures of overseas numbers are taken from annual statistical returns, kept in the University registry. Nominal rolls of overseas students to 1965–66 are in Aberdeen University Library, U 1026/27. The appendix compares these with the *Rolls of Graduates*.
15. E. Boyle and A. Crosland, *The Politics of Education* (London, 1971), p.175.
16. C.A.R. Crosland, *The Future of Socialism* (London, 1956), p.258: 'The school system in Britain remains the most divisive, unjust and wasteful of all the aspects of social inequality'. See Susan Crosland, *Tony Crosland* (London, 1982), pp.147, 194.
17. OVERSEAS STUDENTS & FEES. ABERDEEN UNIVERSITY, 1967–79

	1967/8	68/9	69/70	70/1	71/2	72/3	73/4	74/5	75/6	76/7	77/8	78/9
1	236	216	210	223	218	216	277	335	389	395	427	463
2	5.4	3.8	3.5	3.78	3.7	3.8	4.8	5.8	6.7	7.0	7.6	8.0
3	250	250	250	250	250	250	250	250	320	416	650	705
4	75	75	75	75	75	75	75	75	145	189	500	545

Notes: (1) Total overseas students, Commonwealth & Foreign, full and part time.
(2) Percentage of 1 in total student body.
(3) Annual undergraduate fee in science and medicine.
(4) Annual undergraduate fee in science and medicine, home students.

Sources: Annual Statistical Returns, University Calendars. Figures cited for British universities calculated from Alan Phillips, *British Aid for Overseas Students* (World University Service, London, Feb. 1980) Table 5.

18. Phillips, *British Aid*.
19. Shirley Williams, 'Education for Overseas Students', WUS NEWS, 1979, Spring term. See AU Senatus Minutes, 35, 6 Dec. 1978; 141, 13 June 1979.
20. An extracted list of overseas students (including those domiciled in UK or EC) gives the following figures by country: Botswana 5; Cameroon 5; Ethiopia 16; Gambia 2; Ghana 2; Ivory Coast 1; Kenya 17; Malawi 5; Morocco 1; Nigeria 8; Somalia 2; South Africa 8; Sudan 3; Swaziland 1; Tanzania 5; Uganda 2; Zambia 6; Zimbabwe 7.

APPENDIX

GRADUATES FROM AFRICAN COUNTRIES WHO ENTERED ABERDEEN UNIVERSITY
BETWEEN 1945 AND 1965

		MA	B.Sc.	B.Sc.En.	B.Sc.Fo.	B.Sc.Ag.	MB:	M.Sc.	ArA	Ph.D.	NON
EGYPT	38	2	–	–	–	–	–:	3	2	21	10
SUDAN	31	5	1	–	6	–	–:	9	–	5	5
NIGERIA	75	5	3	18	17	–	19:	3	–	1	10
GHANA	34	2	3	4	6	–	10:	2	–	4	3
SIERRA LEONE	10	1	2	–	–	–	6:	–	–	–	1
GAMBIA	1	–	–	1	–	–	–:	–	–	–	–:
KENYA	25	1	3	1	2	1	7:	2	–	1	7
UGANDA	9	–	1	–	3	–	2:	1	–	–	2
TANZANIA	11	1	–	1	1	–	2:	1	2	–	4
SOMALIA	2	–	–	–	–	–	1:	–	–	–	1
ETHIOPIA	1	–	–	–	–	–	–:	–	–	–	1
LIBYA	1	–	–	–	–	–	–:	1	–	1	–
ZAMBIA	1	–	–	–	–	–	1:	–	–	–	–
MALAWI	3	–	–	–	–	–	2:	1	–	–	–
TOTAL: (excluding Egypt)	242	17	13	25	35	1	50:	23	4	33	44
	204	15	13	25	35	1	50:	20	2	12	34

Ph.D. figures = Science only.   Ara = Ph.D. Arts(1) + M.Litt.(2) +M.Ed.(1)

This table is based on annual returns of overseas students sent by the University to the Association of Commonwealth Universities (U 1027/26). It does not include South Africans, or those whose names suggest European descent. Mauritius is also excluded.

The NON column indicates students on these lists who do not appear in the *Rolls of Graduates*, which are complete to 1970. They are not to be regarded as academic failures. Some took Diplomas, in Agriculture or Statistics, or had come only for short periods of postgraduate experience; others may have transferred, or graduated after 1970.

Achtung! The Black Prince: West Africans in the Royal Air Force, 1939–46

ROGER LAMBO

This contribution constitutes part of a larger study of the role that Black colonial subjects played in the Royal Air Force during the Second World War. It follows the controversy that surrounded the RAF's 'pure European descent' policy with regard to the recruitment and utilization of colonial manpower. It illustrates the attitudes held by both government and Service officials towards the colonies and their people, and the impact these had, on the design and implementation of policy. Finally, it recounts the unique experiences of West Africans who saw active military service in Britain during the Second World War.

At the Battle of Crecy, on 26 August 1346, the English King, Edward III, gave the 'place of honour and greatest danger, commanding the right of the line', to his eldest son, the 16-year-old, Black Prince. As argued by John Terraine, for much of the Second World War, the honour of holding the right of the line in the battle for Europe, went to the youngest of Britain's fighting forces, the Royal Air Force.[1] When in 1941, Akin Shenbanjo, from Nigeria, was eventually allowed to enlist into the RAF, he was grudgingly given, along with a very small, select group of other young West Africans, the privilege of sharing the honour of holding the right of the line. In due acknowledgement of this, Flight Sergeant Shenbanjo later flew in RAF raids over occupied Europe in a Halifax bomber christened 'Achtung! The Black Prince'.

Had Akin Shenbanjo sought to enlist in the RAF, at the very outbreak of war in 1939, the Recruiting Officer would almost certainly have turned him away. Candidates for aircrew duties, apart from having to meet strict educational and medical standards, had to be white. In 1939, the peacetime recruiting regulations, which were issued under the authority of the Air Force (Constitution) Act of 1917, restricted entry into the RAF to men of 'pure European descent'.[2] Under the Act, all 'men of colour' were automatically debarred from enlisting either as officers, or in the ranks. Somewhat contradictorily, Section 95(2) of the Air Force Act did contemplate the voluntary enlistment of 'any inhabitant of any British protectorate and any negro, or person of colour'. While serving in the regular air force, such persons were to have all the privileges of a natural-born British subject. Except that, under Section 95(1) of the same Act, no such 'aliens' were to be promoted above the rank of Non-Commissioned, or Warrant Officer. Section 95(2) of the Air Force Act was, however, solely an enabling provision, allowing for the recruitment of 'non-Europeans', under exceptional, emergency circumstances.

Such was the case, in the First World War, when a relaxation of the colour bar enabled 'non-Europeans', like Sergeant-Pilot W.R. Clarke from Jamaica and Second Lieutenant Indra Lal Roy from India, to fly and fight with the Royal Flying Corps. Second Lieutenant Roy was officially designated an ace, having claimed ten victories, for which he was awarded the Distinguished Flying Cross. Sadly he was killed in July 1918 when his aeroplane was shot down in flames over France. In spite of the distinguished service of men like Clarke and Roy, the 'pure European descent' policy or colour bar, was reimposed as soon as the First World War ended. Although, in the 1920s and 1930s, the policy was challenged on several occasions, it was still firmly in place, by the outbreak of war in September 1939.[3]

Senior RAF officers and Air Ministry officials had always sought to defend the colour bar as expediency, the imposition of which was vital for securing harmony in the corporate life of the Service. In February 1939, the Secretary of State for Air, Sir Kingsley Wood, drafted a reply to the Labour MP, Sir Stafford Cripps, who had threatened to make the colour bar a public issue. In his reply he made clear that in principle 'we are opposed to the idea of discriminating against a British subject on the ground that he is a man of colour'. However, 'adherence to that principle would not justify us ignoring strong feelings of antipathy which are well known to exist and which we are powerless to remove'.[4] The 'strong feelings of antipathy' were felt to derive from a natural reluctance on the part of both Europeans and the members of other races to mingle. In the 'enforced intimacy' of Service life such feelings of antipathy would lead to much friction. As such, the colour bar was framed 'as much with a view to the happiness of the non-European individual as in the interests of the Service'.[5] In such manner, did the officials of Britain's Imperial government and Armed Services, justify the practice of a repugnant policy of racial discrimination. The colour bar, official or otherwise, ensured that Blacks and Whites never interacted in 'close quarters'. Even more to the point, it ensured that a 'man of colour' never occupied a position in which he had the powers of command and punishment over Whites.

I

The preservation of European status in colonial society dictated a system of social segregation that, in British West Africa, was to persist well into the 1950s. As Kenneth Little has stated, British colonial organization 'made for separation rather than amalgamation in the social as well as in the racial sense'.[6] Residential areas, hotels, clubs, hospitals and even, in 1940, the passage-ways at the military headquarters in Lagos were segregated. Although publicly deplored by certain Colonial Governors, and never formalized into official policy, racial discrimination in West Africa, as pointed out by John Flint, was almost entirely the result of government activity.[7]

Ambivalence perhaps best describes the overriding sentiment that most colonial servants in West Africa felt for the peoples under their administration. Sir Alan Burns, whose experience in the region spanned some 23 years, would speak of the traditional rulers of northern Nigeria, with the deepest respect. At the same time, he had, by the end of his term, reached such a degree of mutual understanding with the indigenous elite of Lagos, that even 'the difficult and delicate question of race and colour' could be discussed with frank openness.[8] The same man, however, regarded the younger generation of educated Africans as something of an anathema. In his opinion, education in Nigeria had given rise to 'bad imitations of Europeans', who manifested 'discontent, impatience of control, and an unjustified assumption of self-importance'.[9] Men such as Nnamdi Azikiwe and Wallace Johnson, representative of a younger and more aggressive strain of African nationalism, were regarded with a mixture of contempt and deep suspicion. The events of the 1930s in West Africa – measures to deal with 'sedition', the invasion of Ethiopia and the cocoa 'hold-ups', all argued over in the indigenous press, stimulated the growth of nationalist sentiment. In West Africa, and elsewhere in the Empire, colonial subjects were demanding greater participation in their own affairs. Youth movements, which threatened to disrupt the *status quo*, sprang up in Nigeria, the Gold Coast and Sierra Leone, and demanded social and political reform.

Similar concerns were, at the same time, being expressed in the United Kingdom. In 1938 Lord Hailey published his magisterial *African Survey* which greatly criticized British colonial administration for its failure to employ the 'intermediate' class of African who had received some form of higher education. Because British colonial policy exhibited 'no clear view on the future of the educated African',[10] educational facilities, particularly for secondary and higher learning were woefully inadequate. Such conditions of neglect were not restricted to Africa. In the Caribbean, the violent nature of the disturbances that swept through the islands, between 1935 and 1938, led to an acknowledgement of the discontent and resentment that was festering throughout the Empire. Although the full report of the subsequent Royal Commission of enquiry was not made public until June 1945, the outbreak of war in 1939 made it all the more imperative that Britain be seen to demonstrate concern for the well-being of its colonial subjects. The plight of the colonies made good propaganda for the enemy, and Britain's most essential ally, the United States of America, had always regarded British imperialism with disapproval. Finally, Britain's colonial subjects could not be expected to rally to the aid of the 'Mother Country', if they saw themselves as the victims of discrimination and callous exploitation.

Confronted with these wartime political concerns, the retention of any sort of colour bar in British public life, but particularly in the Forces, became increasingly untenable. As young Black men and women clamoured to enlist in the Services, their cause was taken up by influential personalities and pressure groups. Harold Moody's League of Coloured Peoples and Ladipo Solanke's West African Students' Union (WASU), were two such organizations, which tirelessly appealed for the removal of the colour bar. For the government to have turned a deaf ear to such appeals would have meant exposing itself to accusations of racial discrimination. The Colonial Office, in particular, if it was to maintain any credibility in its dealings with the Colonies, had to ensure that fair treatment prevailed on the vexed question of enlistment into the Forces.

II

On 19 October 1939, the British government eventually announced the lifting of the colour bar in the Armed Services for the duration of the war. According to the statement read out in Parliament, British subjects from the Colonies and British protected persons, who were then in the United Kingdom, were eligible for voluntary enlistment in the Armed Services, and for the award of emergency commissions in those Forces.

In spite of this announcement, however, Black volunteers were, for the first six months of 1940, still being turned away by recruiting officers. In December 1939, officials at the Air Ministry were still confident that the RAF's traditional recruiting grounds at home would continue to satisfy its personnel requirements. An understanding was therefore reached with the Colonial Office, whereby Black volunteers from overseas would be allowed to 'gravitate to the army'.[11] In May 1940, Flight Lieutenant Shone of the Air Ministry was still insisting that 'the RAF did not want and would not absorb Black applicants'.[12] Secret dispatches were subsequently approved by Sir Alan Burns, then an Assistant Secretary at the CO, and sent to all the colonial governors. The circular letter explained that in the RAF 'the coloured problem' was especially difficult. At the time, aircrew were essentially needed to man the heavy bombers. Such crews had at all times to be in the most intimate contact, and it was felt that 'the presence of a coloured man in such a crew would detract from efficiency'.[13]

Throughout 1940, however, a totally different reality was unfolding. Casualties were mounting and it was proving extremely difficult to find replacements. Both the Battle of France and the Battle of Britain cost the lives of almost 3,000 aircrew. A further 96,000 pilots, observers and air gunners were estimated to be required for the period, 1940 to 1942. In short, the manpower situation was fast becoming critical.[14] Therefore, among the decisions taken in June 1940, in order to greatly increase the flow of aircrew candidates, was the launching of the Air Ministry Overseas Recruitment Scheme. Under this Scheme volunteers from the Colonies were invited to enlist in the Royal Air Force. By the middle of the month there were hints of a dramatic reversal of opinion on the part of the Air Ministry. It now seemed that the demands of the RAF would be such that it would, in the future, welcome 'coloured personnel' for training as aircrew.[15]

Once under way, the Overseas Recruitment Scheme could not have been expected to work unless it was opened up to all candidates irrespective of race. In November 1940, therefore, the Air Ministry informed the Colonial Office that it would be prepared to accept Black aircrew candidates from the Colonies. The West African territories, which had previously been omitted from the Scheme, were then included.

The November decision to consider suitable candidates from West Africa had also been prompted by another series of events. Over the preceding months, the Air Ministry had received a number of letters from would-be candidates in Nigeria. One such letter, from a prospective 'aeroplane driver' in Lagos, gave the assurance that if engaged he would be 'ready to die for the British Empire'. Another, from three 'Brave Aspirants', in Kaduna, who described themselves to be of 'black complexion, blue eyes, curly hairs', humbly begged for positions of pilots-in-training. In conclusion they promised that, should 'equity and justice be fairly displayed, in the transaction of this negro touching matter, we will owe an endles gratitude'.[16] Faced with such eloquent expressions of loyalty, the Air Ministry felt bound to enquire from the Colonial Office, as to what possibilities existed in West Africa, for the recruitment of aircrew. The request was subsequently passed on to the then governor of

Nigeria, Sir Bernard Bourdillon. His reply, in September 1940, that 'there is certainly no considerable field of employment here', was thought by the Colonial Office, to apply equally to all the other West African territories.[17]

However, in the following month of October, the whole question of recruitment in West Africa was again examined. This time, it was prompted by an application which could not as easily be disposed of. Charles Woolley, the Chief Secretary to the government in Nigeria, personally forwarded the application of Peter Adeniyi Thomas to London. Peter Thomas, a young Nigerian employee of the Colonial Secretariat, was 'very anxious to enlist in the RAF'. He was the son of J.C. Thomas who, in the words of Woolley, was one of the 'leading lights from the African community in Lagos'. It followed that his acceptance by the Air Ministry would therefore 'have excellent publicity value in Nigeria'.[18] Peter, or 'Deniyi' to those close to him, had all the right qualifications for entry into the Royal Air Force. At the age of 25 he was the youngest member of one of the wealthiest and most influential families on the West Coast. He had obtained his Cambridge School Certificate at the age of 17, and then attended King's College, one of the best secondary schools in Lagos, for another two years. 'A fair long distance runner', Peter was already enrolled in the Territorial Battalion of the Nigerian Regiment at the time of his application. When he eventually set sail for Britain, Peter Thomas was set to make history as not only the first West African to qualify as a pilot, but also, the first to be commissioned in any of His Majesty's Forces.

III

The recruitment of Peter Thomas posed something of a dilemma for the Colonial Office. On the one hand, it had no intention of starting a recruitment drive in West Africa, as had been done in the West Indies and Ceylon. On the other hand, to deny other West African applicants the same opportunity, would have left the government open to embarrassing accusations of favouritism. Accordingly, on 30 November, letters were addressed to all West African governors informing them that the Air Council was willing 'to consider applications from all suitable candidates for training as aircraft crews . . .'.[19] In line with the current recruitment instructions, the same letter informed the governors that the RAF had relaxed both the medical and educational standards for entry. No longer was the School Certificate, or even continuous schooling up to the age of sixteen, required. All that was necessary was a 'reasonable standard of education', and a certain ability in mathematics. Successful candidates, however, had to be 'of a character and personality' that would ensure that they mixed satisfactorily with European personnel. The governors were specifically instructed to send the applications of suitable candidates direct to the Colonial Office, for forwarding to the Air Ministry.

Finally, in March 1941, almost one-and-a-half years after the British government's announcement on the lifting of the colour bar, public appeals for aircrew volunteers were launched throughout West Africa. The appeals were responded to with a great deal of enthusiasm. However, the subsequent handling by the authorities of the applications of prospective candidates was the subject of much controversy. In Nigeria, 500 applications were received from young men throughout the country. Of these, only 271 applications, all from the colony of Lagos, were considered by the Selection Board. All the 48 candidates passed by the Board, were subsequently failed by the RAF Medical Officer, on the grounds that they were infected with malarial parasites.

In the Gold Coast, after recruiting for two-and-a-half months, 58 applicants were examined by the Selection Board. Of these, only four were found fit enough for aircrew duties. All four suffered from minor ailments which required treatment. In the Gambia, only one man met the prerequisite educational and medical standards. The governor of Sierra Leone, Sir Hubert Stevenson, sent the particulars of only five African candidates.[20]

The results of this appeal for aircrew volunteers were very disappointing. In Nigeria, they led to outrage and disbelief. A long editorial in the *West African Pilot*, Nnamdi Azikiwe's newspaper, long suspected for 'creating mistrust amongst Africans of HMG's good faith', denounced the 'whole mess as an eye wash'.[21] In the *Comet*, owned by Dusé Mohamed Ali, another editorial ominously predicted that in the light of the poor recruitment results slight enthusiasm could be expected of Nigerians when asked to subscribe to the purchase of the additional aircraft needed by the Royal Air Force.[22] In the Lagos Legislative Council, Sir Adeyemo Alakija asked the government to clarify the situation with regard to the local recruitment for the Royal Air Force.

The Colonial Office's reaction to the controversy was to denounce any allegations of the practice of a colour bar in the RAF as 'plain nonsense'. Assurances were made that the particularly high medical standards applicable to aircrew candidates, were being uniformly enforced throughout the Empire. All recruits, irrespective of race, had to show that they had been free of malaria for a continuous period of six months. As such, the Colonial Office felt that criticism of a lack of sympathy or encouragement on the part of the West African governments, were in all circumstances, unjustified.[23]

What the Colonial Office had been slow to understand, however, was that the authorities in West Africa were, contrary to instructions, still applying pre-war educational and medical standards. Although already abandoned in Britain, the School Certificate, or its equivalent, was still demanded of West African candidates. Likewise, at the start of 1940 Medical Boards were being asked not to reject candidates with disabilities which, within a period of three years, would not become so aggravated as to render them unfit for aircrew duties. In the case of malaria, the period of non-infection had been reduced to three months. In view of directives that the RAF Director of Medical Services had issued in the past, serious doubts must be cast on the medical examinations which were later conducted in West Africa. As far back as 1936 directives had been issued to the effect that all candidates of 'doubtful European descent', if found to be of borderline fitness medically, should definitely be rejected. They were also not to be given the benefit of any doubt which might have existed. In the case of successful candidates particular care had to be taken not to inform them that they were medically fit.[24]

By 1941, even the Colonial Office was beginning to lose confidence in the sincerity of local authorities about recruiting aircrew in West Africa. In February of that year a frantic telegram was received from the RAF station in Takoradi claiming that no facilities existed in the Gold Coast for the recruitment of the Africans who were inundating them with applications. At the same time a directive from Headquarters Middle East Command stated that only British subjects of pure European descent would be accepted for training as pilots, 'Africans not repeat not suitable for RAF'.[25] Later on in the year, Colonial Office staff were surprised to learn that Sir Alan Burns, by then the governor of the Gold Coast, had chosen to ignore directives concerning the transmission of applications. At the CO W.J. Bigg suspected that the dispatch of applications directly to the Air Ministry, instead of via the Colonial Office, accounted for the West African's lack of success in enlisting for the Royal Air Force. It also appeared to Bigg as if the RAF Medical Officer in Takoradi was in considerable doubt as to what constituted the proper standard for aircrew.[26]

IV

Peter Thomas set sail for the United Kingdom in February 1941, having obtained a passage aboard the *Mary Kingsley*, and was eventually commissioned in mid-1943.[27] In October, the first contingent of Sierra Leonean recruits – Remi Davies, Christo Davies, Adesonya Hyde, Michell Johnson and Johnny Smythe – were given a rousing send-off by the community of Freetown. At a special occasion at the Victoria Park, organized by family and friends, a band of the Royal West African Frontier Force played, and speeches were given. In the *Daily Guardian*, a 'Composition of Free Verse' eulogized the five 'brave and gallant "Creole" boys'.[28] Over the next two years, small groups of RAF recruits periodically sailed from the west coast of Africa. David Oguntoye was an elementary school supervisor in Nigeria, when he heard in 1943 that his application to join the Air Force, made almost a year earlier, had been successful. In June, after spending 35 days in U-boat infested waters he arrived safely in Britain. Two months later, a further batch of eight recruits including V.A. Roberts, N. Akinbehin and Godfrey Petgrave arrived in Liverpool on board the *M.V. Stuyvesant*. The voyage had been perilous, with the convoy coming under aerial attack in the Bay of Biscay.

Other young men, frustrated by the lack of encouragement they were getting from the West African authorities, made for Britain under their own steam. On occasion, this meant having to resort to quite unconventional means of transport. In 1941 Claude Foster-Jones of Sierra Leone, undeterred by failing the medical examination in Freetown, left for Lagos. There he joined a UK-bound Elder Dempster boat as an assistant in the engine room. Upon arrival in London, he was granted an audience with the Secretary of State for the Colonies, to whom he complained of the treatment being given the West African volunteers. Eventually, he succeeded in joining the RAF as an engineer.[29] William Leigh, having failed to enlist in Freetown, this time on the grounds of age, also decided to work his passage abroad. Upon getting to England in 1941, he was accepted by the RAF as a wireless operator/air gunner (WOP/AG). After four weeks he was selected for pilot training in Canada.[30] In 1943, Robert Nbaronje upon obtaining his School Certificate in Onitsha, Nigeria, proceeded to Lagos to study pharmacy. There he decided to postpone his studies in favour of joining the RAF. Arriving in Freetown he stowed away in the coal bunker of an England-bound steamer. After ten days of hunger, thirst and coal dust, he gave himself up, and was immediately put to work painting and shovelling coal. Upon getting to England, however, he achieved his ambition of joining the Air Force. For Emmanuel Oluwole, however, the gods were not so kind. In May 1944 he pleaded guilty before a Sierra Leoneon magistrate of being a stowaway. According to his testimony, his journey to Britain, to join the RAF, had started in Lagos. For seven days, he had paddled through the coastal creeks in a canoe, and then caught a lorry bound for Accra. There, he had hidden aboard ship, and got as far as Freetown before being discovered. Because of having suffered the last number of days, working hard at shovelling coal, the Magistrate was decent enough to discharge him with only a stern warning.

Upon their arrival in Britain, aircrew candidates passed through a series of Receiving Centres, Initial Training Wings, and Elementary Flight Training Schools before being selected for particular trades. At the time, the majority of aircrew were needed to man the heavy four engine bombers. The bombers – Stirlings, Halifaxes and Lancasters – carried a crew of seven which included a pilot, navigator, bomb aimer, flight engineer, two air gunners and a wireless operator, who was also a trained gunner. A crew would undergo several months of training in their individual trades before meeting up at an Operational Training Unit and then being posted to a squadron.

Pilots and navigators did a good part of their training overseas in Service Flying Training Schools, which had been established in Canada, the USA, and southern Africa, under the Empire Training Scheme. Training was long and, depending on the demand for aircrew, could be subject to much delay. As many as eighteen months to two years could go by before a raw recruit was ready for operational flying. Because of the delays and lengthy training, some of the men who had joined in 1943 never reached the operational flying stage of their RAF careers. By the time both Bankole Oki and David Oguntoye returned to the UK in May 1945, having been trained as navigators in Canada, the war in Europe was over.

There were other West Africans, however, who finished their training in time to join the major bombing offensives of 1943 and 1944. During this most intensive period of operations, Bomber Command lost a total of 19,000 men. At the height of the aerial offensive against Germany, aircrew stood only a one in four chance of surviving the war unscathed. Throughout the entire war, Bomber Command lost 47,268 men killed in action; that is about 70 per cent of all RAF losses.

Flying Officer (later Flight Lieutenant) Johnny Smythe was, by November 1943, a navigator with 623 Squadron at Downham Market. At the time the Squadron was equipped with the Stirling which had the slowest speed and the lowest ceiling of all the heavy bombers. In the early evening of 18 November a force of 395 aircraft took off to bomb the German industrial town of Ludwigshafen-on-Rhine. German night-fighters successfully intercepted the raid, and Johnny Smythe, and his crew, who were only on their third operation, were shot down. Johnny Smythe parachuted safely from the aircraft but was captured and incarcerated in a prisoner-of-war camp for the rest of the war. In Stalag Luft I, at Bad Vogelsang, Johnny Smythe surprisingly received slightly better treatment than his fellow European prisoners. The hope, vainly held by the Germans, was that he could be used for propaganda purposes. As a result of the losses incurred by Stirling crews, Air Chief Marshal Arthur Bomber Harris, C-in-C, Bomber Command, decided in the last week of November 1943, to no longer use the Stirling against targets in Germany.

Bankole Vivour, a Nigerian bomb airmer, joined 156 (Pathfinder) Squadron at the height of the winter offensive of 1943–44. On the night of 24–25 March along with 148 other men in his Squadron, he took part in Bomber Command's last determined effort to destroy Berlin. The raid was not a success and the attacking force suffered the loss of 72 bombers. Bankole Vivour survived, to take part in an attack on Essen two nights later. On 30 March 1944, 156 Squadron's Lancasters again took off from their Cambridgeshire base of Upwood. This time the target was Nuremberg deep in the south of Germany. Nuremberg was Bomber Command's most disastrous raid of the entire war. German night-fighters decimated the attacking force and one of the 545 men who died that night was Sergeant Bankole Vivour. Of his crew of seven men only the pilot survived. Nuremberg effectively marked the end of Air Chief Marshal Arthur Harris's 'Main Offensive' against Germany. For the next six months Bomber Command concentrated on targets in France in support of the invasion of Normandy. For many of the crews this provided, at least initially, a welcome respite from German night fighters. However, they still had to contend with heavy concentrations of ground-based anti-aircraft fire.

Flight Sergeant Akin Shenbanjo served a full tour of 30 operations with 76 Squadron as a wireless operator/air gunner (WOP/AG). Whilst bombing the rail marshalling yards of Lille in April 1944, he had a narrow escape when an anti-aircraft shell passed through one of the engines of the aircraft without exploding. The pilot, a Canadian, was able to nurse 'Achtung! The Black Prince' home on three engines. Akin Shenbanjo was awarded the Distinguished Flying Medal in September 1944. Later he was promoted to Warrant Officer and survived the war.

Like so many young men, Adesanya Hyde from Murray Town, Sierra Leone, joined the RAF because he wanted to fly. In May 1944, he began what was to be an eventful tour of operations as a navigator with 640 Squadron, which, along with an Australian squadron, was based at Leconfield in Yorkshire.

On 27 June 1944 Flight Sergeant Ade Hyde and his crew were lucky to walk away from their Halifax bomber after it had crashed on take-off. On 9 August they set out in daylight to destroy a flying bomb site at Les Chatelliers. The weather was fair with broken cloud and as the attacking force approached the target black puffs of anti-aircraft fire could be seen amongst the aircraft. A fragment from a shell, that burst right in front of Hyde's aircraft, missed the bomb aimer by inches, but caught the navigator in the right shoulder. Ade Hyde refrained from telling his captain of his wounds until the target had been bombed. In spite of being in pain he refused any morphine and insisted on staying at his station until they were safely within reach of the English coast. Only then did he retire to the rest position where he collapsed. Ade Hyde's injuries put him in hospital for three months, after which he returned to his Squadron to complete his tour. For his 'tenacity and unfailing devotion to duty' an immediate Distinguished Flying Cross was awarded to Ade Hyde in June 1945.[31] Prior to that, in December 1944, he was commissioned to the rank of Pilot Officer. Pilot Officer Ade Hyde took part in operations until V.E. Day. He then transferred to Transport Command and flew on duties that took him to India and the Middle East.

Although the majority of aircrew were lost on operations, about 8,000 men, including two West Africans, were killed in training accidents. In July 1944 a Nigerian, Sergeant Akinpelu Johnson was training on Stirlings as a flight engineer. On the night of the 4th the bomber in which he was flying struck a tree on take-off. With both the left elevator and tail-plane torn off the aircraft the pilot lost control and crashed. There were no survivors. Flight Lieutenant Peter Thomas, whose recruitment back in 1940, had been considered as 'excellent value' was killed towards the end of the war. In January 1945, while flying a Proctor out of Madley he descended through cloud and hit high ground to the west of the field. Although his companion survived, Peter Thomas was killed instantly by the impact of the crash. At the time, in anticipation of the war's end, he had already been admitted as a law student at the Middle Temple.

For those West Africans who joined front-line squadrons, the surreal world of bomber operations over Germany, became an ever-present reality. By night they embraced the enemy in a ghastly dance of death and destruction. By day the survivors had but a few hours of calm in which to savour a good meal and the company of compatriots, before being thrown back into the fray. Casualties were horrendous and it was not unusual for aircrew (such as Johnny Smythe and Bankole Vivour) to have been with their squadrons for only a few days before being lost in action. Fear, the 'eighth passenger', was for all bomber crews a constant companion.[32] The extreme danger that they all faced however, engendered a bond, which in many instances, has survived until today. The average bomber crew, usually composed of different nationalities, was a very tight unit of men in which the need for solidarity left little room for any form of bigotry. Godfrey Petgrave likened his crew to a family and learnt that the key to survival lay in having, at all times, a good sense of humour. Johnny Smythe spoke of 'all the lads in the Services' as being decent and sincere.

The Air Ministry, in a Confidential Order issued in 1944, remarked upon the ease with which most Black aircrew had settled into their respective squadrons. It regretted the absence amongst the ground staff of the spirit of tolerance and broadmindedness that existed among aircrew. Incidents of racial prejudice did occasionally occur but for the most part were limited to off-duty encounters with white American servicemen. In one incident a West African fighter pilot was beaten up and thrown out of a 'pub' by the very American bomber pilots he had a few hours previously escorted into battle.[33] Other incidents of racial abuse occurred when Black airmen were posted to overseas commands in regions such as West Africa, which, right throughout the war, remained untouched by the liberal racial attitudes of the Metropolis. In early 1943 the Nigerian, Valentine Oke, and four other West African airmen were posted to Sierra Leone. Trouble erupted when the men were refused service in the Army canteens in Freetown. After having been severely roughed up by RAF police, they were repatriated to the United Kingdom.

Another incident occurred in mid-1943 when Sergeant Audifferen, who had worked his passage to Britain to join the RAF, arrived in the Gambia as a member of a bomber crew. Within a few weeks he was ordered back to the UK. When he and his crew protested they were told by the commanding officer that it was not imperial policy for coloured servicemen to serve in West Africa. This 'humiliating' experience for Sergeant Audifferen angered the CO which referred to the incident as a perilous policy blunder.[34] As late as 1946 other unpleasant experiences were had by Black servicemen returning home on leave. For this reason restrictions were imposed on the posting of Black servicemen to Overseas Commands, such as West Africa and the Middle East, where they might come into contact with South African personnel. The same restrictions applied to postings to Transport Command, where duties entailed the ferrying of troops.[35]

In Britain, however, complaints of unfair treatment within the RAF on the grounds of colour discrimination were rare. On the whole the West Africans, like their West Indian compatriots, were accepted on their own merits. According to the RAF race did not prove to be any handicap in training, in the performance of duties, and to service and social relationship within the ranks.[36] The only unfair proviso included in the report was that Africans were not deemed suitable to become captains of aircraft. Unfair because this proviso was based on the only known incident that occurred throughout the entire war where an all-white crew refused to fly with a Black captain. Even then, the captain in question went on to successfully complete his tour with another crew. In spite of this, however, the incident was to serve as a major justification for later terminating the recruitment of black aircrew candidates altogether.[37]

V

To West Africans like Peter Thomas, who had already 'travelled the high seas', Britain held no surprises. Most, however, had never been to Britain before. Among Robert Nbaronje's first impressions were the lack of fruit and the long cold summer days which made sleeping difficult.[38] On the train from Liverpool to London, V.A. Roberts remarked to his friend N. Akingbehin on the low grey overcast sky that hung above them like some predestination of doom. Sammy Bull, an air gunner from Sierra Leone, was impressed by the surprisingly high standard of food, not realizing that this was a privilege only given to operational aircrew.

In spite of the war, life in Britain held many attractions for the off-duty serviceman. Leave, which was approximately seven days every six weeks, might be spent either with the family of a fellow crew member or exploring the delights of London. In London the West Africans liked to stay at the Victoria League Club where they could read newspapers from home and enjoy the company of fellow West Africans. The office of the Victoria League's Colonial War Services Committee was established in March 1943 with the express aim of looking after the welfare of African men and women in the services. It did good work in providing woollen clothing and other amenities, and in arranging for men such as Bankole Vivour and Claude Foster-Jones to spend week-ends with British families.

When not on RAF duties, the West African airmen were kept busy, attending social functions organised by the Victoria League and the West African Student's Union. They made broadcasts on the BBC's 'Calling West Africa' programme, and featured in propaganda films for the colonies. Peter Thomas, whose interests extended to social welfare and labour problems, undertook other responsibilities on behalf of the Colonial Office. When West African social science students arrived in Britain for training, he took part in meeting the trains, and welcoming them.

For many of the West Africans, service in the RAF and their stay in Britain, enabled them to meet men and women from different parts of the Empire. They served alongside Canadians, Australians and West Indians under the most demanding conditions. When off-duty, they were members of a community that included radical and not so radical Black activists, like George Padmore and the members of the League of Coloured Peoples, Black American soldiers, and African and West Indian students. Towards the end of the war, and while still in the Service, a few, such as Claude Foster-Jones, became students themselves and spent the best part of their free time studying.

To many of the West Africans, the British at home were a pleasant contrast to those in the colonies. They appeared refreshingly liberal with respect to race. Also they genuinely seemed to welcome the contribution that the colonial peoples were making towards the war effort. One Sierra Leonean, who broke his leg in an accident during the Christmas of 1944, recounted how taxi drivers would take him to his destination free of charge in appreciation of the contribution that the 'coloured chaps' were making.[39] Johnny Smythe, in giving his impressions of the British people, spoke of their strong sense of justice and the 'guts' with which they were prepared to fight for it. If anything disappointed him, it was the ignorance that most people displayed with regard to the colonies. Visitors to Africa had brought back images of Africans as 'savages', and there was the tendency to regard all educated Blacks as coming from the West Indies. He was, however, of the opinion that the average Britisher proved to be a very fine and decent person once he had got to know the African. For some Servicemen contact with the British at home led to relationships which in West Africa would have been unthinkable. Flight Sergeant David Oguntoye fell in love and, despite all the efforts to keep them apart, married a girl serving in the Women's Auxiliary Air Force in November 1946.[40]

Towards the end of hostilities many of the West African servicemen began to make preparations for their post-war careers. By March 1946, M.O. Audifferen, having left the RAF as a Flying Officer, was working in London and was hoping to train for the police force in Nigeria. As mentioned earlier, some of the men, for example, Foster-Jones and 'Archie' Williams, had begun their studies, whilst still in the Service. A surprising number of ex-aircrew, men such as Bankole Oki, David Oguntoye and Emmanuel Dadzie, later took advantage of grants provided by the government to study law.

After his release from prisoner-of-war camp in 1945, Johnny Smythe returned on leave to a hero's welcome in Freetown. Back in the United Kingdom after six weeks he became, along with David Oguntoye, a liaison officer under a welfare scheme established jointly by the Colonial Office and the Air Ministry. Under the scheme West Indian and West African officers gave counselling to the large numbers of West Indians who had been recruited in 1944 to serve in various ground trades. Since the work involved representation at Courts Martial and the preparation of defence briefs for airmen in trouble with the authorities, it was for both David Oguntoye and Johnny Smythe valuable experience towards their future training as lawyers.

The majority of West Africans, having satisfied their thirst for adventure, travel and education, returned to their respective countries. In the years following independence, they were to play prominent roles in the domestic and international affairs of their countries. Adesanya Hyde became Sierra Leone's ambassador to the United States from 1968–69.

Emmanuel Dadzie held a number of ambassadorial posts for the Ghanaian government and was elected a member of the International Law Commision in 1978. Johnny Smythe, apart from running a successful private legal practice, was the Solicitor-General of Sierra Leone from 1961 to 1963. Other West African airmen, after their service, chose to remain in the United Kingdom where they settled down to more private and, in some instances, equally satisfying careers.

VI

In retrospect, the Air Ministry failed to make full use of local manpower in the colonial territories. In West Africa neither the local colonial governments nor the RAF were entirely sincere about recruiting West Africans. The little recruitment that did take place was motivated more by political considerations than by any real appreciation of the true manpower potential of the region. Not even the Colonial Office had any intention of initiating a recruitment exercise on a scale similar to that in the West Indies and Far East. As it was only about 50 West Africans were recruited into the Royal Air Force throughout the entire war. Several reasons were advanced for this low number. In the early stages of the war it was argued that aspirants to the RAF would make a far better contribution to the war effort by joining their local defence establishments. Furthermore, it was pointed out that ample opportunity for combatant service existed for West Africans in the Royal West African Frontier Force. However, the RWAFF was hardly an attractive Service for the more educated elements of West African youth.

In comparison to the West Africans, many more West Indian (about 500 members of aircrew and 6,000 ground personnel) served in the RAF. In Britain it was argued that West Indians were better educated and in sounder health than their African compatriots. There was some truth in this, but not to the extent of the differences in policy towards recruitment and the disparity in numbers enlisted. By 1943, and in spite of the war, more West Africans than West Indians began arriving in Britain for higher education. At the same time both regions were producing comparable numbers of secondary school students.[41] Standards of nutrition and health were generally poor in the West African colonies but also in Jamaica. In 1941 the League of Coloured People reported that the health of the working class male population of Jamaica was so bad that 'one out of every five (was) unfit for hard and continuous work', and, it continued, the health of the Jamaican middle-class worker was no better 'for of the nearly fifty volunteers who satisfied the intelligence test requirements of the RAF, only 17 were medically fit for such service'.[42]

Certainly in the West Indies the issue of race was more acute than it was in West Africa. When it came to recruiting for the RAF, great care had to be taken to ensure that all racial groups were equitably treated. For these reaons, the West Indian governors displayed far greater enthusiasm than their West African colleagues for the recruitment of 'non-Europeans' into the Service. Nothing in West Africa compared to the support that would-be recruits in the West Indies received from local government and business interests and influential lobby groups such as the West India Committee in London.

In March 1941, just as notices calling for aircrew volunteers were appearing in the West African newspapers, the Air Ministry took the decision to 'slow down' the recruitment of all 'non-Europeans' from the colonies. After much remonstration by the Colonial Office, a compromise solution was to restrict further recruitment to a pitiable 234 'non-Europeans, of which 48 would come from West Africa'. The decision to entirely suspend the recruitment of aircrew volunteers from the Colonies was taken in May 1944. Shortly after, in July 1944, the debate on the post-war fate of the 'pure European descent' policy was reopened. Ostensibly for the purpose of securing harmony in the corporate life of the RAF, senior Service officers and Air Ministry officials favoured the re-imposition of the colour bar after the war. In doing so they chose to ignore the exceptional service given by Blacks. In addition they dismissed the harmony that had existed among aircrew of different races, arguing that the 'rough and tumble' and general common effort of wartime conditions were not applicable to normal peacetime circumstances.

The position of the Colonial Office on the question of the colour bar was, however, quite clear. Any attempt to reimpose the colour bar would be 'flatly contrary to the avowed policy of His Majesty's Government'.[43] It held that after 'coloured' men had shown themselves to fight as officers in war it would be impossible to ever again consider them unfit to hold such commissions in peacetime. Finally, the Air Ministry, in order to resolve the impasse, decided to quietly drop the 'pure European descent' clause from the Act and allow a process of 'natural selection' to run its course.[44] In future, the commissioning, etc. of Blacks would be left to the discretion of Selection Boards 'who (would) be instructed verbally as to the course they should pursue'. As such 'on paper coloured troops (would) be eligible for entry to the service, but the process of selection (would) eliminate them'. Although it was realized that such a course of action was deceitful and dishonest, the alternative was considered injurious to the Service. In any event, 'the application of this unwritten rule (would) require great tact and diplomacy'.[45]

Of this, the Secretary of State for Air, Viscount Stansgate, was only too aware, when, on 19 November 1945, he triumphantly informed George Hall, Secretary of State for the Colonies, that the Air Council had decided not to 'reintroduce the colour bar *in the form in which it existed before the war into any of our regulations*' (author's italics). For those West Africans who served Britain, in her hour of greatest need, not even such a thankless tribute as this, could erase the memories of what was one of the most vivid experiences of their lives.

NOTES

1. John Terraine, *The Right of the Line* (London, 1988).
2. Regulations governing entry into the RAF are to be found in Public Record Office, Kew (PRO) CO AIR 10/965, 'Recruiting Regulations, Air Publication 948', 1923; *Air Force Act. Manual of Air Force Law* (London, 1939), pp.196–206. In spite of these regulations, one should always be aware of the many instances in which actual practice with regard to enlistment, posting, etc. deviated from the rules.
3. On racial discrimination in the Army see David Killingray, 'All the King's Men? Blacks in the British Army in the First World War, 1914–1918', in Rainer Lotz and Ian Pegg (eds.), *Under the Imperial Carpet: Essays in Black History 1780–1950 (Crawley, 1986), pp.164–81; and 'Race and Rank in the British Army in the Twentieth Century', Ethnic and Racial Studies*, Vol.10, No.3 (1987), pp.276–90.
4. PRO AIR 2/3936, 'Nationality Regulations for Candidates Enlisting in the R.A.F.'. This letter was never sent, as Sir Kingsley Wood decided to have a quiet word with Sir Stafford Cripps in private.
5. PRO AIR 2/3936. 'National Regulations', memo of R.S. Cranford, Personal Secretary to Air Member for Personnel.
6. K.L. Little, *Negroes in Britain. A Study in Racial Relations in English Society* (London, 1948), p.215.
7. John Flint, 'Scandal at the Bristol Hotel: Some Thoughts on Racial Discrimination in Britain and in West Africa and Its Relationship to the Planning of Decolonization', *Journal of Imperial and Commonweath History*, Vol.XII, No.1 (Oct. 1983), pp.74–93.
8. Sir Alan Burns, *Colour Prejudice (With Particular Reference to the Relationship between Whites and Negroes)* (London, 1948), p.12.
9. Sir Alan Burns, *History of Nigeria* (London, 4th edn., 1948), p.243.
10. Lord Hailey, *An African Survey: A Study of Problems Arising in Africa South of the Sahara* (Oxford, 1938), Ch.XVIII.
11. PRO AIR 2/4166, 'Recruitment of British Subjects Resident Outside the United Kingdom', Report of meeting 22 Dec. 1939.
12. PRO CO 323/1729/19, 'R.A.F. Recruitment', Colonial Office memo, 24 April 1940.
13. PRO CO 323/1729/19, 'R.A.F. Recruitment', Circular letter to all governors, 30 May 1940.
14. PRO AIR 41/65, 'Manning Plans and Policy 1939–45', pp.145–6.
15. PRO CO 323/1729/40, 'R.A.F. Volunteers', Colonial Office memo, 15 June 1940.
16. Both these letters are to be found in PRO CO 323/1729/26, 'R.A.F. Recruitment (Nigeria)'.
17. PRO CO 323/1729/26, Sir Bernard Bourdillon's cable of 19 Sept. 1940.
18. PRO CO 323/1729/26, C.C. Woolley's letter of 23 Oct. 1940.
19. PRO CO 323/1828/28, 'R.A.F. Recruitment (Nigeria)', Colonial Office letter of 30 Nov. 1940 addressed to all West African Governors.
20. The replies of the West African governors are to be found in PRO CO 323/1828/28, 38 and 39, 'R.A.F. Recruitment'.
21. PRO CO 323/1828/28, 'R.A.F. Recruitment', which also includes the article from the *West African Pilot* of 18 Sept. 1941.

22. Editorial, Comet (Lagos), 16 Aug. 1941.
23. PRO CO 323/1828/28, 'R.A.F. Recruitment', Colonial Office memo, 12 Dec. 1941.
24. PRO AIR 2/2248, 'Aircraft Apprentices – Candidates of Doubtful European Descent 1935–37', Letter of Director of Medical Services, 11 June 1936.
25. PRO CO 323/1828/38, 'R.A.F. Recruitment (Gold Coast)', Cable of 19 Feb. 1941 from R.A.F. Takoradi.
26. PRO CO 323/1828/38, 'R.A.F. Recruitment (Gold Coast)', Colonial Office memo, 1 Jan. 1942.
27. See West African Pilot, 24 and 29 Oct. 1943; Colonial Review, June 1943, p.35. Thomas's commission was the subject of a film made for use in Africa by the Colonial Film Unit.
28. Daily Guardian (Freetown), 18 Oct. 1941.
29. PRO CO 323/1828/39, 'R.A.F. Recruitment (Sierra Leone)'.
30. West Africa, 15 Sept. 1962, p.1013.
31. PRO AIR 2/9059, Sheet 40, 'Citation Award to Pilot Office Adesanya Kamina Hyde'.
32. Miles Tripp, The Eighth Passenger – A Documentary Account of a World War 2 Bomber Crew (London, 1985).
33. Peter Abrahams, 'Colour in Khaki', Daily Worker, 20 Sept. 1943. The story in all probability relates to a West Indian as no record has been found of a West African pilot in Fighter Command.
34. PRO CO 968/74/14504/41/3, 'Manpower – West Africa'.
35. '5 West African Airmen are Discriminated Against in Ship in W. African Waters', West African Pilot, 11 July 1944. Other similar incidents of racial harassment were reported in the Daily Guardian (Freetown) of 13 March 1946. Restrictions were imposed on the postings of Black RAF servicemen well into the 1960s.
36. PRO AIR 2/6876, 'Coloured R.A.F. Personnel: Report on Progress and Suitability'. See also PRO AIR 2/6876, 'British Non-European Aircrew in the RAFVR: Commissions, Decorations and Casualties'.
37. Papers relating to this incident are to be found in PRO AIR 2/8269, 'Drafting of British Non-European Airmen Overseas'.
38. Accounts of the experiences of RAF ex-servicemen were obtained from personal interviews and a variety of documentary sources, including newspapers.
39. This episode was reported in Edward Scobie, Black Britannia (Chicago, IL, 1972). In all probability it refers to Sammy Bull as he was the only Sierra Leonean to have broken a leg in an accident at that time.
40. Dulcie Oguntoye still vividly remembers her Commanding Officer tearfully pleading with her to break offer her engagement to the young West African airman.
41. According to the Report of the West Indies Committee of the Commission of Higher Education in the Colonies (Cmd. 6654, June 1945), in 1943 there were 9,800 secondary school students in Jamaica, Trinidad, British Guiana, and Barbados. In 1942, throughout British West Africa 11,670 pupils were enrolled in secondary schools and classes Report of the Commission on Higher Education in West Africa (Cmd. 6655, June 1945).
42. L.C.P. Newsletter, No.26, Nov. 1941, 'Public Opinion'.
43. PRO AIR 2/13437, 'Conditions of Entry into the Post-War Air Force: Nationality Rules and Admission of Candidates Not of Pure European Descent', Air Council Paper No. A.C.37(45).
44. The correspondence in PRO AIR 2/13437, 'Enlistment in the Post-War Air Force: Nationality Rules, 1944–51' serves as a distressing testimony of bigotry and deceit. In this regard, the memorandum of 16 Aug. 1945, written by Air Chief Marshal Sir John C. Slessor, then the Air Member for Personnel on the Air Council, takes the prize. His comments on the unsuitability of the gentleman with a name like 'U-ba or Ah Wong', or who 'looks as though he had just dropped out of a tree' are shocking, coming as they did, from a man of such stature.
45. PRO AIR 2/13437, 'Enlistment', Air Ministry memo of 23 Aug. 1945.

Kwame Nkrumah: The London Years, 1945–47

MARIKA SHERWOOD

Kwame Nkrumah is one of the most important figures in the history of modern African nationalism. Returning to the Gold Coast from London in 1947 he created the Convention People's Party and mobilized disenfranchised people to successfully challenge British colonial rule. In ten years Nkrumah's CPP won three elections and led to independence the new state of Ghana. Nkrumah spent two-and-a-half years in London which were of great significance to the development of his political experience. Relatively little is known of his activities other than the limited partial account given in his Autobiography. *This contribution, a resumé of a longer study, looks at the political groups and Black activists with whom Nkrumah associated in Britain and suggests the part that they played in shaping the political talents that he was to deploy with such remarkable effect in the Gold Coast.*

Chronicling and discussing the few years spent in London by such a highly controversial figure as Kwame Nkrumah is fraught with difficulty. Yet if we are to begin to understand the events in the Gold Coast after Nkrumah's return home in November 1947, it is important to describe what came before. The task is made infinitely more difficult by the paucity of evidence; Nkrumah's and George Padmore's papers, by all accounts, were burnt at Flagstaff House, Accra, in the course of the 1966 coup; the British government will not release to the Public Record Office any of the files on Nkrumah; and I have been able to meet only one or two of the very few people still alive who knew him in those years.

Many researchers have used Nkrumah's autobiography as an unquestioned source for his activities while in the United States and in Britain.[1] It clearly is a partial source, dictated at a time when Nkrumah was Prime Minister and negotiating to take the Gold Coast into independence. Can we expect a man in the throes of such politics to paint anything but a highly self-aggrandizing picture of himself? The very title he chose – *Ghana* – and the date of publication, 6 March 1957, the day that the Gold Coast became independent, surely indicates that the book was intended as a propaganda exercise. The many chroniclers of Nkrumah, who were contemporaries, either wrote hagiographies or attempted to denigrate him; hence they also have to be read with as much caution as the autobiography.

The Kwame (or Francis as he was then known) Nkrumah who arrived at Liverpool in June 1945 was neither young nor innocent. He was probably in his mid-thirties and had spent the previous ten years struggling to pay his way through various universities in the United States where he was involved in Afro-American and pan-African politics. In his time in the US Nkrumah had formed many friendships and made many acquaintances among his fellow students, his teachers, political figures and the local Black population. It was one of those friends, C.L.R. James, the Trinidadian writer and veteran political activist then living in the United States, who provided Nkrumah with an introduction to his fellow-countryman, George Padmore, who was in London.

George Padmore, WASU and the Situation in England

George Padmore had been in the UK since the mid-1930s. An ex-communist, he had wide organizing and publishing experience and earned a precarious living as a journalist, writing for African and diaspora newspapers and for the Independent Labour Party's *New Leader*. With a very wide circle of acquaintances and correspondents in the colonial and anti-imperialist worlds, by 1945 he had established himself as a mentor to those African and West Indian students who were interested in the politics of independence. In 1935 he worked with C.L.R. James, I.T.A. Wallace Johnson and others in the International Friends of Abyssinia. This organization was transformed into the International African Service Bureau (IASB) in 1937. The IASB was an anti-imperialist lobbying, information and educational association, whose aim was to support all colonial peoples struggling for democratic rights, civil liberties and self-determination. In late 1944 the IASB was merged into a newly created organization, the Pan-African Federation, which listed 13 constituent associations. The Federation's aims were to demand self-determination and independence for all colonial peoples and to secure 'equality and civil rights for African peoples and the total abolition of all forms of racial discrimination'.[2] Among Padmore's colleagues in these organizations were Ras T. Makonnen of British Guiana, Jomo Kenyatta (to become first President of independent Kenya) and I.T.A. Wallace Johnson, the Sierra Leonean trade union organizer and founder of the West African Youth League.

The West African Student Union (WASU), founded in 1925 by the

Nigerian lawyer Ladipo Solanke and Dr Bankole Bright of Sierra Leone, had been a social, political, residential and debating centre for the more radical of the African students in Britain. Solanke, as early as 1927, had written of the necessity for Africans and Africans in the diaspora to join in order to build a future, and for the necessity for a united West Africa – an 'impregnable whole'. He intended WASU to serve as the 'training ground for practical unity and effective co-operation between all West African students'.[3] By the 1940s, WASU had on its own, or in co-operation with other 'Black' organizations, lobbied parliament, protested to the Secretary of State for Colonies, held public meetings on political issues, called and participated in conferences, hosted political figures such as the Colonial Secretary Lord Lloyd, and the Deputy Prime Minister Attlee, and established a study circle. Its hostel served as a useful base for Africans from all over Britain, from Africa and from the Americas and proved a haven for many an impecunious student. In 1944 Ladipo Solanke, the warden, and his wife left on a fund-raising tour of West Africa. During their absence, WASU deteriorated; there was growing dissension among the students and an increasing organization along regional lines: for example, Ibo and Yoruba Unions were formed and in 1945 Obafemi Awolowo, then a law student and not a WASU member, formed the Yoruba nationalist organization, Egbe Omo Oduduwa.[4]

In 1945 there were a number of 'Black' organizations in the UK besides the IASB and WASU. The League of Coloured Peoples, for example, an organization akin to the National Association for the Advancement of Coloured People (NAACP) in the United States in that it admitted European members and believed in the legalistic approach and diplomacy to bring about change, was also heavily involved in the welfare problems of London's 'coloured' population. In at least Cardiff, Manchester and Liverpool there were local welfare organizations, while Cardiff also had a history of political organizing. There were also nationalist organizations: for example, the India League had been in existence for many years; the Somali Youth League (whose aim was the independence and unification of Somalia) was just coming into existence under the leadership of, among others, Mohamed Said, an old colleague of George Padmore's.[5]

February 1945 saw the preliminary meeting of the World Federation of Trade Unions (WFTU) in London. As a number of colonial delegates attended, Padmore and his colleagues seized this unique opportunity. They called a meeting at which it was decided to hold a Pan-African conference later in the year when colonial delegates would again (or still) be in Europe for the first meeting of the WFTU.[6] By May, when Francis Nwia-Kofi Nkrumah arrived in London, preparations for the Pan-African meeting were under way.

Political Activities, London, 1945

Before Nkrumah left the United States, C.L.R. James had given him an introduction to George Padmore. In his *Autobiography* Nkrumah claims that he had written in advance, asking Padmore to meet him at Euston Station; Padmore duly met him and took him to the WASU hostel. However, accommodation at WASU had been reserved by Peter Carter from Bishops Stortford, who had written to Solanke on 3 May asking for a bed for 'my friend Francis Kofi Nkrumah, whom I met when I was teaching at Lincoln'.[7] Joe Appiah, then a student and activist in the Padmore circle, recalls that he and Padmore met Nkrumah together and 'to give him a foretaste of our work . . . took him straight from the station to this meeting [Appiah was due to address a railway union meeting] and introduced him to our friends'.[8]

Finding permanent accommodation in war-damaged London where the colour bar was practised by many landladies was not easy. However, with the aid of a fellow Gold Coast student from the US, Ako Adjei, who had come to Britain in 1944 to qualify for the bar, Nkrumah found a room at 60 Burghley Road in Tufnell Park. This was not too far, about one and a half miles, from where a number of radical West Africans were living in Primrose Gardens; it was about the same distance to the WASU hostel in Camden Square, and not much further from Padmore's flat in Cranleigh Gardens.

Nkrumah quickly became absorbed in the activities and discussions taking place around him. These were exciting days. The war was drawing to a close. The Labour Party, whom WASU supported, was about to win the next general election. How could the students and activists influence the shape of the post-war world? Would the freedoms promised by the Atlantic Charter, which Attlee had told WASU 'apply to all peoples of the world . . . We in the Labour Party have always demanded that the freedom which we claim for ourselves shall be extended to all', be honoured?[9] Among Nkrumah's immediate involvements was helping Padmore with the organization of what was now styled the Pan-African Congress, to be held from 13 to 21 October, in Manchester. Nkrumah, calling himself 'Kwame', was made the regional secretary of the Pan-African Federation (PAF); in this capacity, using his private address on the 'PAF Regional Council – Southern Section' letterhead, he sent out letters of invitation to Padmore's world-wide contacts. (The Regional Administrator was K.O. Larbi, another Gold Coaster, then a barrister in London.)[10] Undoubtedly Nkrumah would have participated in activities such as the demonstrations and meetings called by the WASU and the PAF in support of the strike in Nigeria in July, and the September publication by the PAF of 'An Open Letter to the Prime Minister' which demanded, *inter alia*, 'the immediate right to self-determination'.[11]

Nkrumah must also have become immediately and deeply involved also in the affairs and activities of the WASU as he was elected Vice-President at the Union's October elections. He only held this post for one year; in 1946–47 he was a member of the Union's Executive.

Nkrumah's circle of acquaintances was not confined to the WASU and PAF groups. Among the WASU supporters were British progressives such as Fenner Brockway, Ben Riley MP and Reginald Sorensen MP. Padmore was well-known in socialist and Independent Labour Party circles. Naturally, the new arrival would have been introduced. More importantly perhaps, Nkrumah must have met those delegates who had stayed on in Britain between the two meetings of the WFTU in February and September. Among these were I.T.A. Wallace Johnson, representing the Sierra Leone TUC, who had unequivocally demanded that the WFTU should endorse 'the principle of self-determination for Colonial peoples . . . (and) declare a time limit when the principle shall be translated into practice'. Another African delegate, Annan of the Gold Coast Railway Union, asked for WFTU support for wide-ranging reforms while calling for 'unity among working-class people (in Africa) . . . to form a regional association of the four countries of West Africa'.[12] At a meeting in February organized by the Fabian Colonial Bureau, J.S. Annan had argued that all restrictions on trade unions must be removed directly the war was over 'otherwise there would be a violent reaction'.[13]

Perhaps emboldened by these contacts and the militancy of the trade union delegates, Nkrumah appears to have begun to introduce himself to people of importance on the Gold Coast. Only one letter has come to light but it would have made sense for him to have written to others in West Africa. Nkrumah was said to be well known by the managing proprietor of the *Ashanti Pioneer*, John Tsiboe.[14]

In September Nkrumah wrote to the well-known writer and political activist Kobina Sekyi stating that he hoped to enter journalism in the Gold Coast where a 'politically fearless and militant newspaper is more than a necessity'; the imperialists' strategy of divide and rule must be counteracted by unity. Sekyi replied in October, congratulating Nkrumah on his academic achievements and approving his and Padmore's meeting with Ashie Nikoi, the representative of the Gold Coast Farmers' Association, then in Britain. Sekyi's letter concludes with: 'When are you coming home to enter the lists?'[15]

But Nkrumah was not yet ready to return home. While still attempting to study, he was becoming more and more involved in London activities. For example, he attended and addressed some meetings of the Coloured

Workers' Association which had been started by a Sierra Leonean, Ernest Marke, in 1944.[16] There was also the Pan-African Congress to help organize. It was held in Manchester as Ras T. Makonnen's restaurant there solved the problem of the colour-bar then operated by many eating-houses. As hotels also generally excluded people of African descent, accommodation must have been offered to the delegates by the Manchester hosts: besides Makonnen, Dr Peter Milliard, the president of the PAF, was a long-standing Manchester physician. Accommodation must also have been solicited from other 'Black' Mancunians and the local organization, the Negro Association, whose members were mainly educated West Indians.[17]

Some 200 people, mainly Africans and those of African descent, attended the Congress, including W.E.B. DuBois and Mrs Amy Ashwood Garvey, the widow (first wife) of the great Marcus Garvey. Though sixth in the line of pan-African congresses, this was the first meeting with numerous Africans and the first attended by workers and trade unionists. European organizations, including the International Labour Office and the Colonial Office, were asked to send observers only.[18]

W.E.B. DuBois, the 'father' of pan-Africanism, was honoured by being declared International President of the Pan-African Congress (PAC). Nkrumah, an old acquaintance of DuBois, was appointed rapporteur of the two sessions on 'Imperialism in North and West Africa' held on 16 and 19 October. This put him in a highly responsible position as he had to present the resolutions arising out of the discussions at the two sessions. The congress gave unanimous support to the members of the West African delegation in declaring 'that complete and absolute independence is the only solution to the existing problems'.[19]

Nkrumah also wrote one of the two major declarations of the Congress. (The second, 'Declaration to the Imperial Powers of the World', was drafted by DuBois.) The 'Declaration to the Colonial Peoples of the World' approved by the Congress, called for freedom, self-government and for the unity of workers, farmers and the intellectuals, as well as for all colonial peoples to unite in the struggle against imperialism.[20] Not content with this, the West Africans at the Congress also sent a telegram to the Secretary of State for the Colonies, which demanded the revocation of the Richards Constitution in Nigeria and the withdrawal of Sir Arthur Richards; the repeal of various ordinances, Acts and Bills; the abolition of racial discrimination and the lifting of the ban on 'progressive literature'.

The Congress had not only given Nkrumah a high profile as a rapporteur – it also allowed him to meet political and trade union activists in the capacity of one of the recognized organizers of the Congress. Among the delegates at the Congress were many Africans who were to assume leadership positions in the future: those who became most eminent were Dr Hastings Banda and Jomo Kenyatta who led their countries into independence; Obafemi Awolowo, Garba Jahumpa and Jaja Nwachuku who became ministers of state; J.S. Annan, Kamkam Boadu, Eddie DuPlan and Ako Ajei, all to serve in the Nkrumah Administration, as well as Joe Appiah and Dr Karankyi Taylor who later became Nkrumah's adversaries. Nkrumah was named the secretary of the working committee (under DuBois' presidency) set up after the Congress to give 'effect to the programme' drawn up at the Congress and to establish a headquarters. It was envisaged that this office would keep in contact with and serve as a 'clearing house for the various political movements that would take shape in the colonies'. In a letter to the Aborigines' Rights Protection Society (ARPS), Nkrumah, signing as the secretary of the Federation's International Secretariat, promised that he would 'do everything in my power to make this organization an effective weapon in the fight for Colonial Freedom and Justice'.[21]

As if to follow Makonnen's advice that being a (full-time) rebel was as good a profession as any, before the year was out Nkrumah was heavily involved in a new organization. He became the secretary of the West African National Secretariat (WANS) which must have grown out of the discussions held by at least some of the West Africans at the PAC. According to the pamphlet published by WANS, 'Aims and Objects of the West African National Secretariat', the organizing of WANS was suggested by the Sierra Leone Branch of the West Africa Youth League and the Aborigines' Rights Protection Society. Of those mentioned in the *Autobiography* as being founder members, G. Ashie Nikoi had represented the ARPS at the Congress, Wallace Johnson the Youth League, and Bankole Awoonor-Renner the Friends of Africa Freedom Society. Bankole Akpata and Kojo Botsio, the other two men named by Nkrumah, are not among the list of delegates at the PAC, but that does not mean they did not attend.[22]

At a meeting held in London on 14 December, under the chairmanship of the veteran revolutionary Wallace Johnson, it was decided that the functions of WANS were to be:

> to maintain contact with, co-ordinate, educate and supply general information to . . . progressive organisations in West Africa with a view to realising a West African Front for a United West African National Independence
>
> to serve as a clearing house for information . . . and to educate the

peoples and the working class of the imperialist countries concerning the problems of West Africa

to foster the spirit of unity and solidarity among the West African territories

to work for unity and harmony among all West Africans who stand against imperialism

to publish a monthly paper and other literature.

The pamphlet concludes by affirming that the Secretariat would 'strive to make West Africans the true interpreters of their various desires, wishes, sufferings, hopes and aspirations for themselves and their prosperity. WEST AFRICA IS ONE COUNTRY: PEOPLES OF WEST AFRICA UNITE!'[23]

Whether it was before or after the formation of WANS that Nkrumah started what a PAF colleague, Peter Abrahams described as 'a secret society, the Circle', is unclear.[24] The Circle was formed from among the student supporters of WANS. It became

the vanguard group . . . membership cost seven guineas and only those who were believed or known to be genuinely working for West African unity and the destruction of colonialism were admitted. Members began to train themselves in order to be able to commence revolutionary work (in Africa) . . . They were like a special service group . . . who directed the programmed and activities of the National Headquarters and took the lead in calling meetings and conferences and arranging lectures and discussions.[25]

Members had to 'pledge and swear to live up to the aims of the Circle', to infiltrate organizations in order to propound the Circle aims of national unity, independence and a Union of African Socialist Republics. Members had 'formally' to accept the 'leadership of Kwame Nkrumah', who presumably would have assumed the leadership of the political party which was expected to evolve out of the Circle, 'embracing the whole of West Africa, and whose policy then shall be to maintain the Union of African Socialist Republics'.[26]

That Kwame Nkrumah already saw himself as the future leader of a Union of Socialist Republics, on a continent he had left 12 years previously, appears to indicate not only his burning ambition for African freedom, independence and unity, but also a personal ambition that many saw in him. Certainly, he appears to have been convinced of his own destiny. There is, however, also an air of unreality, a lack of 'groundedness': he appears to be ignoring the contemporary realities of West Africa, divided not only by the European powers but also by language, custom, pre-invasion history and the personal ambitions of its leaders. Did he really believe that his great zeal and conviction, and a handful of student supporters from the UK could overcome both European and local vested interest?

Political Activities, London, 1946

It seems likely that Nkrumah neglected his duties as Pan-African Federation working party secretary in order to devote himself to WANS, as I have not been able to discover any indications of further involvement with the Federation. Nor does he appear to have become involved in the British Centre Against Imperialism: no WANS personnel are listed as attending the inaugural meeting in February.[27] Did Nkrumah believe that the future he had cherished since his US days, of a free, independent and united West Africa, were more realizable within an organization in which he held the most senior post? Did he perceive George Padmore as an obstacle to his own ambitions? He would certainly have received ample support for such a belief and such a tactic from Bankole Awoonor-Renner's and his own contacts within the Communist Party of Great Britain. In his *Autobiography* Nkrumah comments that the Party was 'fortunate in having among its leaders personalities such as Emil Burns [sic], Palme Dutt and Harry Pollitt'. Emile Burns became and remained a 'close friend'; what Nkrumah's relationship was with Dutt and Pollitt I have not yet been able to discover. The Communist Party, of course, perceived the renegade ex-communist Padmore as an arch-enemy.[28]

WANS swung into action quickly. Office space was obtained from the lawyer Koi Larbi, who had also been at the PAC. The first public meeting was held on 1 February 1946 and called upon the newly formed United Nations Organization to guarantee the liberation of 'the oppressed people of the Colonies immediately . . . to help West Africans achieve a free, united, independent and democratic West Africa . . . to bring about the complete liquidation of the Colonial system'.[29]

On 27 March another meeting was held and new resolutions approved for desptach to the UN. Direct representation for colonial people at the UN was demanded, as well as the 'liquidation' of the colonial system; the UN Secretary General and the Trusteeship Council were called upon to 'affect the speedy realization of complete independence for the peoples of the colonies'. The international body was chastised for permitting the compromises which left colonial peoples in the same position as they had been in thirty years earlier, and for not allowing colonial people the right to choose whether they wanted to come under the Trusteeship Council or become independent.[30]

Not satisfied with this, Nkrumah went to Paris to meet the African members of the French National Assembly – Sourous Apithy, Leopold Senghor, Lamine Guèye, Félix Houphouët-Boigny and others. The discussion, according to Nkrumah, focused on planning a union of West African socialist republics.[31] Apithy and Senghor promised to attend the next WANS meeting in London. Nkrumah also maintained a correspondence with Kobina Sekyi, asking Sekyi to write for the Secretariat's journal (he refused on the grounds of ill health), seeking suggestions for the by-laws and declaring that a governing council of West African leaders was contemplated.[32]

The first West African conference, held from 30 August to 1 September, was organized jointly by WANS and the West African Students Union (WASU). The conference discussed a proposal for the calling of a constitutional convention for the people of Africa to formulate their own constitution, and called for a programme of political action to further this aim. WANS was mandated to rally the 'masses' and to initiate territorial councils. It warned educated Africans against returning home to form a bourgeoisie which would play into the hands of the imperialist powers; the anti-imperialist movement must have a socialist basis. The conference concluded with a 'resolution and plan of action read by Mr Nkrumah. It demanded among the objectives the creation of a politically independent and united West Africa and the holding of a congress in West Africa within the next year, to promote their aims.' According to Padmore, the conference also rejected 'the British Tory doctrine of trusteeship and the Fabian thesis of "gradualism" and endorsed the programme hammered out at the Pan-African Congress'.

In the meantime, WANS, with fewer than 100 members, in March began to publish a monthly journal, *The New African* headlined with the motto 'For Unity and Absolute Independence'.[33] The first issue carried articles on the formation, aims, resolutions and activities of WANS; the cocoa monopoly; the situation in French Cameroun; and exhorted African women to join with the men in working for self-determination and independence. True to the concept of unity, one article was in French. An article was reprinted from the *New Times* (Moscow) on the Trusteeship question. The second issue continued the discussion on trusteeship, attacked the new Nigerian Lands Acquisition Bill, printed a South African resolution to the UN, and also the Gold Coast and Nigerian Farmers' delegation's letter to the Colonial Office. The May issue dealt with racial discrimination in Britain and WANS' and Nkrumah's activities. Issue number four was also concerned with racial discrimination in Britain and with African soldiers' experiences in India; it noted the meeting in Accra called by Dr Nanka Bruce, Sekyi, G.F. Molore, and J.B. Danquah in an attempt to resuscitate the defunct National Congress of British West Africa. The withdrawal of British troops from Egypt was heralded as marking the beginning of the end of British world power. The July issue again attacked racial discrimination (this time by another Russian author) and the Labour Party's 'nominal' condemnation of the colour bar.

There appear to have been no further issues. There must have been an appeal for funds for, though the ARPS seemingly made no attempt to sell the copies of *The New African* sent in March, in August Sekyi sent £150 for publishing the journal. Nkrumah promised to repay within six months.[34] An undated circular which listed Nkrumah as editor and Bankole Akpata Managing Editor, apologised for the interruption in publication and promised an enlarged journal from January 1947.[35]

There was a widespread attempt to publicize the Secretariat and its paper. West African organizations, addressed as 'Dear Comrade', were circularized and asked to 'rally with their fullest support behind WANS . . . Apply for your sponsorship and affiliation and let us work hard for the building up of a West African National Unity for a United West African National Independence', Nkrumah wrote. *The New African* was offered at a subscription rate of five shillings a year.[36] It was advertised in the 23 February issue of the Independent Labour Party's journal, *New Leader*. As I have found WANS material in the NAACP files, it is probable that Nkrumah also contacted his other US acquaintances.

West African leaders visiting the UK were also approached. Overtures were made to the National Council of Nigeria and the Cameroons (NCNC) delegation led by Nnamdi Azikiwe. According to Padmore, who served as press secretary to the NCNC, 'a close personal relationship was established between the younger West African nationalists . . . a working alliance . . . Dr Azikiwe endorsed the decisions of the Fifth Pan-African Congress and the West African National Secretariat to work for immediate self-government and the realization of a United West African Federation.'[37] Subscriptions and articles were sought from men such as Sekyi and Dr J.B. Danquah, who was also invited to address a WANS meeting held at the WASU in November.[38]

West African newspapers were naturally informed of WANS and its activities. Of those papers available to me, it appears that the *West African Pilot*, despite editor Azikiwe's endorsement, did not wish to report WANS. The *Ashanti Pioneer* (9 February 1946) reported its inauguration and recommended it 'to the serious patronage of all progressive Africans in West Africa'. The *Gold Coast Observer* reviewed *The New African* on 3 May 1946; Nkrumah and Akpata wrote articles for the *Observer* on WANS activities. For example, in his report on the August WANS meeting (14 February 1947) Nkrumah concluded by exhorting the 'People of West Africa: your future is in your hands. The eleventh hour has struck for all West Africans to join in the common struggle for unity and complete independence.' Other tactics were tried: for instance, a letter from K.A. Taylor (presumably Karankyi Taylor, who had attended the PAC) was published (13 June 1947) recommending WANS (among other organizations) to Gold Coast students going to the UK. The only publication of the 'WANS Press' appeared in May 1946. It was a pamphlet by Awoonor-Renner, called *West African Soviet Union*, consisting of letters by Renner which had been published in various newspapers since 1937. The preface asserts that 'only a united and independent West Africa . . . could ensure security, happiness and prosperity for our unfortunate country'.[39]

Significantly in pan-Africanist terms, WANS telegramed President Truman protesting at the lynching of seven 'Negroes' and demanding that lynching should be made a federal offence.[40] WANS co-operated with other London-based Black organizations on some campaigns. Thus when a West Indian aircraftman was accused of murder, WANS co-operated with WASU, the PAF, the League of Coloured People and the Federation of Indian Organisation to secure his release. The year ended with a joint WANS/PAF/LCP meeting with the Transvaal Council of Non-European Trade Unions in the LCP's offices: it was decided to send a telegram to the United Nations demanding that South Africa should surrender its mandate over South-West Africa to the Trusteeship Council and that South Africa should abide by the principles of the UN Charter in its treatment of African peoples.[41]

In April 1946 Nkrumah spoke at a Fabian Colonial Bureau conference, where about 50 of the 100 participants were Africans and West Indians. The debates were apparently acrimonious: the colonials felt betrayed by the Labour government and the Bureau. Nkrumah castigated the Labour government, which, while in opposition had promised so much, but was now apparently intent on retaining the empire. Furthermore, the Bureau, which had once been the Labour Party's socialist anti-colonial think-tank, was now supporting and defending an imperialist party.[42] The participants and the Bureau decided that the major speeches at the conference should be prepared for publication as the first in a new series to be called the 'Controversy' series. In the first pamphlet, *Domination or Co-Operation?*, Nkrumah repeated the resolutions on West Africa promulgated at the Pan-African Congress in 1945. He concluded by saying

> you can shackle the hands of men, you can shackle the feet of men, you can even shackle and enslave the bodies of men, but you cannot shackle and enslave their minds. There is justice behind every

historical necessity. Colonial individuals and institutions may
retreat and hide. The leaders of the colonial world may also retreat
and hide but the masses of the colonial people have nowhere to
retreat. They have only one battle-cry 'Advance and destroy
Imperialism'.[43]

Political Activities, London, 1947

The furious pace of activities must have continued, though I have been
able to find less evidence than for 1946. As Joe Appiah comments,
'Nkrumah impressed all of us as a very hard worker who enjoyed hard
labour and needed very little or no rest',[44] although there is no evidence
to substantiate Nkrumah's claims that he paid 'fairly regular visits to
Liverpool, Manchester and Cardiff . . . to help (Africans) find a job, or
failing that, to find ways and means of getting them repatriated . . . I used
to sit and listen to their problems.'[45] This was a somewhat unreal claim as
such problems were dealt with by Black organizations in those cities in
any case.

Sometime during the year WANS sent out a circular appealing for
£25,000 for the proposed All West African National Congress, to be held
in Lagos in October 1948.[46] The circular stated the aims of the Congress as
'the Self-determination and National Independence of all West African
peoples, leading eventually to the Democratic Federation of all West
African Territories'. Recipients were exhorted to form 'territorial' Congress Committees 'to discuss the aims and organization of the Congress,
to publicize it and to collect the money needed for the organization'. Each
of these Congress Committees would send delegates to the Lagos Congress; their aim would be to set up National Councils to carry on the work
of the Congress. The Congress would also elect a Supreme Council,
consisting of representatives from each National Council; this Council
would elect a Secretary General and a Secretariat, and delegate 'such of
its powers as it may choose to the Secretariat'. It was hoped by WANS
that every West African 'territory' would send delegates.

The covering letter, signed by Nkrumah, noted that WANS had
'already launched an appeal in the West African press for a fighting fund
of £25,000'. The people of West Africa were asked to respond to 'this
clarion call . . . to work and act in unity . . . The future of West Africa
and her peoples rests with every one of us. We cannot escape from our
duty and our destiny.'[47] In the few West African newspapers for these
years in the British Library I have not been able to find any mention of this
appeal. However, a few months later the *Gold Coast Observer* carried a
photograph and a long article on Nkrumah, forecasting that he would

'play a great role in the future of West Africa . . . He devotes all his energies in working with many others towards the national liberation of African people . . . He is now preparing for the All West African National Congress.'[48]

In April a 'further copy of the Congress Appeal fund' was sent to the West African press in April, with a copy to 'Dear Mr Danquah', for 'your information'. 'Political power is the only key to freedom of any sort', the circular, addressesd to 'Fellow Men and Women of West Africa' by Kwame Nkrumah, stated. 'West African nationalism does not preclude African nationalism . . . a united free and independent West Africa is the political condition for Africa's redemption and emancipation . . . (and) for the emancipation of the Africans and peoples of African Descent throughout the world'. The All West Africa Congress would meet this challenge. All territories should follow Nigeria's example and form national councils. The Congress 'will carry on the struggle for a united free and independent federal union of West African Republics'.[49]

Perhaps not surprisingly, these appeals did not elicit a great response. The WANS plans were very grandiose and very complex, though those interested in the scheme must have taken some comfort from the attempt to define the previously nebulous rhetoric of West African unity. £25,000 was a vast sum of money to even dream of raising by an appeal in the media. Ladipo Solanke, the warden of the WASU hostel, who was touring West Africa at this time in an attempt to raise money for the hostel, only managed to collect £6,000 out of a projected £50,000.[50]

In April, Nkrumah addressed the Study Group at WASU on 'Philosophies of Our Time'. Unfortunately no report appears to exist of this talk. In September, Nkrumah was among those who addressed a rally at Trafalgar Square in support of the campaign against the Richards constitution, which was attended by some 400 people. In October, Nkrumah wrote to Ako Adjei, who had returned to the Gold Coast in April, that 'we had raised hell here with regard to Padmore's book – the West African National Secretariat led the attack – and we are glad to know that you have got them at last'.[51] This refers to Padmore's *How Russia Transformed Her Colonial Empire*, which had been banned by the colonial government.

Also in October, after an approach by Nkrumah and Awoonor-Renner, the Conference of British Missionary Societies (CBMS) agreed to meet with the WANS representatives. At the meeting on 29 October held at the YMCA, Nkrumah explained the Secretariat's aims and asked the missionaries to keep out of the forthcoming struggle. After a two-hour discussion, the CBMS promised to issue a statement as the church 'will always support the principle that the backward nations must be guided and led to rule themselves'. The CBMS could not campaign, these racist missionaries informed Nkrumah and Awoonor-Renner, but could use their influence to 'inspire friendship, goodwill and honesty on both sides'. Once the statement was agreed, it would be sent to the Secretariat. It was not until August 1949 that the churchmen managed to agree the wording, which stated that the CBMS regarded 'with deep sympathy and understanding . . the nationalist movements which aim at freedom and self-determination by constitutional methods'. It would draw attention to 'injustices and denials of freedom . . . welcome government reforms . . . assist Europeans and Africans to develop the moral and personal qualities essential to the well-being of individuals and communities'.[52] I have not been able to discover whether something particular prompted WANS to make this approach, or if it was simply a piece of prescient political manoeuvering in the light of Nkrumah's imminent return to the Gold Coast.

There were also plans afoot for further publications. Nkrumah had written some pamphlets and it was also planned to bring out a quarterly magazine to be called *African Digest*, which was to concern itself with academic and cultural isuses.[53] Neither the pamphlets nor the magazine were ever published.

Meanwhile, WANS was broke. Despite the £150 from Sekyi, *The New African* had not reappeared. The situation was so desperate that Nkrumah wrote to the ARPS, pleading for help. WANS's debts were £150 and some creditors were threatening to sue.[54] It is probable that other supporting organizations were also asked for donations, and that at least some helped, as in November a circular promised *The New African*'s reappearance. A new scheme for its survival was proposed: under Nii Odoi Annan, the new Business and Circulation Manager, the enterprise was to become a publishing co-operative, with £1 shares. However, *The New African* did not appear.

Money was a constant problem. Padmore and Nkrumah both comment on how difficult it was to buy coal to keep warm in the winter. Without the 'ever ready offer of help by several English girls – most of them of good class families – (who) used to come and type for hours on end in the evenings and they never asked a single penny for their work', the organizations could not have survived.[55] As Padmore explained to Professor St. Clair Drake: 'Lack of money is our handicap, for unlike in America, we have no rich ones among us . . . all the work that has been done all these years has been done on a purely voluntary basis (which) avoids a lot of corruption . . . (but) men must eat . . .'.[56]

However, ignoring WANS' financial problems, Nkrumah obtained the funds to privately publish a pamphlet, *Towards Colonial Freedom (TCF)* in 1947. At least one of Nkrumah's close colleagues was more than a little miffed by this individualistic (if not self-aggrandizing) behaviour: 'how could you get money for printing your *TCF* and none for WANS?', Bankole Akpata wrote to Nkrumah. 'I agree that *TCF* is needed before the Congress, but it's WANS that's organising the Congress. I have tried everything to raise money here for WANS.' The Secretariat was so poor that it could not pay the rent or its secretary, Margot Parrish.[57]

Nkrumah claims in the Foreword to *Towards Colonial Freedom* that he had begun drafting it in 1942, while in the USA: 'I was so revolted by the ruthless colonial exploitation and political oppression of the people in Africa that I knew no peace', he wrote.[58] Unfortunately he does not explain why he became so particularly revolted in 1942; was this some watershed in his understanding of the situation in Africa? In 1945, he goes on to explain, he was 'stimulated to complete the booklet (by) the determination of student bodies fighting and agitating for colonial freedom'. The pamphlet – it is 43 pages – begins with an economic and Leninist analysis of colonialism and imperialism. Nkrumah then goes on to surmise that 'unless there is a complete national unity of all the West African colonies it will be practically impossible for any one colony to throw off her foreign yoke' (p.33). He then advocates the 'Organization of the Colonial Masses; the abolition of political illiteracy . . . through mass political education'; the preparation (through both technical and political education) of 'agents of progress'; and the ownership of its own press (pp.41–2).

TCF concludes with what Nkrumah calls a programme, but which is in fact a series of proposals and demands, for complete and absolute independence, the establishment of a democracy and 'social reconstruction', that is, 'freedom from poverty and economic exploitation, and the improvement of social and economic conditions'. The concluding sentence is very reminiscent of the British Communist Party's propaganda materials: 'PEOPLES OF THE COLONIES, UNITE: The working men of all countries are behind you' (p.43).

On 14 November, Nkrumah and his friend Kojo Botsio left London in order to return to the Gold Coast. Curiously, I have not been able to find their names in the passenger lists published regularly in those days.

Nkrumah and Padmore

What was the relationship between the two men during these years? C.L.R. James's introduction to Padmore described Nkrumah as talking 'a lot about imperialism and Leninism and export of capital, and talk(ing) a lot of nonsense'. 'George', C.L.R. James wrote, 'this young man is coming to you. He is not very bright, but nevertheless do what you can for him because he's determined to throw the Europeans out of Africa.'[59] Padmore obviously took James at his word by taking Nkrumah under his wing. The fact that Padmore offered the new arrival the very responsible post of regional secretary of the Pan-African Federation, as well as subsequently making him rapporteur of the sessions on West Africa at the Pan-African Congress, indicates Padmore's positive opinion of Nkrumah and the growing trust and friendship between the two men during Nkrumah's first few months in London.

Yet, in Abrahams' words, 'Nkrumah drifted away from us (the PAF) and started his own West African group'.[60] There is corroborating evidence for this drift, despite Nkrumah having spent 'endless hours discussing colonial issues' with Padmore, or as Drake put it, 'getting some political education from Padmore'. Murapa notes that similar views were expressed by Makonnen and Abrahams in interviews.[61] What were the reasons? They were probably twofold; Padmore was against the regionalism represented by a purely *West* African organization. He was also concerned about Nkrumah's group being dominated by people who though not necessarily card-carrying Communist Party members, were certainly communists or had communist sympathies. It is stated by former members of the CPGB that it was party policy not to issue membership cards to those whom such cards might endanger, such as 'colonials'. St. Clair Drake, a US 'Negro' sociologist researching in the UK during these years, was 'struck by the uneasy feeling that existed between the PAF group and Nkrumah and his WANS'. When Drake asked Padmore if the Colonial Office knew that 'communists are mixed up with WANS', Padmore replied that of course the Colonial Office knew: there was a 'dossier' on Awoonor-Renner and there was 'Stalinist literature all over the place (in the WANS office). And that magazine (*The New African*) anybody who knows communist language could tell it'.[62]

Padmore's close colleague Ras T. Makonnen noted that the 'alignment of Kwame and the communist boys seemed quite clear at that time . . . we discovered that Kwame was playing with the communist boys in King Street (the CPGB's headquarters) and developing the very alliances we had outlawed . . . he was double dealing between pan-Africanism and communism'. Makonnen says that the PAF Central Committee questioned Nkrumah about his involvement with the communists and his 'stewardship' of his position with the Federation. It was pointed out to Nkrumah that the Colonial Office would use any evidence of communist involvement to 'damn the movement'. The meeting appears to have been inconclusive: all Makonnen says is that it was 'embarrassing' for Nkrumah.[63]

To Padmore, an avowed Marxist, pan-Africanist and anti-Stalinist, the presence of Awoonor-Renner, Bankole Akpata and Margot Parrish in the WANS Executive and office would have been an anathema. (Awoonor-Renner, educated in the USA and the USSR in the 1920s, an ex-colleague of Wallace Johnson's and currently studying law at Lincoln's Inn, was certainly regarded at that time as a communist. Bankole Akpata, then studying for his B.Sc., was at least a communist sympathizer, judging by his letters to Nkrumah. Margot Parrish, WANS' irregularly paid secretary, was a CPGB member.) Emile Burns, as previously indicated, one of the CPGB's inner circle and deputed by the Party to run classes for students at the WASU, became a life-long friend of Nkrumah's. Moreover, Padmore believed that as a political tactic 'in this business you don't want to let anybody put any kinds of labels on you'.[64]

When answering questions at the Watson Commission Enquiry, Nkrumah confirmed that he had 'adopted communist opinions, but had not joined the communist party . . . (he) had discussed colonial questions with Palme Dutt . . . the idea of a West African Congress might have arisen at this meeting'. He had turned to West African unity after the Pan-African Congress, where he had realized that Pan-Africanism was an 'ideal with no realism'.[65] According to Peter Blackman, then a staunch member of the CPGB, 'Nkrumah did not belong to any department of the Communist Party'.[66]

How deep this rift was at the time is not possible to tell as neither man ever wrote about it. However, as Padmore was one of the men Nkrumah consulted when he was offered the secretaryship of the United Gold Coast Convention, we have to presume that even before Nkrumah left London to return home the two men had begun to reconcile their differences.

The London Years – Private Life

Very little is known of Kwame Nkrumah's personal life during his London years. However, despite the tremendous pace of activity, there was time for a private, social life. Joe Appiah relates that he and his flat-mates from Primrose Gardens often hosted racially-mixed social gatherings which Nkrumah attended. He also appeared at the dances and social occasions at the WASU hostel, but 'was too shy to talk to white girls or to dance with them or even to get too close to them'. So the Primrose Gardens 'gang' decided that he needed a white girl-friend. Nkrumah was introduced to 'Diana P. [sic], herself a revolutionary Marxist'. The two got on so well that Diana accompanied Nkrumah to the Congress in Manchester.[67] However, Ernest Marke, who attended many socials at WASU, doubts Appiah's assessment: 'Nkrumah was certainly not of a shy nature . . . his reluctance to dance was because what was uppermost in his mind at that time was to bring his dream into reality . . . enjoyment was no part of it'.[68] WANS also organized social get-togethers. For example, during the August 1946 conference, there was a dance at the Holborn Town Hall and a social evening at the WASU hostel.[69]

Diana P. was not the only 'girlfriend' Nkrumah had in London. From the evidence of one of the letters found on him when arrested, Nkrumah's landlady, Mrs F.M., did not long remain exclusively in that role. Nkrumah clearly wrote to her regularly at least during the first few weeks of his return to Ghana and she expected to join him in the Gold Coast. As far as I have been able to discover, the only trip Mrs M. made to Africa was to Ghana's independence celebrations. She was one of the many English girls who worked without pay in the WANS office. 'At most all they got was the price of their bus ticket home. Yet they never flagged or complained', Nkrumah later remembered.[70] In a 1973 interview Mrs M. said: 'Nkrumah fasted every Friday . . . he spoke at Hyde Park at least once'.[71]

Nkrumah registered as a Ph.D. candidate in Anthropology at the London School of Economics (LSE) in October 1945. According to an LSE official, the few remaining papers indicate that he 'decided he did not want to do Anthropology' and withdrew after one term.[72] In October 1946 Nkrumah registered at University College London (UCL) as a Ph.D. student for the 1946–47 session. He was expected to re-register for the following two academic years but as he failed to attend his registration was cancelled. In June 1948 Nkrumah wrote to UCL that 'circumstances beyond his control forced him to come to his home in the Gold Coast'.[73] His dissertation topic had been 'Knowledge and Logical Positivism'. His supervisor, Professor A.J. Ayer recalled that he did not think that Nkrumah was 'a first-class philosopher. I liked him and enjoyed talking to him but he did not seem to me to have an analytical mind. He wanted answers too quickly. I think part of the trouble may have been that he wasn't concentrating very hard on his thesis. It was a way of marking time until the opportunity came for him to return to Ghana.'[74] Nkrumah had also been admitted as a 'student member of Gray's Inn in November 1946 . . . his degree exempted him from the preliminary examination. He was later fined for not keeping his dining terms (the sum of £12) which he later paid. He does not appear to have been Called to the Bar.'[75]

Why had Nkrumah abandoned all thoughts of a Ph.D. or of becoming a barrister? Was Professor Ayer's analysis correct? At least some of Nkrumah's new colleagues actively discouraged him from this path. Ras T. Makonnen, Padmore's friend and the general secretary of the PAF, recalled that 'we pooh-poohed the idea (of Nkrumah taking legal qualifications) . . . being a rebel was as good a profession as any . . . Lawyers take a constitutional approach . . . C.L.R. James had sent him to us . . . when one met him, one could see that he would become some kind of leader; he had the mark on him.'[76] So Nkrumah spent much time sitting in Padmore's 'small kitchen, the wooden table completely covered by papers', discussing Congress preparations, political tactics and politics.[77] He was acquiring the education he lacked: the practical side of mass-organizing. Towards the end of 1947, Nkrumah suffered another attack of the pneumonia which had ravaged him in Pennsylvania. Found severely ill in bed by the 'gang' from Primrose Gardens, he was saved by the hastily summoned Dr Hastings Kamuzu Banda, then a physician with a large practice in North London.[78]

Nkrumah and the Colonial Masters

The UK, without a Freedom of Information Act, is probably the most secretive society in the Western world: the government's departmental files on the 'subversives/communists' of the 1930s and 1940s are witheld indefinitely. Until very recently the very existence of MI5 (the arm of Military Intelligence which gathers information and keeps people within the UK borders under surveillance) was denied by government spokes-men of all political parties. However, there is enough evidence to indicate that many 'colonials' were under sporadic surveillance and the activists were watched constantly.[79] That the snoopers often still 'got it wrong' testifies to the solidarity among the activists.

As Joe Appiah relates,

> one morning Kwame went to the office as usual to discover that all the files and drawers had been turned out . . . Nothing had been stolen . . . the police had their station some ten yards away, oppo-site to our office building . . . We went and reported the matter to the police . . . the sergeant's only comment was 'Curious, ain't it?' . . . The police knew and we knew perfectly well who had broken in to try and find out what the 'colonial conspirators' were about![80]

Not that Nkrumah attempted to keep at least some of his activities from the authorities. Undoubtedly he had learned from Padmore, who sent invitations to the 1945 Congress to the Colonial Office, that this was the best tactic. Nkrumah certainly put the Colonial Office on notice that he intended to bring its days of supremacy to an end.

From the few correspondence registers open to researchers (not from the files for which *no release date has been set*) we learn that the Colonial Office probably opened its files on WANS in 1946. The Nigerian governor wrote requesting information on the organization as *The New African* had appeared, followed by a WANS circular. By 1947 at least some people in Britain with whom the Secretariat had been in contact felt honour bound to inform the Colonial Office: the Rev. Harold Grace of the Conference of British Missionary Societies informed the Colonial Office of his meeting with Nkrumah and Awoonor-Renner. This resulted in telegrams to the West African governors, as did the arrival from WANS of the 'special conference edition of *The New African*' in October 1947. At the end of November the Colonial Office received a report on a WANS meeting held on 11 November from 'National Secret', which, one has to presume, is the pseudonym of MI5.[81] In a previous report from 'Robinson' the CO had been advised that Nkrumah held 'extreme political views (and) has been attempting to enlist help from Mr Rogerson of the Communist Party of Great Britain for the West African Congress proposed for Lagos in 1948'.

Nkrumah and WANS were certainly under surveillance. For example, in the material preserved in the Watson Commission Enquiry files we learn that the Gold Coast Police Commissioner had written at length to his counterpart in Sierra Leone, who had already been warned to expect the arrival of Nkrumah. 'Nkrumah is well known', the Commissioner wrote. 'While in the UK he had come under the notice of MI5 in connection with his activities with the British Communist Party . . .'. The report is full: it mentions some of Nkrumah's activities in the United States and his association with Padmore and Makonnen. It gives details of the WANS August 1946 conference and of Nkrumah's contacts with communists such as William Rust, editor of the *Daily Worker*, Michael Carritt of the CPGB's Colonial Section and M. Rogerson, who had been in charge of the colonial delegates to the CP's Empire Conference in February 1947. The report suggests that it was with 'Rogerson and others' that Nkrumah had discussed the plans for a West African Congress.[82]

The reports from Britain had apparently focused on Nkrumah's communist contacts. Kenneth Bradley, the Acting Colonial Secretary of the Gold Coast, in a long report to the Colonial Office on the United Gold Coast Convention, expected that when Nkrumah arrived, he would make contact with French West African communists. He warned that Nkrumah held 'extreme political views' and that his political associates in the UK had been mainly 'communists and the other extremist groups'.[83]

WANS and Nkrumah were causing consternation around the world. The Americans were concerned. The US Consul in Accra wrote to his superiors in the State Department in December 1947 giving a detailed biography of Nkrumah and stating that the British officials considered him a communist without any real basis for this belief. He anticipated that Nkrumah 'will do his best to make it (the UGCC) a more radical organization'.[84]

The Consul kept the State Department fully informed of events as they unfolded. So did the Embassy in London, whose reports are based at least partially on discussions with J.K. Thompson of the West Africa department at the Colonial Office. The Embassy's report for March 1948 gave lengthy biographies of Nkrumah and Awoonor-Renner, whom Mr Thompson considered 'the most dangerous'. However, Awoonor-Renner had recently fallen out of favour with the Communist Party, as the Party had not considered that 'the time was ripe for the UGCC to make its bid', and had told Awoonor-Renner it was annoyed with WANS over this 'premature and unsuccessful affair', the Gold Coast riots of February 1948. All of this must be seen against the background of the developing cold war and British official concern at the possible spread of communism in Africa.

In March 1948 the British Consul-General in Leopoldville in the then Belgian Congo, reported to the Foreign Office (FO) that the Director-General of the Belgian Congo police had questioned him about Nkrumah and WANS. The Director complained that the 'natives' were receiving seditious literature from WANS, about WANS' aims and the proposed West African Congress. He asked for WANS to be investigated. He was sending copies of this despatch to the British embassies in Paris, Brussels and Lisbon and to the Nigerian and Gold Coast governors.[85] The Foreign Office asked the Colonial Office for information. D.G. Pirie replied that Nkrumah was 'strongly suspected of communist connections and of political aspirations which differ radically from the purely Gold Coast nationalism of the UGCC, but these are individual to himself and to a perhaps limited personal following and there is at present no firm ground for thinking that the Convention as such has any connection with communism'. This information was communicated at least to the French Embassy in London.[86]

By the end of the year the FO's concern was increasing. It was decided to prepare a paper on communism in Africa; unfortunately, if a copy has been preserved it is not available to researchers. Information was gathered from MI5 and from 'other sources' about Nkrumah's movements in West Africa. Concern by the British Embassy in Brussels about the narrow, 'local' view of the Colonial Office in not prohibiting the proposed Lagos Congress led to a meeting between the two British government departments in October 1948.[87]

The apparently blasé attitude displayed by the Colonial Office to the Foreign Office regarding the Lagos Congress was probably no more than a matter of guarding 'turf'. Certainly the CO was concerned. The internal memoranda in one of the few files dealing with political activities open to researchers (on the UGCC), but from which all MI5 reports have been removed, notes Nkrumah's communist connections and expects that he might become a 'channel for communist infiltration'. Internal memoranda prophesied that 'Nkrumah is most likely to emerge as a real leader' and warned that the WANS was 'a violently secessionist' organization.[88]

Some months before its meeting with the FO, the Colonial Office had asked for fortnightly reports on communist activities from all colonial governments. The reports date from the two weeks ending 4 June 1948; the last report available, the 14th, covers the end of December. The reports from West Africa found no communist activity: Awoonor-Renner's return to the Gold Coast is mentioned and that the 'communist protagonist' Nkrumah had visited French West Africa and announced the postponement of the Lagos Congress.[89] From November 1948 the CO also began preparing intelligence summaries – one can presume that this is one of the outcomes of the FO/CO meeting in the previous month.

The quality of surveillance had also been improved in the colonies – without any pressure from the FO. In the first fortnightly report on communism it is stated that 'senior members of the Secret Service from the UK on a recent visit put the Special Branch work on a more efficient basis; officers will be going to the UK for training soon'.[90] In May 1948, in another file it is advised that there should be close collaboration between the Police Intelligence Services and the Military commanders. 'The current visit of Mr Kellar of MI5 to West Africa is likely to result in a permanent posting of an MI5 representative.'[91]

Colonials in Britain, not just the colonies, were causing unease in the Colonial Office. In mid-1947 the Office discussed how to implement a memorandum by George Cartland which had made suggestions for the 'educated classes (whose) appearance has upset our calculations and disturbed the even tenour [sic] of political development among the slow moving masses'. Cartland advocated more contact between African students and 'cultured English men and women . . . the objective presentation of facts to achieve a balanced political understanding . . . authentic information' on the British government's colonial policies and more visits to places of interest.[92] A few months later the CO received a report from MI5 on a Fabian Colonial Bureau conference, at which it seems colonial students were quite free in their expressions of 'suspicion and distrust'. During the discussions on the report Mr Rees Williams complained that after he had spoken at student gatherings 'communists gather, counter-saying . . . I hear too that Communists are working through prostitutes in London and other big cities to get their policies across.'[93] Keith, in charge of the Welfare Department at the CO was much more astute: 'events in

Africa influence students more than discrimination here', he minuted; 'they want democratic government and their experience of democracy and free speech in Britain only fuels this desire'. Hilton Poynton agreed with Keith: 'No action is possible . . . this is one of the factors to take into account when working out the general political future of the colonies'.[94]

Conclusion

What are we to make of Nkrumah's years in London? Formative they certainly were. Nkrumah arrived in Britain with a 'Christian and African mystical orientation'.[95] He had been a 'serious student . . . not rushing off to Philadelphia to spend weekends with girls'.[96] In fact, he had spent many Sundays during his last years preaching in Baptist churches in the Philadelphia–Washington area, an excellent training for a platform politician.

From George Padmore, the London-based guru of colonial revolutionaries, he received an 'injection of Marxism', though apparently Padmore 'always considered religion a major weakness in Nkrumah during 1945–47'.[97] Padmore and his colleagues however obviously appreciated the potentialities of Nkrumah, who was already 'consumed by the passion for the emancipation of Africa'.[98] Peter Abrahams remembered that his erstwhile colleague 'had quickly become part of our little group . . . joined our protests against colonialism . . . He was much less relaxed than most of us . . . he was consumed by a restlessness that led him to evolve some of the most fantastic schemes. His name then was Francis.'[99]

It is of interest, I believe, that Nkrumah retained the Christian name of 'Francis', occasionally adding either the initials 'N–K' or the full 'Nwia-Kofi', until about the time of the formation of the West African National Secretariat. Does it denote a clinging to Christianity? A retention of a foot in the door of Western academia and 'respectability' or 'acceptability'? Was the dropping of the name a symbol of total commitment to African nationalism? And why did he, when he reverted to a Ghanaian forename, adopt 'Kwame'?

By all accounts, including his own, Nkrumah was thoroughly educated by Padmore. This education was not confined to Marxist theories. Padmore was a veteran, a seasoned organizer, writer, agitator. From him Nkrumah could learn the techniques of organizing – in fact, Padmore obviously insisted that he did so by involving him in the organizing, administration and reporting of the Pan-African Congress of 1945. Nkrumah also gained many valuable contacts through Padmore with anti-imperialist politicians in Britain and of course the trade union leaders and others attending the Congress. Padmore's contacts were world-wide and his knowledge of colonial affairs encyclopaedic. Through the West African Students' Union, Nkrumah met others whose acquaintance would prove useful.

Yet it appears that Nkrumah turned away from the Pan-African Federation by founding a purely regional organization, and came to some extent under the influence of the Communist Party of Great Britain. Why did he do this? Was this a way of gaining leadership within an organization of his own? Though Murapa maintains that Padmore believed the struggle for the independence of Africa would begin in East Africa, where 'a confrontation between the African and white settlers was imminent', it is unlikely that Padmore would have been inflexible on this issue.[100] After all, the revolution had to begin *somewhere*. Had the Communist Party of Great Britain promised Nkrumah some kind of support? I would argue on the evidence presently available, that Nkrumah's ambition, so amply demonstrated in the Circle document, and his appreciation of the presence of a number of West Africans in London, communist, non-communist or anti-communist, but certainly pro-independence, led him to make his bid for West African leadership by setting up the Secretariat.

Was he personally ambitious? I would suggest that he was ambitious for African independence and unity; that he saw himself as a man with a destiny to fulfil, as being inseparable from the idea of independence. He was not an ideologue but a romantic. As he expressed it to the President of Lincoln University, 'I seem to almost hear the cry of my people for me to hurry for they do need me. My soul answers this cry because I realise there is so much to do and at the most there is so little I can do in a life span'.[101] A romantic with a definite sense of his own role and destiny, and a shrewd political sensibility. Who but a man with such a character would ask a friend/secretary to write his biography when his student days were barely behind him? Margot Parrish refused, writing to Nkrumah that she had not known him long enough. In any case, 'is the time ripe', she queried; 'Shouldn't a few years of work in the Gold Coast elapse?'[102]

It is impossible to determine how much influence the Communist Party of Great Britain exerted on Nkrumah and WANS. As mentioned above, at least one member of the WANS executive and the secretary were communists (Awoonor-Renner and Margot Parrish). Nkrumah had known a number of communists in the United States where in the 1930s the communists had taken one of the leading roles in anti-racist struggles. Padmore and many other 'colonials' had been attracted to the communists by their advocacy of freedom for the colonies. In Britain Nkrumah was at least acquainted with the CPGB's leadership and was sufficiently close to one leading member, Emile Burns, to maintain a long-lasting friendship. Did the CPGB hope to take control of WANS and to use it as an entry into British West Africa? If so, it did not succeed. Nkrumah was probably too much of a pragmatist and an opportunist in the best sense of that word, to be committed to any theory or political party. His idealism, his consuming passion was for freedom – for all Africa, West Africa, or just the Gold Coast – whichever could be attained the soonest under his leadership.

Perhaps the greatest achievement of WANS lies in shaking the British government's racist complacency. But the Colonial Office and its officials as well as the Foreign Office apparently could not conceive of Africans struggling for independence without the 'outside agency' shibboleth. The myopia bred by a society suffused with class and racial hierarchies was all too evident in the Colonial Office. So the CO searched for communist influence. Unable to see students from Africa, most of whom were much older than the usual age for even postgraduate students, as anything but students, the CO sought to improve their living conditions in Britain. Yet they were clearly worried: why else set up a committee to deal with the 'political significance' of students three months after Nkrumah's return home?

Moreover, by 1948 it had become evident even to the Colonial Office that old tactics would no longer serve. During the war, Wallace Johnson had been imprisoned and Zik's press temporarily silenced. In Britain attempts were made to intimidate activists. Why else search WANS' office so blatantly? Why else imprison Ernest Marke for activities (running a gambling club) which previously had invariably been dealt with by paying the usual fine?[103] Once at home, Nkrumah and his UGCC colleagues were gaoled – but not for long. The imprisonment was questionable, the protests loud, and within the CO the proponents of economic development and more rapid constitutional and political change for the colonies were in the ascendant. Negotiation was to be the new tactic, as well as new forms of economic control which many now might call 'neo-colonialism'.

One lesson for the historian is that autobiographies cannot be taken literally, or certainly not those of politicians in mid-career who must necessarily consider the effect of their words on their adherents and thus on their political future. Nkrumah's autobiography, written while he was Prime Minister, glorifies his own exploits in the United States and Britain. He was not, for example, one of the founders of the African Students' Association of America, nor its first president. In Britain it is unlikely that he could have played any kind of welfare role at least for the first few months after his arrival: he would simply not have known the 'ropes'.

Later, once he had learned his way about London, he would still have been a stranger in other cities, where, in any case, local Black organizations were doing all that could be done. It is much more likely, if he travelled about at all, that it was to recruit for WANS and to meet West Africans, both the students and the seamen, who could give him up-to-date information about conditions and events in West Africa.

A politician's autobiography is also bound to ignore or underplay matters which the voting public would find questionable or distasteful. Thus Nkrumah plays down his communist acquaintances and ignores the rift with Padmore, who by the 1950s was well known as his close adviser. And he does not mention his sources of income!

NOTES

1. Kwame Nkrumah, *Ghana: The Autobiography of Kwame Nkrumah* (London, 1957). See also Carlos Nelson, 'Kwame Nkrumah: A Study of His Intellectual Development in the U.S.A., 1939–45', unpublished Ph.D. thesis, Temple University, 1985.
2. The work of the Black organizations in Britain has not been documented. On some of the organizations in Cardiff, see Marika Sherwood, 'Racism and Resistance: Cardiff in the 1930s and 1940s', *Llafur*, Vol.5, No.4 (1991), pp.51–70.
3. Ladipo Solanke, *United West Africa* (London, 1927).
4. So far there is only one brief study of the WASU, by G.O. Olusanya, *The West African Students' Union* (Ibadan, 1982). See also forthcoming Ph.D. dissertation by Hakim Adi (SOAS, 1993).
5. For the little information at present available on the Somali Youth League see Sherwood, 'Racism and Resistance', pp.63–5.
6. The Pan-African Congress held in Manchester in 1945 is described by George Padmore in his *Pan-Africanism or Communism?* (London, 1956), Ch.IX. See also George Padmore (ed.), *Colonial and Coloured Unity, a Programme of Action* (Manchester, 1945), reprinted as *History of the Pan-African Congress* (Hammersmith, London, 1963). On the WFTU see George Padmore, *The Voice of Coloured Labour* (Manchester, 1945).
7. WASU Papers, University of Lagos. Box 18, Peter Carter to Ladipo Solanke, 3 May 1945. When I looked at these papers they were still unsorted; hence it is possible that once the cataloguing is complete, the box numbers may be different.
8. Joe Appiah, *The Autobiography of an African Patriot* (New York, 1990), p.163.
9. Attlee is quoted in *West Africa*, 23 Aug. 1941.
10. Rhodes House Library, Oxford (RHL), Mss.Br.Emp.s.19, D8/6. Circular letter on Pan-African Federation letterhead, 2 Oct. 1945.
11. See report of meeting and demonstrations in two US newspapers, *Chicago Defender*, 21 July 1945 and 28 July 1945, and in the *Pittsburgh Courier*, 28 July 1945. 'An Open Letter to the Prime Minister' is in the W.E.B. DuBois Papers, University of Massachusetts, Amherst; microfilm reel 57, frames 1076–8.
12. J. MacIntosh and S. Ireland, *Report of the World Trade Union Conference, County Hall, London, February 6–17th* (London, n.d.), pp.155, 169.
13. The Fabian Colonial Bureau's meeting with the colonial delegates to the WFTU is described in ILO Archives, Geneva (ILO). NL1/25/6, 'Meeting of Colonial Delegates with the Fabian Colonial Bureau'.
14. *Ashanti Pioneer*, 19 Feb. 1946.
15. National Archives of Ghana, Cape Coast (NAG, CC). ARPS Correspondence, Acc.77/6, file 5; Nkrumah to Sekyi, 18 Sept. 1945, and Sekyi to Nkrumah, 1 Oct. 1945.

16. By early 1946 the original Colonial Workers' Association (CWA) had be
over a dispute between Ernest Marke and the secretary, E.W. Matthews. ~~
continued to speak in Hyde Park and to solicit funds in the name of the Association,
much to the annoyance of Ernest Marke. Matthews was not a political person; his
speeches focused on 'the grey offspring of Blacks and whites who would eventually
take over Britain'. He was very abusive to his audience who took delight in heckling
him, so I was told by Billy Strachan; interviews in London, 17 Jan. 1991 and 20 Sept.
1991. There were two placards on Matthews' soapbox: one for the Association and the
other for the Biological Socialist Movement – according to a photograph loaned to me
by Don Bateman from Bristol. Thus it is hardly likely, despite Nkrumah's claim in his
Autobiography, pp.48 and 52, that he travelled Britain on behalf of the Coloured
Workers' Association, unless it was for Matthews' version of it, which seems improb-
able. Mr Marke is adamant that Nkrumah's only connection with the CWA was at the
irregular Sunday meetings, some of which Nkrumah was invited to chair. Interviews
with Ernest Marke, 27 Feb. 1991 and 15 March 1992. See also ASACACHIB *Newsletter*
2 (1991), pp.11–12.

17. Eyo Ita Ndem, 'Negro Immigrants in Manchester', unpublished MA thesis, University of London, 1953. Ndem estimated that there were about 300 Black residents in
pre-war Manchester. Some had settled there after the First World War. He found a
social schism between those Blacks with some Western education and those without,
which generally meant a division between West Indians and West Africans.

18. On the Pan-African congresses see, for example, Colin Legum, *Pan-Africanism. A
Short Political Guide* (London, 1962); Imanuel Geiss, *The Pan-African Movement*
(London, 1974); P. Olisanwuche Esedebe, *Pan-Africanism* (Washington, DC, 1982).
That the Colonial Office was invited is evident from Public Record Office, Kew (PRO)
CO 974/22/14814/20, Register of Correspondence. Though the file has been destroyed,
the entries in the Register note that an invitation to attend had been received on 2 Oct.
1945. See also ILO, D117-1, W. Benson to C.O.J. Matthews (London representative
of the ILO), 28 Sept. 1945.

19. Padmore, *Colonial and Coloured Unity*, p.56.

20. 'Declaration to the Colonial Peoples of the World', in Kwame Nkrumah, *Towards
Colonial Freedom* (London, 1947). See also Esedebe, *Pan-Africanism*, p.170.

21. NAG, CC. ARPS papers, Acc. 78/64. Nkrumah to the Secretary of the ARPS, 23 Nov.
1945, on PAF letterhead with 60 Burghley Road (his then home) as the address.

22. Nkrumah, *Autobiography*, p.45. The 'Aims and Objectives' of WANS are in the
Library of Congress, Washington, DC. National Association for the Advancement of
Colored People (NAACP) papers, Group II, Box 44. Bankole Awooner-Renner was
probably still a communist in the 1940s. He had been educated partly in Moscow. In an
interview in the *New Statesman and Nation* (London), 7 Aug. 1943, he advocated the
formation of a united West Africa or at least a united self-governing British West
Africa with Dominion status.

23. 'Aims and Objectives', pp.8–9.

24. Peter Abrahams, 'Nkrumah, Kenyatta and the Old Order', in Jacob Draschler (ed.),
African Heritage (New York, 1963), p.139. It is possible that Abrahams' recollections
are not strictly accurate; not only was he recalling events which had taken place about
15 years before, but his political views had changed in the interim. See also his *A
Wreath for Udomo* (London, 1956), a fictionalized and somewhat vituperative depic-
tion of these tumultuous years.

25. Nkrumah, *Autobiography*, p.50.

26. See Nkrumah, *Autobiography*, Appendix 8, pp.303–4.

27. *New Leader*, 16 Feb. 1946 and 9 March 1946.

28. Nkrumah, *Autobiography*, p.43. Letters from Dr Marca Burns, Emile Burns's
daughter, 16 June 1991 and 28 Aug. 1991. Dr Burns, who confirms that most of her
father's correspondence has been destroyed, wrote to me that Nkrumah had attended
the class for students taught by her father. Emile Burns was the President's guest at
Ghana's independence celebrations. My views, after an examination of the CPGB

archives and reading their publication for these years, are that the Communist Party had little interest in the colonies, except for India. Though the few Black members were kept busy collating cuttings about the colonies, these resulted in more rhetoric than action. Some of the articles in the CPGB's journals contained racist statements. There was more interest shown in the colonies from 1945 onwards.

29. *The New African*, March 1946, p.14; *West Africa*, 2 Feb. 1946, p.151. In an editorial commenting on the WANS' letter, *West Africa*, criticized the Secretariat 'for ignoring the reality of the divisions in West Africa', and suggested that they should campaign for 'genuine local self-government' (p.147).

30. The text of the resolution is reprinted in *The New African*, May 1946.

31. Nkrumah, *Autobiography*, p.57.

32. NAG, CC. Sekyi papers. Acc. 111/65. Nkrumah to Sekyi, 28 Jan. 1946, 12 Feb. 1946 and 21 Feb. 1946.

33. S.K.B. Asante, 'Kwame Nkrumah and Pan-Africanism: The Early Phase, 1945–1961', *Universitas* (Legon), Vol.3, No.1 (1973). Most writers give membership of WANS as around 100, which is the number suggested in the Watson Commission papers. I would suggest 42, on the basis that the unassigned WANS membership card found on Nkrumah at the time of his arrest was no.43. There could not have been many students or non-professional workers who could afford the seven guineas membership fee, a large sum in 1946.

34. NAG, CC, Sekyi papers, Acc. 111/65. Sekyi–Nkrumah correspondence.

35. NAG, CC, ARPS papers, Acc. 78/64, file 6, Circular.

36. PRO CO 964/24, WANS circular.

37. George Padmore, 'Pan-Africanism and Ghana', *United Asia*, Vol.9, No.1 (1957).

38. PRO CO 964/24, WANS to J.B. Danquah, 4 Aug. 1946, and Bankole Akpata to Danquah, 19 Nov. 1947.

39. Bankole Awooner-Renner, *West African Soviet Union* (London, 1946), p.3.

40. *Gold Coast Observer* (Accra), 20 Sept. 1946; see also *New Leader*, 31 Aug. 1946.

41. The League of Coloured People's *Newsletter* (London), Dec. 1946.

42. The Bureau had called the conference because it was disturbed by the growing criticism of the Labour government's colonial policies; see D. Goldsworthy, *Colonial Issues in British Politics* (Oxford, 1971), p.132.

43. Fabian Colonial Bureau, *Domination or Co-Operation?* Controversy Series No.1 (London, 1946).

44. Appiah, *Autobiography of an African Patriot*, p.164.

45. Nkrumah, *Autobiography*, p.48.

46. According to information given by the Colonial Office to US officials, the CO had been sent a copy of this circular in Oct. 1947; see National Archives and Records Administration, Washington, DC (NARA). RG59: 848N.00/3-1848, Despatch No.715, 18 March 1948, US Embassy, London, to State Department, Washington, DC.

47. PRO CO 964/24, exhibit 19. Copy of undated letter signed by Nkrumah on behalf of the Secretariat.

48. *Gold Coast Observer* (Accra), 24 Oct. 1947.

49. PRO CO 964/24. Copy of letter from Nkrumah, 21 April 1947.

50. Olusanya, *West African Students' Union*, p.73.

51. PRO CO 964/24, exhibit 19. Nkrumah to Ako Adjei, 2 Oct. 1947.

52. School of Oriental and African Studies Archives, University of London, CBMS papers, A/G23, Box 257, 'Africa Committee – Political'. Notes on Meeting held at the YMCA, 20 Oct. 1947. The final version of the statement, issued as a pamphlet, is also in this file. The discussions on the wording are in A/G1, Box 235, 'Africa Committee Minutes and Committee Papers 1942–49'.

53. PRO CO 964/24, exhibit 36. The plans for publications are mentioned in Akpata's letter to Nkrumah, 22 Nov. 1947.

54. NAG, CC, ARPS papers, Acc. 78/64, file 6. Nkrumah to ARPS, 29 Sept. 1947.

55. Nkrumah, *Autobiography*, p.46.

56. Padmore to St Clair Drake, 28 Oct. 1949, quoted in Rukudzo Murapa, 'Padmore's

role in the African Liberation Movement', unpublished Ph.D. thesis, Northern Illinois University, 1974, p.215.

57. PRO CO 964/24, Akpata to Nkrumah, 8 Feb. 1947.
58. Nkrumah, *Towards Colonial Freedom*, p.ix.
59. C.L.R. James, quoted in Asante, 'Kwame Nkrumah and Pan-Africanism'. Ivor Cummings, a Welfare Officer at the CO in the 1940s, who knew all the African students, spoke to me of Nkrumah in similar terms: 'I thought him a nice fellow . . . wasn't an intellectual, but a man of considerable vision – and a natural politician.' Interview 11 March 1992.
60. Abrahams, 'Nkrumah, Kenyatta and the Old Order', p.138.
61. Murapa, 'Padmore's Role', p.218.
62. Murapa, 'Padmore's Role', pp.175–6, 221.
63. Ras T. Makonnen (with Kenneth King), *Pan-Africanism From Within* (Oxford, 1973), pp.262–3.
64. Murapa, 'Padmore's Role', p.176.
65. PRO CO 964/30. The interrogation of Nkrumah in the Daily Summary of the Watson Commission of Enquiry.
66. Interview with Peter Blackman, 5 Nov. 1991.
67. Appiah, *Autobiography of an African Patriot*, p.164. The Primrose Gardens (*sic* – actually Primrose Hill Gardens) 'gang' were Akpata, L. Anionwu, Kamkam-Boadu, and Afolabi Ocebiyi (Electoral Register, 1947). The Gardens was a very cosmopolitan street; besides these African residents, there were a number of Indians, one Arab and numerous European names listed in the Electoral Register.
68. Mr Marke's written comments to the draft of this study.
69. *West Africa*, 14 Sept. 1946, p.845.
70. PRO CO 964/24, exhibit 46, Mrs M's letter; and exhibits 36, 39–45, letters from Akpata and Parrish reporting on her distress at Nkrumah's departure. The comment on English girls is from Erica Powell, *Private Secretary (Female) Gold Coast* (London, 1984), p.50. That Mrs M worked in the WANS office I learned from June Milne, Nkrumah's literary executor; interview, 13 Sept. 1991.
71. Dabu Gizenga's interview with Mrs M, 28 June 1973, is in the Dabu Gizenga papers, Howard University Archives, Washington DC. MSS. 128, Box 128-5, folder 77.
72. Letter from London School of Economics, 23 Sept. 1991, and subsequent telephone conversation, 2 Oct. 1991.
73. Letter from Registrar, University College London, 16 Sept. 1991. In a subsequent telephone conversation the Registrar confirmed that the papers do not reveal the reasons for the transfer from the LSE.
74. Professor A.J. Ayer, quoted in Basil Davidson, *Black Star: A View of the Life and Times of Kwame Nkrumah* (London, 1973), p.47.
75. Letter from the Honourable Society of Gray's Inn, 23 Oct. 1991.
76. Makonnen, *Pan-Africanism From Within*, p.154.
77. Nkrumah, *Autobiography*, p.52.
78. Appiah, *Autobiography of an African Patriot*, pp.169–70.
79. For example, PRO CO 323/1517/7046/3. Minute by Howard, 3 Oct. 1937: 'We can safely leave it to MI5 to notify us of any further activities of the Bureau' (that is, Padmore's International African Service Bureau).
80. Appiah, *Autobiography of an African Patriot*, p.167.
81. PRO CO 555/33851. West Africa, Register of Correspondence 1946–47; the actual files have been 'destroyed under statute'. I have not been able to find a copy of this issue of *The New African*. See also CO 1018/19, 'Report of the All-Ewe Conference, 1947'.
82. PRO CO 964/7, Report of the Gold Coast Police Commissioner, 9 Dec. 1947.
83. PRO CO 537/3559/2, Report by Kenneth Bradley, 12 Dec. 1947.
84. NARA, RG59: 848N, 00/12-1947. Report of US Consul, Accra, to State Department, 19 Dec. 1947.
85. PRO FO 371/72936/Z3350/4. British Consul General, Leopoldville, to FO, 7 March 1948.

86. PRO FO 371/73037/Z4049/39/72. D.G. Pirie, Colonial Office, to J.W. Blanch, Foreign Office, 11 May 1948 [*sic*] – I believe this date is incorrect; it should probably be 11 April 1948.
87. PRO FO 371/72938/Z9688/3771/4/G. Reports on Nkrumah. FO 371/72936/Z8070/3350/4. British Embassy, Brussels, to FO, 4 Oct. 1948.
88. PRO CO 537/3559. Minutes by T.K. Lloyd, Assistant Under-Secretary of State, 29 Dec. 1947, and J.K. Thompson, Principal Officer, 24 Dec. 1947.
89. PRO CO 537/2638. Awooner-Renner is mentioned in the 6th and 7th reports; Nkrumah in the 10th.
90. PRO CO 537/2638/14322/30/2, First report on Communism in the Colonies, 4 June 1948.
91. PRO CO 537/2760/14873, Report of the Defence Department, 2 May 1948.
92. PRO CO 537/2574/11020/30/2. Undated, unsigned memorandum, folio 5. The discussions are in CO 537/2572/11020/30/2.
93. PRO CO 537/2574/11020/30/2, D.R. Rees Williams, Parliamentary Under-Secretary of State, to T.K. Lloyd (now Sir Thomas), Permanent Under-Secretary of State, 13 Feb. 1948.
94. PRO CO 537/2573/11020/30/1, memorandum by J.L. Keith (Head of Welfare), 6 June 1948, and minute by Hilton Poynton (Social Services and Welfare). See also CO 537/5138/9680/1, which ends with a plaintive minute over the indecipherable initials of a CO official: 'this file is a perfect example of failure to get anything done'.
95. Murapa, 'Padmore's Role', p.316.
96. Interview with Dr Robert Lee, who was a student at Lincoln University at the same time as Nkrumah, 20 June 1988, Accra.
97. Murapa, 'Padmore's Role', p.317.
98. C.L.R. James, 'Notes on the Life of George Padmore', mss. at Northwestern University, Evanston, IL. It should be noted that not everything James writes regarding events in Britain is accurate; he was living in the United States during the war years when mail was strictly censored. See C.L.R. James, *Nkrumah and the Ghana Revolution* (London, 1977), p.39.
99. Abrahams, 'Nkrumah, Kenyatta and the Old Order'.
100. Murapa, 'Padmore's Role', p.222.
101. Horace Mann Bond papers, University of Massachusetts, Amherst. Group III, Box 68, folder 289A. Nkrumah to President Wright of Lincoln University, 8 March 1944.
102. PRO CO 964/24, Margot Parrish to Nkrumah, 13 Feb. 1948.
103. Mr Marke attended the Pan-African Congress in Manchester in his capacity as the founder of the Coloured Workers' Association, at whose Sunday gatherings Nkrumah had spoken a number of times. He explained to me that all the gambling-club owners had an arrangement with the local police whereby they were raided every three months or so; the owners pleaded guilty when arraigned in the Magistrate's Courts and paid a fine. Then they returned to their clubs and business went on as usual. It was unheard of for a club-owner to be imprisoned. Interview with Mr Marke, 11 Nov. 1991.

The Impact of Seretse Khama on British Public Opinion 1948–56 and 1978

NEIL PARSONS

Seretse and Ruth hit the headlines after their 1948 marriage, as he was deposed from chieftainship in Africa and exiled in Britain. British colonial power had given way to white racist pressures from South Africa and Rhodesia. The public storm in Britain against both Labour and Tory governments encompassed left, right and liberals in support of Seretse's inheritance and human rights, until the couple were allowed home in 1956. The storm drew public attention to the iniquities of apartheid in South Africa, to the stirrings of nationalism in Africa, and to black immigration into Britain. Many years later, in 1978, President Khama of Botswana was briefly the butt of less favourable British press and media attention.

The story of Seretse Khama and his wife Ruth gripped the British and international press in 1949–50, and continued to periodically excite interest until the couple left England in 1956. Seretse was the heir to the most important chieftainship in Bechuanaland (colonial Botswana), a British imperial protectorate squeezed between South Africa and Rhodesia. It was evidently pressure from those white-ruled states that induced first a Labour government and then a Conservative government to bar Seretse from succession and then to exile him in Britain. The story of Seretse helped to bring into British public consciousness an awareness of the juxtaposition of Black Africa and White Africa in the years before Ghana and *apartheid* hit the headlines. Seretse also lived in Britain between 1945 and 1956 – the period of increasing Caribbean immigration into Britain. To some extent, therefore, the well-publicized story of Seretse may have both reflected and helped to predispose British public opinion towards the black population of Britain itself.

I

Seretse Khama graduated with a B.A. degree in law and administration from Fort Hare University College in South Africa at the end of 1944. He was then admitted to Oxford University for further studies. His uncle

Tshekedi Khama, who had been acting as regent for Seretse for the previous 19 years, was particularly anxious for Seretse to overcome the 'anti-white' Africanist prejudices he had picked up at Fort Hare. In Britain Seretse was put in the care of his uncle's friends, notably various divines of the Congregational Church and establishment individuals such as Professor Sir Reginald Coupland at Oxford, but also the prominent black leader, Dr Harold Moody, at whose house in Peckham Seretse spent his first few nights. But Seretse's antipathy to the study of Latin, and the incompetence of Coupland as director of studies in arranging an unexaminable combination of subjects, resulted in Seretse leaving Oxford in 1946. He enrolled instead for legal studies at the Inns of Court in London. Here he cut himself off from his uncle's friends, though he remained in a Congregationalist-linked international student hostel, and fell among friends of his own age and gender, mostly from Africa and the Caribbean. It was also in this hostel, at a small reception in a warden's flat, that he first set eyes on Ruth Williams in June 1947.

They married in London on 29 September 1948. Tshekedi Khama failed to stop the marriage despite his considerable influence on the Commonweath Relations Office in London, which was responsible for Bechuanaland's colonial administration. The CRO was given the advice that marriages could only be stopped on racial grounds in Romano-Dutch law as in Scotland and not in Common law as in England.[1]

Seretse flew back home to explain himself to Tshekedi and his people. From this moment on, the press began to take an interest in events. The Johannesburg press trailed Seretse back home to Serowe. The London press pestered Ruth, and began the annoying habit of referring to her as a London 'typist'. (A libel on a secretary who actually employed a typist, which has resulted in her resisting learning to type ever since.) For the next 17 months Seretse and Ruth assiduously avoided all comment to the press, making them all the more intriguing to the British and South African press – especially after Seretse's people proclaimed him Chief in June 1949 in overt defiance of the British and South African governments. In late 1949 and early 1950 the couple lived with international journalists, led by Noel Monks of the London *Daily Mail* and John Redfern of the London *Daily Express*, camped around them in Bechuanaland – and shepherded by Nicholas Montserrat the local press minder for the British authorities. Eventually, in February 1950, the famous American photo-journalist Margaret Bourke-White persuaded them to sit for photographs. She said it was more difficult than getting a photo-opportunity with Joe Stalin. Her two photo-features on Seretse and Ruth in *Life* magazine took the love story to an enormous new audience in America where the press had previously been fairly uninterested. As Monks

wrote, 'there's a wave of sympathy for Ruth and Seretse that no Government decree can kill'.[2]

Seretse was summoned from Bechuanaland to London for official
discussions in February 1950. The Commonwealth Relations minister,
Philip Noel-Baker, asked Seretse to voluntarily relinquish his chieftainship, flirting with the idea of letting Seretse into his confidence by 'frank
discussion of race relations in the Union'. However, as one CRO official
remarked to another, it was hard enough for 'a Socialist' to admit to himself, let alone to other people, 'that his motive in sitting on Seretse was
unwillingness to offend South Africa'.[3]

Seretse was then left to stew by himself in a West End hotel, while the
British government busied itself with a general election. Noel-Baker was
replaced by an ambitious young man, Patrick Gordon Walker, who
accepted the resolution of the Seretse affair as the price of a seat in Cabinet.
Walker made a clumsy and – to Seretse – highly offensive, attempt to get
Seretse to abandon his wife, and then slapped a ban not only on Seretse as
Chief but on their returning home for five years. Seretse broke the news
to Ruth in a pithily worded telegram: 'Tribe and myself tricked by British
Government. I am banned from the whole protectorate, Love Seretse'.[4]
Then he broke his self-denying ordinance on talking to the press. He
'called a press conference on his own, blew the gaff, and therefore spoiled'
all the well-laid plans of the government for spiriting his wife out of
Bechuanaland similarly unsuspecting:[5]

> I am kicked out, and my wife is kicked out with me; that is the sum
> of it. I maintain it was because the British Government wanted to
> appease Dr Malan [S.A. prime minister], and to keep the Union of
> South Africa in the Commonwealth that they have done what they
> have done . . . It hurts a lot.[6]

The next morning, the British press, itself predominantly Tory-
supporting and gunning for the re-elected Labour government, had a field
day airing Seretse's highly justified indignation. The government for its
part began to fear the reactions of what the *New York Times*, remarking
on the importance of the Seretse débâcle, called the 'wider problem of
Native feelings throughout Africa . . . heaving under the same disturbing
forces that have transformed Asia since the war'. The Colonial Office
cabled all British governors in Africa to stand by for a parliamentary
statement.

Gordon Walker stood up in the House of Commons on 8 March, and
uttered a bare-faced lie: 'we have had no communication from the Government of the Union [of South Africa] . . . There have been no representations and no consultation in this matter.' In the flush of presentation he

had made the planned statement a trifle too categorial, but the South African prime minister was to assure 'all possible discretion so as to avoid embarrassment to Gordon Walker'.[7]

The first body to protest on Seretse's behalf was a group of 2,000 women meeting in London to celebrate International Women's Day. They condemned his exile 'for apparently no other reason than that he married a White woman'. Fellow African students and Afro-Caribbeans were particularly conspicuous supporters of Seretse. One of the first protest letters addressed to the prime minister, Attlee, was from the West African Student's Club at Oxford University, signed by its president E.A. Boateng, in later years a distinguished Ghanaian geographer. The leader of the Caribbean community in Britain, the famous cricketer Learie Constantine, who had himself been the victim of a well-publicized case of racial discrimination by a Russell Square hotel, brought together a Seretse Khama Fighting Committee to organize protests.

Seretse attended and spoke briefly at a meeting of 800 people held by the Fighting Committee in Dennison Hall on Vauxhall Bridge Road in London on 12 March. Constantine presided, and the meeting carried a motion calling for Seretse's return to his people and for the report of an official enquiry that had been kept secret (and was to be kept secret for another 30 years). He also had to attend yet another protest meeting that night.[8] The issue was taken up by a Campaign Committee on South Africa and the High Commission Territories among students at the London School of Economics. Other bodies that came to Seretse's aid included the National Council for Civil Liberties and the League of Coloured Peoples.[9]

The Fighting Committee presented itself to the new Colonial minister, James Griffiths, on 17 March, with Gordon Walker in attendance. They had already accused Gordon Walker of being a well-known 'Negro-phobist'.[10] Constantine, whom the CO accepted as a man of 'a certain standing', even suggested that 'coloured British subjects' would be prepared to provide an army to defend the High Commission Territories from South African aggression.[11]

Support for Seretse Khama was surprisingly strong in Scotland. A Seretse Khama Defence Committee was founded in Edinburgh by a Nigerian student and a young lecturer in colonial history. After petition-ing the Colonial Office, they held a protest meeting in Oddfellows Hall. The Scottish National Party proudly announced that it had elected Seretse Khama as one of its vice-presidents.[12]

Gordon Walker began to waver under the onslaught, but British government resolve was strengthened by General Jan Smuts, the former South African prime minister, held in high respect as a war hero by the

British, who threatened to personally intervene. Smuts feared black rebellion in South Africa if Seretse were allowed to return home as Chief.[13] The Afrikaans newspaper *Die Burger* in South Africa thought the most disturbing new phenomenon revealed by the Seretse 'affair' was 'the existence in Britain of a strong clamourous and uninformed mass on conditions and problems' of Southern Africa.[14]

The West African press responded vigorously. 'Not Cricket, Sir!' and 'Et Tu, British' were the headlines in the Lagos *Daily Service. The Nigerian Eastern Mail* attacked the White Paper 'as a monument of insincerity . . . a slap in the face for all moderate Africans who have . . . urged co-operation with Britain and confidence in her promise to lead us on the road to self-government'. The Freetown *Evening Dispatch* in Sierra Leone thundered in more characteristic old coastal style: 'Is this democracy or is it a demonstration of Hitleric power? The African cosmos shakes, the African ground trembles and from the four corners of the African horizon comes out the words . . . "Let justice be done though the heavens should fall".'[15] In India, a Calcutta newspaper claimed: 'For every white man placated in South Africa, a hundred Indians and Pakistanis have been affronted'. Krishna Menon, a former Labour political figure in Britain, made representations over Seretse, first as India's high commissioner to London and then as India's UN representative in New York. Far more disturbing for the British government was a burst of concern from the United States of America, fuelled by Ruth and Seretse featuring twice in *Life* magazine in two months. David C. Williams of Americans for Democratic Action (national chairman, Hubert H. Humphrey) privately contacted Gordon Walker. He forwarded a letter from a senior American trade unionist, who had written:

> It would be difficult to exaggerate the repercussions of the Seretse affair among some quarters here . . . The Negro press – which is a highly influential medium – is full of the Seretse debacle . . . un-happy conclusion: our discrimination, our jim crow ain't really so bad . . . I wish you could hear some of the union Negro leaders talk about the Labor Govt now.[16]

Seretse himself was receiving offers of legal partnerships ranging from the Gold Coast to as far as Brazil. Journalists in Bechuanaland were now gratified to be received, with a choice of teas, by Ruth Khama, who 'has emerged from the role of mystery woman to one of the most publicised women in the world'. She was quoted calling the officials of her government 'little nitwits', but the British government was obliged to allow Seretse a temporary visit back home to join his pregnant wife and settle his affairs.[17] Seretse and Ruth met again in Bechuanaland with cameras flashing around them in the early hours of Sunday 16 April. Once again Seretse was dogged in his tracks by the world press corps and Nicholas Montserrat.[18]

On their arrival for exile in London in August 1950, the Khamas were greeted as celebrities, the press cooing over baby Jacqueline with drinks provided by Seretse at the Grosvenor House Hotel in Davies Street, Mayfair. He had no qualms in accepting a generous monthly allowance from the British government, and shipping of his household furniture and big green Chevrolet at government expense, though he met with racist insolence from dock-workers unloading his car, offended by the thought of a mere 'nigger' with such opulence.[19]

CRO officials were delegated to befriend Seretse, and to persuade him not to push and complete his barrister studies too fast. The couple were resigned to five years' exile, and Seretse talked of becoming a barrister in West or East Africa. Ruth told one such official that she was a 'true blue' Conservative, while Seretse was a Socialist. The evidently rather stuffy official took the couple to a Hungarian restaurant, and they then took him to the Sugar Hill Club, off Duke Street in St James, which was frequented by blacks and whites. They introduced him to the Jamaican athelete Macdonald Bailey. The official reported back that he was impressed by Serete's sense of the comic, and noticed that he suppressed any sign of bitterness. Above all he had 'an honesty and directness in dealing with people, and a right judgment of them'. 'It would be to my mind a tragedy if these qualities were to be frustrated by bitterness, or inactivity, or neglect.'[20]

Seretse's uncle Tshekedi came to Britain between March and August 1951, to lobby unceasingly in Westminster and Whitehall and among his friends in libertarian and humanitarian bodies.[21] His aim was to overturn the Labour government's two-wrongs-make-a-right policy of deposing and exiling (though within Bechuanaland) him as well as his nephew. The South African government also sent its most senior civil servant to London to lobby the Labour government over the centrality of South Africa to its economic and defence policies. The result was a long debate in the Commons at the end of June, lasting from 3.45 until 10 that night, in which Government and Opposition front-benches combined to steer debate away from the South African factor into the human rights of Seretse and Tshekedi and domestic politics of the Bangwato people:

> Attlee: I think it is all to the good that, in the midst of present world affairs, the House should devote a day to the affairs of a small tribe in Africa, and concern ourselves with the rights of individual citizens.

> Churchill: We have had a deeply interesting debate and I think I
> may say that I have rarely listened to a debate which has caused
> more heart searchings on both sides of the House than this . . . all of
> us want to give a right, honest, sincere, truthful opinion upon the
> issues which are before us.[22]

Tshekedi's presence in London resulted in some supporters abandoning him. For example, the radical lawyer Dingle Foot, who had been a prominent supporter, now declined to be Seretse's legal tutor. But Seretse and Ruth were fêted by their parliamentary supporters, and became fashionable accessories in radical *chic* circles. Tom Driberg of the Labour Party invited them to his bizarre wedding reception on the riverside terrace of the House of Commons. This was one of a number of recorded occasions when Seretse made humorous play on the embarrassment of white people unthinkingly using the racist expression 'nigger in the wood-pile'. The offender was Kingsley Martin, editor of the *New Statesman*.[23]

When the Conservatives took office in October 1951, it was decided to make 'the ban on Seretse . . . permanent', rather than just for five years, and to orchestrate the election of a new Chief to replace both Seretse and Tshekedi. The 'main policy' of continued 'appeasement' of South Africa was justified on the grounds that 'the future happiness and well-being of 1,000,000 Africans' depended on it, that is, the populations of the imperial protectorates who might be attacked and invaded by South Africa if Seretse became Chief.[24] This rationale, of sacrificing one good man to save a million, was adopted by the new Commonwealth Relations minister Lord Ismay. It was given a note of desperation by the quickly hushed-up 'revolt' of colonial officials in Bangwato country, in January 1952, protesting at the duplicity of British government policy.

The CRO first warned Seretse that his monthly allowance would be docked if he continued to make public statements calling himself 'Chief'. Secondly, Ismay tried to use his charm on Seretse before he turned over his ministerial post to Lord Salisbury, the ultra right-wing peer. He told Seretse that his undoubted talents needed a fresh start – in the colonial service of Jamaica – and for this he must abdicate his hereditary position for ever. Seretse replied that the post should go to a Jamaican. As for himself he had long made clear that he was quite prepared to abdicate on condition that he was allowed to return home and exercise his full rights as a private citizen. At this point Ismay was almost won over, but Salisbury took over the negotiations and made it clear that 'renunciation but retention of full political liberty was unacceptable'. Salisbury drew the meeting to an abrupt end with the announcement that 'the decision to bar Seretse and his children from the Chieftainship was now permanent'.[25] Seretse returned to his rented house in Chipstead, Surrey, 'and buried his face in his hands and said: "To think that I can never go home again. Never, ever".'[26]

After Seretse's fate was announced in parliament, on 27 March, it was the *Daily Express* which most clearly caught the growing mood among the British public, regardless of political affiliation. It attacked Salisbury's decision as 'a bad deed which should arouse shame and anger throughout the country'.[27] Lord Beaverbrook, the Canadian press baron who owned *Express* newspapers, took up the cause of Seretse and Ruth, as an echo of the cause of Edward VIII and Mrs Simpson which he had supported 16 years earlier.

A flood of letters from the public began to pour into Lord Salisbury's office. Of the 140 odd still preserved in CRO files, a mere dozen were hostile or indifferent to Seretse. The sentiments of Seretse's supporters are reflected in the following statements:

> British sense of fair play has been outraged . . . to appease the Malan-ists and the anti-Negro section of South Africa (R.B. Harrington, West Bridgford, Notts.);

> The Tories were not elected to continue the bad policies of the stupid Socialists. What we want is justice & freedom from all the tomfool controls of bloated bureaucrats! If you don't agree to let Seretse return to his tribe when they want him to – then resign! If you continue in your post you must put Britain and Empire first! (A.E. Southernwood, New Cross, SE14 – all in capital letters);

> Who do you think you are? . . . Seretse's people want him back & I hope they defy you in every way to get him & I'm glad to know Seretse refuses your bribe of a job in Jamaica & hope he fights you and wins. Freedom! My foot, where is it? You're another Mussolini and not fit for your job! (no signature);

> To Hell with Dr Malan (F. Wilkinson, Ely, Cambs);

> I think it is now high time that public opinion takes up the cudgels on behalf of Seretse Khama . . . How I admired Fenner Brockway for his championship of this educated African chieftain . . . We had much in common for in our young days our lives were fired with missionary zeal . . . My protest [is] as an Englishwoman against this tyranny (Mary R. Varley, Huddersfield);

> Our name in Africa will be mud after this low down dirty trick, which is what can only be expected from a Tory (C. Smith, Poulton-le-Fylde);

I, among many millions I should imagine, have been dismayed (Arthur Devon, Queen's Gate, SDW7);

Swallow your pride, be a man, and send them their King back (C.J. Hopkins, Brighton, Sussex);

The bilge you people put out about the Commonwealth being a family of nations would look a little less hypocritical if our Government dropped its racial prejudices (Secretary, Amalgamated Engineering Union, Rainham Branch No.59);

YOU ARE WRONG (Cank, Blackburn – telegram);

No wonder we are hated by most of the world (P. Wilson);

To back down in hope of pleasing a crowd of semi-Nazi Dutchmen in South Africa is not only foolish but suicidal (Robert Tate, Columbia University, New York);

I have always previously voted Conservative, but my faith is broken, in view of the pompous, unEnglish, unjust cowardly policy adopted towards Seretse Khama (Fred C. Worley, Reigate).

Reports were received that substantial numbers of people were resigning from the Conservative Party over the issue in more than one constituency. A number of critics pointed to the 'violation of justice and human rights'. They were referring to Article 13 of the 1950 Universal Declaration of Human Rights – the right of freedom of movement within one's own country, and to be able to leave or return to it. However the United Kingdom, while subscribing to the Declaration had crossed its fingers and toes with an exclusion clause for its colonies and protectorates. (The CRO was happier with the dilute European Convention on Human Rights currently being negotiated in 1952–53.)[28]

One of the dozen letters hostile or indifferent to Seretse was from E. Okagoo-Farmer (Bruce House, Kemble Street, London EC), who greeted a 'very wise decision . . . which meets the approval of all right-thinking Africans', and refused to believe that South Africa had had any influence. The CRO minute on the side reads – 'an African who approves HMG's policy in Bechuanaland!' Letters against Seretse included:

Forgive an old lady . . . We don't want an African St. Seretse (Grace Duff, ex-Ilorin, Nigeria – now Eastbourne);

It is quite clear to the meanest intelligence – except to the editor of the 'Daily Express' – that only a pure negro can command complete and utter respect from everyone of the tribe (Dr F.R. Leblanc, Ipswich);

> A negro spurned and insulted negresses by marrying a white female
> . . . His lordship is authorised to oppose Mongrelism (Imperial
> Evolution Movement, London);
>
> It may encourage you to know that the majority of people want
> you to handle this man firmly! . . . Just a few generations back
> Seretse's forbears were eating each other! . . . this white woman is
> an adventuress . . . willing to sell her body (and soul) to such a man!
> . . . The way people talk about the Fatherhood of God and the
> Brotherhood of Man is canting humbug . . . No! My Lord, please
> relegate this sordid case to the background, & *never* yield to clamour
> of irresponsible people (M.A. Bushell, Chiswick, W4).

Some of the dozen really hostile letters appeared to be from white
South Africans, though one at least destroyed its own case:

> I am 100 per cent English, & am praying with my Heart & Soul that
> the Good Loving Almighty God will make a Third War & Blast the
> Cursed Filthy British Isles into the darkest corner of Hell . . . Get
> every cursed Nigger and Bastard out of Britain, before God sends
> an Earth-Quake. Seretse Khama & the filthy White creature
> married to him have no right in Britain . . . May the good God Bless
> Dr Malan and his Cabinet. He, like Hitler, is trying to cleanse God's
> beautiful world . . . the devil will rule, & Britain will be brought to
> nought in one Hour.[29]

Many of the letters were from organizations in Britain and abroad.
Foreign organizations writing in support of Seretse included the African
National Congress of South Africa (ANC), despite both its president and
treasurer, James Moroka and S.M. Molema, being in-laws and close
friends of Tshekedi. Others, many of them forwarded by the Seretse
Khama Fighting Committee, included: the Kingston & St Andrew's
Taxpayers of Jamaica, the Connolly Association of Irish in London, the
Coloured Republicans Assembly of Trinidad, the National Council of
Nigeria and the Cameroons, the Kenya African Union, and the South
African Indian Congress.[30]

It was two letters sent to Churchill and his deputy, Anthony Eden,
which received the most attention. A 24-year-old American ex-army
veteran being trained as a teacher at the University of Cincinatti addressed his plea to Churchill:

> I ask you sincerely, *how can I defend* this action of the 'Mother of
> Democracy', when asked by my eager *and interested* young students
> to explain it? . . . England has betrayed in part my respect for her as

a nation . . . do not minimize or shrug off the importance of the 'Seretse affair' . . . it threatens the very groundwork and fundamental theories . . . from which the United States also derived its democratic principles.[31]

Eden meanwhile was approached by the upper class opera, ballet and theatrical designer Oliver Messel, who was 'wildly distressed' at the 'injustice' shown Seretse Khama. Describing himself as 'a staunch Conservative supporter', he criticized 'weakly pandering to the policy of South African colour discrimination'.[32]

Among British organizations, the body that had to be given most credence was the British Council of Churches, which raised the issue of Seretse Khama at length in a Belfast meeting. A delegation led by the Archbishop of Canterbury, Geoffrey Fisher, in person, eventually arrived at the CRO on 9 May. Salisbury was put to pains to answer five detailed points, each one being turned to justify the government's action. The delegates were told that the 'tribe' threatened to 'collapse' if Seretse returned; and that Seretse 'might in time be allowed back, first for visits' but was unlikely to ever settle back there because of 'his European tastes'.[33]

The arrival of six Bangwato leaders at London's Heathrow airport on 9 April 1952, gave further impetus to the activities of the Seretse Khama Fighting Committee which had resurfaced under the name of the Seretse Khama Campaign Committee. Seretse himself held back from public involvement, ostensibly to give the Bangwato delegates a chance to make their case. More to the point, no doubt it was a private reaction of grief and fury against the secret agenda of the Bangwato leaders, who pleaded with Seretse to divorce Ruth, in the harebrained political belief, encouraged by Paramount Chief Sobhuza of Swaziland, that this would clear the way for him to become Chief.

It was not until 15 April that Seretse appeared at a protest rally in London's Caxton Hall. The meeting was held by a recently formed group known as Racial Unity, which included Clement Attlee's sister among its leaders. Seretse requested that the meeting concentrate on Bechuanaland's future rather than himself, before agreeing to speak.[34] The meeting was chaired by the president of the Women's Liberal Federation, and Seretse's was preceded on the platform by his Ghanaian friend Joe Appiah, who was himself to win temporary fame by marrying an English woman, the daughter of the former Labour minister Sir Stafford Cripps, a year later.[35] With the six Bangwato sitting behind Seretse, obliged to remain silent until they had seen Lord Salisbury, Seretse spoke briefly and ironically about his position to the mainly white, female audience.

After the six Bangwato had seen Salisbury at the CRO, and been dismissed as mere 'country hayseeds', Seretse was freer to speak. On 2 May, the Seretse Khama Campaign Committee arranged a meeting in a London hall, at which both Seretse and an elderly Mongwato delegate, Mongwaketse Mathangwane, spoke.[36] Seretse also attended one of the committee meetings of the Campaign Committee, possibly that of 7 May in the campaign's headquarters at 45 Brondesbury Villas, West London, with the local physician Dr Hastings Kamuzu Banda probably in attendance.

On 10 May Seretse attended a prestigious meeting in the Anti-Slavery Society's Denison House. Mathangwane and the others threatened to renew their boycott of colonial administration back home. Fenner Brockway, the left-wing Labour MP and campaigner against colonialism, described Seretse's banishment as an intolerable crime against humanity, an outrage against democracy, and a blow to the development of Bechuanaland. By refusing to accept Seretse and his marriage, Britain had missed the chance to show South Africa an alternative future of racial equality. Canon John Collins, the campaigning cleric otherwise associated with Tshekedi, attacked South Africa's 'master race' threat to world peace. Seretse was reported to be 'dryly ironic in his comments on the attitude of both the Labour and Conservative parties', using 'the colonial peoples . . . only as play-things – or rather, as sticks with which to beat political opponents'.

On the next night Seretse Khama went to a meeting in Birmingham Town Hall, attended by 2,000 people, which the *Birmingham Post* ignorantly referred to as 'the biggest audience of his life'. The meeting was organized by the Midlands branch of the United Nations Association, chaired by Daniel Lipson, the former MP who had been one of the British government's 'observers' sent to Bechuanaland in 1951. Turning upside-down Ismay's conceit about sacrificing one for a million, Seretse 'asked whether the British government was prepared to sacrifice the friendship of 60,000,000 Africans for the doubtful friendship of Dr Malan'. As for himself, 'I have been here two or three years now and during that time I have been a very good boy. But where has it got me?'[37]

There was also wide publicity given in the next day's newspapers to a sermon given in St Paul's Cathedral, on the invitation of Canon Collins, for his new movement called Christian Action. Rev. Dr Marcus James from Jamaica compared Malan ('the world's high priest of racial hate') with Hitler, and called on Christians to crusade against 'racial idolatory' rather than against communism.[38] The British government was made aware of increasing public sentiment in Britain against racialism at home and colonialism overseas.

One can argue that, at least in England, the issue of Seretse Khama was the way in which the public first, though albeit indirectly, got to grips with the issue of *apartheid* in South Africa. In Scotland the main issue, fuelled by the Scottish churches with missions in Nyasaland, was the impending Central African Federation, which was to be dominated by the white settlers of Southern Rhodesia. The issue of Federation was seen as overlapping with that of Seretse Khama. Both Seretse and the Federation were also issues being addressed by the Colonial Bureau of the Fabian Society and the new Africa Bureau, political pressure-groups and information services in London, run by the sort of British intellectuals with an interest in Africa who had supported Tshekedi Khama since the 1930s. From 1952 onwards, however, their attention was grabbed more and more by news of the Gandhian-style 'defiance campaign' in South Africa.[39]

Cabinet discussed Seretse's speaking in public, and decided not to withdraw his allowance, for breaking its terms of required political silence, for fear of being 'accused' of muzzling free speech and persecuting Seretse'.[40] But no doubt such hints were somehow communicated to Seretse, who quietened down again. He remained remarkably silent during and after dramatic events back home in June. By July the Seretse Khama Campaign Committee was acknowledging that he had only attended one of their committee meetings. The Campaign Committee frightened the CRO because of its communist connections. Its secretary was Billy Strachan, in later years referred to as a 'veteran C.P. hack' by the magazine *Private Eye*: and the Communist Party newspaper, the *Daily Worker*, gave the committee plentiful publicity.[41] A CRO minute in May observed that 'Seretse is not the instigator, but is a pawn in the hands of the "woolly-woollies"', and raised the possibility of 'any action which the CRO could properly take to damp down agitation in the UK in favour of Seretse'. One may therefore speculate about the role of British government agencies in setting up the alternative to the Seretse Khama Campaign Committee, which was to appear in July 1952. Sir Percy Sillitoe, the head of MI5, had been alerted to possible communist connections with Seretse by Tshekedi's lawyer Buchanan when he had visited Cape Town two years earlier.[42]

Supporters of both Seretse and Tshekedi in Britain were brought together in the aftermath of a bloody riot in Bechuanaland, on Sunday 1 June 1952, caused by the Bangwato delegates arriving back home empty-handed. Both Seretse and Tshekedi were needed back home to fill the political vacuum, and to help develop new political structures in the British protectorates, which would ward off and ultimately challenge the dominance of the Union of South Africa. Michael Scott at the Africa

Bureau (of which Tshekedi was honorary president) wrote to Tshekedi in July 1952 that he was being invited to join a Council for the Defence of Seretse Khama and the Protectorates, including all parties *except* communists. Scott complained about the confusion of committees supporting Seretse, not only the old Campaign Committee and its new Bamangwato People's Defence Fund offshoot, but also Canon Collins's Racial Unity and his new body called Christian Action.[43]

The Council for the Defence of Seretse Khama and the Protectorates held its first formal meeting after the re-assembly of parliament in September 1952. Most of its members were parliamentarians. Its chairman was the anti-imperialist Labour MP Fenner Brockway, the son of an LMS missionary in India. Its vice-chairman was the Liberal MP Jo Grimond, while its most prominent Conservative supporters were Lords Hailsham (Quintin Hogg) and Boyd Orr. Three Labour MPs were particularly keen advocates of Seretse and Ruth – Reginald Sorensen, Jenny Lee, and Anthony Wedgwood-Benn (Tony Benn). Learie Constantine was recruited from the old Campaign Committee, together with the West Indian sprinter Macdonald Bailey, and Seretse's friends Joe Appiah and Charles Njonjo. Other supporters included Kingsley Martin and Bertrand Russell, Lady Megan Lloyd George, the painter Augustus John, the playwright Christopher Fry and the novelist Sir Compton Mackenzie, the actors Alec Guinness and Michael Redgrave and the more notably 'political' Dame Sybil Thorndike. Seretse and Ruth were photographed with the main members of the council in the Palace of Westminster. But, to the satisfaction of the CRO, 'there is nothing to show yet that he is actively connected with the new council', and the council seems to have been little more than a parliamentary lobby group in 1952–53. Seretse stuck to his pledge not to make press comments on events back home, but did not keep entirely quiet. He addressed meetings such as his local (Redhill) branch of the United Nations Association, while taking care not to arouse controversy.[44]

The issue of Seretse Khama seems to have run out of steam as far as the British press was concerned by the end of September 1952. But in March 1953 Fenner Brockway held a press conference to publicize a nation-wide petition in Britain for Seretse's return home as Chief, which had started to collect signatures in the previous September. Seretse spoke briefly to the press in a committee room of the House of Commons. He explained the hereditary nature of Bangwato chieftainship, and added: 'so long as it is the desire of the tribe that I should be chief – and information from Bechuanaland indicates that this is so – I am ready to serve them to the best of my capacity'.[45]

The petition was not notably successful, collecting less than 11,000 signatures over the next year. The Council for the Defence of Seretse Khama and the Protectorates published a pamphlet, but Seretse's case seems to have faded as a public issue. Support of Seretse, led by Fenner Brockway, continued as an issue of Labour back-bench MPs, as much against their own front-benchers as against the government.[46]

On 22 May 1953, the House of Commons debated the issue on a motion initiated by the Labour MP Eirene White. It was a characteristic Commons performance of the type which gave both encouragement and frustration to Seretse, who often sat in the visitors' gallery. By this time there was remarkable silence about Bangwato affairs on the Tory back-benchers. It was left to Labour back-benchers to make their mark on the debate. The maverick libertarian Sir Richard Acland began by warning the whites of Africa that they were doomed to disaster by all the rules of Christ, Freud and Marx. The diarist Nigel Nicolson stood up to note that the Commons had expended 20 hours and 450 columns of the Hansard record of debates on Bechuanaland. Jennie Lee then pointed out that the Labour front-bench had absented themselves from the debate in shame. Michael Foot pointed out the immorality of both Labour and Conservatives towards Seretse and Tshekedi. Fenner Brockway spoke of his vision of a 'future race . . . from the intermingling of peoples and colours', and the historical importance of popular Bangwato acceptance of the marriage. Jennie Lee added that human beings held values and principles above mere material interests, and would always fight injustice.[47]

II

By June 1953 the public campaign on behalf of Seretse Khama in Britain had therefore quietened, though the parliamentary campaign was to continue and the threat to the High Commission Territories by South Africa was by no means a dead issue. Overseas public attention on Africa had turned to plans for the new Central African Federation, the beginnings of the Mau Mau emergency in Kenya, and the first black government in British Africa on the Gold Coast under Kwame Nkrumah. The campaign for Seretse Khama gave way to other issues pursued by Canon Collins's Christian Action, Fenner Brockway's Movement for Colonial Freedom, and ultimately by the Anti-Apartheid Movement. But South Africa, despite the ANC's 'defiance campaign', received relatively little attention from the international press until 1956. Churchill's statement in the House of Commons on 13 April 1954, warning off 'Dr Malan and his Government' from 'needlessly' bidding for transfer of the High Commission Territories, was not deemed particularly controversial at the time. But it encouraged people in Bechuanaland to think of alternatives. By

1955, in a pamphlet published by the Africa Bureau in London, Tshekedi was pressing the British government to decide between Bechuanaland's future either as a separate state like Nigeria and Uganda, or as 'an African Territory within a neighbouring state – that is, with the Central African Federation.[48]

Seretse and Ruth and their two children moved into a house of their own at Addiscombe, on the eastern side of Croydon in Surrey, in late 1953. Slow to anger, Seretse shrugged off periodic silly rumours of impending divorce as wishful thinking in Southern Africa or London. Their suburban neighbours were in general friendly and uncomplaining about their stream of visitors, including West Indians, Africans, Indians, Arabs and Americans.

In December 1953, the British exiled another highly educated monarch from Africa, the young Kabaka Mutesa II alias 'Freddie' from Uganda. A somewhat more extravagant and colourful character than Seretse, playing up his background of Eton and the Guards, 'Freddie' and his wife none the less became firm friends with Seretse and Ruth. Their stories became so intertwined in the minds of newspaper readers that Seretse and 'Freddie' are often still confused in the public memory in Britain.

In December 1954 Seretse's annual allowance from the CRO was increased from £1,100 to £1,375 per annum, subject to tax. His law studies became more and more sporadic, though he held to vague plans of entering a law partnership as a barrister in Africa, possibly in Nigeria. As late as September 1956 he was still talking of the possibility of taking bar exams that December. As the five-year mark of Seretse's original exile by the Labour government approached, Fenner Brockway raised the issue of Seretse Khama as a 'gross denial of human rights', at the annual conference of the Labour Party in September 1954. The Labour Party therefore delegated its Commonwealth and Imperial liaison officer, the journalist John Hatch, to investigate and report back. The CRO was blunt: 'reinstatement in a position of authority, on the Union's door step, of an African with a white wife and half-breed family would unite and inflame against us all the white population of the Union'. Rather more persuasive, to Hatch, were the continuing quarrels between Tshekedi and Seretse over such matters as cattle.

Meanwhile writers were at work to bring back the attention of the world to the saga of Seretse's exile. Nicholas Monserrat was at work on a lengthy novel, *The Tribe that Lost Its Head*, satirizing the journalists who had covered the affair in 1949–50, and adding a good measure of steamy jungle tribal-sexual mumo-jumbo.[49] Noel Monks of the *Daily Mail* had already published his autobiography. John Redfern of the *Daily Express* was writing a book which he was to entitle *Ruth and Seretse: 'A*

Disreputable Transaction' – the subtitle being a quote from Churchill in the Commons in 1950. Redfern also wrote a play, which was all set to be produced on the London stage by Brian Rix. It told of the duplicity of the ministers of Her Majesty's Government and, for that reason, the play was totally banned by the Lord Chamberlain, Britain's theatrical censor. No script is known to survive, but an idea of its contents may be gathered from the chapter titles of the book, including 'Cold (Clerical) Feet'; 'What Crime?'; 'Snub for History'; 'The Mean Marquis'; 'Case of Conscience'; and, finally, 'An Appeal'.

Ruth and Seretse was published in July 1955 by the publisher Victor Gollancz. Together with Hatch's visit to Bechuanaland, it helped to bring the case of Seretse Khama back to international public attention. British newspapers and journalists, and Redfern himself, with their readers in mind, not unexpectedly concentrated on the British woman involved – Ruth Khama. There was surprise in the CRO at the good press given to the book in Britain: 'This is, I am afraid, further evidence that a guilt complex where Seretse is concerned is very widespread.'[50]

On 27 July 1955, John Hatch's report, giving hope of full reconciliation between Tshekedi and Seretse, was considered by the national executive of the Labour Party in London. Seretse and Ruth were invited to attend the annual conference of the Labour Party at Blackpool in October 1955. They were loudly cheered in the public gallery when pointed out to the delegates by the chair, Dr Edith Summerskill. But the chair stopped Brockway from speaking about them, on grounds of time. The Sunday *Observer* newspaper, owned by Tshekedi's friend and ally David Astor, had already called for Seretse's return home as a private citizen. The issue was raised again in the Commons by Fenner Brockway on 27 October 1956, though once again it was fobbed off by the government's reply. Pains were taken to disassociate the case of Seretse Khama from that of Kabaka Mutesa II, who had just been permitted to return home to Uganda from exile in Britain.[51] An enterprizing journalist travelled down to Addiscombe to gauge Seretse's reaction. She found that Seretse had no high hopes of following Kabaka 'Freddie', but he was excited by the economic prospects of his country which were opening up. He added: 'It is very difficult to do nothing at all when there is so much to be done.'

In a subsequent interview, in February 1956, Seretse was anxious to correct the impression of slothfulness. He had travelled all over Britain busy lecturing, telling British people about Bechuanaland and its people and problems, in Glasgow and Edinburgh, in Leeds and Sheffield, and in Port Talbot and parts of Wales. (He could have added talks in London, such as a Foyle's literary luncheon, then considered the height of chic.) 'I have no doubt', added Seretse, 'that if it rested with the ordinary British people, I should be back [home] any time. But it is the British Cabinet that must give the decision.' By now he was getting letters urging his return from Bangwato in nearly every mail delivery. 'I feel restless – an urge to get back to where I rightly belong.'

Seretse's friends back home were supplying Fenner Brockway with details of judicial and administrative abuses in Bechuanland, which were written up and published in three issues of the weekly pacifist newspaper, *Peace News*, in May–June 1955. The articles were then prepared as a pamphlet of the Movement for Colonial Freedom, titled *Bechuanaland – What Serete's Exile Means*.[52] But publication of the pamphlet was to be overtaken by events.

Naught for your Comfort by Father Trevor Huddlestone, a devastating critique of South African race policies, was published at Easter. For the first time, the immorality of *apartheid* became a hot public issue in Britain. Huddlestone's speaking engagements at Bristol in June generated public support for the High Commission Territories as shop windows of British 'multi-racialism' for South Africa. There were also the beginnings of regular anti-*apartheid* demonstrations outside South Africa House in Trafalagar Square. It was hardly surprising that Strijdom proved to be so defensive when be came to London for the Commonwealth prime ministers' conference at the end of June. He appealed to British self-interest as 'Britons, proud of your British race and heritage . . . which like ours is white and European', not to force his people into 'race suicide'.[53]

Tshekedi arrived in London in July 1956, ostensibly on a private visit without political overtones. Public attention was enveloped by the Suez Crisis, with Nasser's announcement of Egypt's unilateral nationalization of the Suez Canal on 26 July. The issue of Seretse's return home, raised officially by the Labour Party was debated once again in the House of Commons on 1 August. Seretse's closest ally, Anthony Wedgwood-Benn, compared the fame of Seretse Khama – as an issue, 'debated and discussed wherever intelligent thinking people meet in any part of the world' – with the fame of Miss Autherine Lucy, who had recently made news as the first black student to enter the University of Alabama. Conservatives as well as Labourites now began to call for the development of democratic institutions in Bechuanaland. The House had, after all, been discussing the merits of self-government for colonies in West Africa. But the call for Seretse's return once again met with the predictable government rebuff.[54]

Tshekedi and Seretse decided to take advantage of the temporary diplomatic breach that had opened up between Britain and South Africa, and now prepared a joint case for their return to Bangwato politics as private citizens. This time they avoided all Labour and Conservative politicians and took into their confidence Clement Davies, the leader of the

Liberal Party, which had most consistently supported both of them.[55] On 15 August 1956, Seretse and Tshekedi appeared before the Commonwealth Relations minister, the Earl of Home, with a signed joint renunciation of the Chieftainship to return home 'as free citizens with as full political rights as anyone else, and to be allowed to serve our people in any capacity to which they may wish to elect us'. Home leapt at the opportunity to solve once and for all the intractable case of Seretse Khama, which had dogged British governments for seven years. Going against the received wisdom of his officials, he ordered an urgent review of the case. The official announcement of Seretse's renunciation of Chieftainship, and of his impending return from exile, was made on 26 September, though the news had 'leaked' two days earlier.[56]

The British press and establishment were enthusiastic about the return of Seretse as a return to honour over a disreputable affair. But the attention of the British public was stuck elsewhere with the Suez Crisis and the Soviet invasion of Hungary. Seretse Khama came to symbolize an 'all our yesterdays' age in British politics that was lost and replaced by new concerns at the very moment of his return home. The words 'Seretse' and 'Tshekedi' were still being shouted among parliamentarians as taunts, questioning the moral integrity of their opponents, as late as 1963–64. But Seretse Khama himself, even after he began his political career as prime minister and president of Botswana in the mid-1960s, was to find that old acquaintances in Addiscombe had not heard of him or his country since 1956.

III

On 9 November 1976, President Sir Seretse Khama of the Republic of Botswana had a permanent stand-by pace-maker inserted in his heart. This was his second major medical breakdown as president, the previous occasion having been in 1968, when the effects of diabetes had drawn him near to death. Possibly from 1976, and certainly from 1978, Seretse Khama had intimations of imminent mortality.

On his return home from the heart operation, the president was greeted at Gaborone airport by university students angrily demonstrating over their government's passivity in the face of Rhodesian military incursions. Rhodesia had recently slipped back into the civil war that was to lead to its independence in 1979–80, and Rhodesian forces were following in 'hot pursuit' of refugees into Botswana. Botswana's other borders were threatened by South African forces seeking the children of Soweto who were escaping to join guerrilla movements based further north. Seretse received the moral support of the other Front-Line presidents, notably Kaunda and Nyerere, but Botswana was bereft of physical force to resist its aggressive white racist neighbours. In December the Botswana government outlined its concerns before the UN Security Council. A total of 36 incursions by Rhodesian forces were designed to 'intimidate the Government of Botswana into changing its present policy of giving refuge and assistance to victims of oppression'.

Botswana had no army until March 1977 when the Botswana parliament established a Botswana Defence Force, consisting of two companies of 140 men and 160–180 men respectively. The refugee problems grew more acute. In the first half of 1977, an estimated 15,000 rural dwellers crossed into Botswana from Rhodesia. Hot pursuit raids continued. Though the British and other European governments began to express support for Botswana, the foreign press almost without exception took its cues from correspondents stationed in South Africa and Rhodesia, who supplied stories of secret guerrilla camps in the desert. On an official visit to Brussels during June 1977, Seretse was taxed by the press on the issue of guerrilla camps.

The sense of insecurity was increased by South African army units camped on and periodically infiltrating across Botswana's other borders, and by refugee youths fleeing South Africa into Botswana in the wake of the Soweto uprising of June 1976. There was the threat of guerrilla retaliations on the first anniversary of Soweto, which would give South Africa the pretext for invasion. Botswana was obliged to systematically search refugee homes for firearms to maintain its own security. South Africa was also, from June–July 1977 onwards, putting pressures on Botswana to recognize South Africa's Tswana Bantustan ('Bophutatswana') as an independent state in December 1977.

By September 1977, Rhodesian forces were massed at Pandamatenga on the Botswana border, and Seretse was openly talking of 'war psychosis' in southern Africa and of the 'white death wish' driving it onwards. In February 1978 the South African and international press made much of an 'innocent' South African mercenary arrested on a Botswana train, wearing military uniform and carrying a completed application form for Rhodesia's notorious 'contra' force the Selous Scouts. Then, at the end of February, a Rhodesian force crossed the border at Leshoma, north of Pandamatenga, at the end of February and gunned down 15 Botswana soldiers and two young boys travelling in land-rovers on the main road inside Botswana.

It would be difficult to overstate the sense of national shock and anger in Botswana that followed the massacre of its young and inexperienced soldiers at Leshoma. The anger was compounded by the comparative indifference of the international press and media, which concentrated instead on the court proceedings against the white mercenary arrested on the train.

Such bitterness helps to account for an incident in mid-March in the Tuli Block near the point where the borders of Rhodesia, South Africa and Botswana met. (An area where South African soldiers had not long before been court-martialed for gang rape of a pregnant woman on the Botswana bank of the Limpopo.) Two white South African game-rangers and a British youth were arrested by a BDF patrol, and were then shot dead while 'attempting to escape'. The South African press went wild. So too did the British press about the British youth, one Nicholas Love, out in South Africa on holiday from Britain. Ironically, in the same month as Seretse was awarded the international Nansen Prize for humanitaran assistance to refugees, he became an international press ogre. Seretse was now being blamed for the very situation of inter-racial strife that he had warned about for so long, and which he had spent many years of his life trying to avoid. Assassination threats poured in through the mail from abroad, while hot-heads at home wanted the offending soldiers to be declared heroes for revenging the nation's honour.

The processes of military and judicial enquiry into the Tuli Block incident ground slowly onwards, while the British government, under pressure from its Rhodesia lobby in parliament, pressed for an explanation. Seretse was scathing in private about the double standards of those who ignored the Leshoma 'murders': 'They were merely Africans that were killed, so their deaths are dismissed as of no importance.'

All this threatened to disrupt Britain's final apology to and reconciliation with Seretse Khama, for the events of 1949–56, in the form of an official visit by Seretse to a Labour government in London. There were matters for discussion with James Callaghan, the Prime Minister, which ranged from Rhodesia and Namibia to British aid and Botswana's beef exports to the EEC. Seretse was also obliged to go to London for medical reasons, to have his chest opened once more, now that a trip to medical facilities in nearby Johannesburg was impossible for diplomatic reasons.

Seretse and his party, including Ruth Khama, arrived in London on 16 May 1978. He immediately came under pressure to visit the family of Nicholas Love, which he resisted on the ground that he had not visited the families of the 17 people killed at Leshoma. He did not talk directly to the press, but consented to give what he thought would be an uncontroversial interview on BBC television. The interview was recorded during the day on 17 May. That evening Seretse and Ruth, and other official delegates from Botswana, were entertained to dinner at No.10 Downing Street. The evening was particularly relaxed and friendly. During an impromptu speech, Seretse put a hand on his wife's shoulder and said: 'I am very happy to be, once again, a guest of the Government of the United Kingdom. I recall that the first time I was invited to London, I was kept here for six years. I hope that this time I can go home when I please.'

The gentle sweetness of such revenge, at the British prime minister's table, was tempered by the bitter edge of the television interview that was transmitted later that evening. Seretse, untrained in the art of television presentation, looked like a crook in his dark glasses donned against the bright studio lights. The glasses may have been fashionable photo-sensitive ones which turned darker in bright light. He may have not been helped by the fact that 'Seretse' was also the name given to a black gangster in a late night detective series on television. Seretse appeared to squirm under the unexpectedly sarcastic technique of the interviewer, as he hesitated in formulating the correct reply to the request of Nicholas Love's father to see him.

Sir Peter Fawcus, Britain's last major colonial proconsul for Botswana, wrote a letter of protest at the discourtesy shown to Britain's official guest, which he mailed to the editor of *The Times*. The editor referred him instead to the editor of the BBC radio and tv guide, the *Radio Times*.

NOTES

1. The precedent being forestry workers from British Honduras prevented from marrying Scottish women in the Second World War – Public Record Office, Kew (hereafter PRO) DO 35/4113, record of telephone call from J.L. Keith, 25–27 Sept. 1948.
2. PRO DO 35/4119; *Life* magazine (New York), Vol.28, No.10 (March 1950), pp.95–7 and subsequent readers' letters; Noel Monks in *Daily Mail* (London), 13 Feb. 1949; Noel Monks, *Eyewitness* (London, 1958), p.282; Nicholas Montserrat, *Life is a Four-Letter Word, Book Two: Breaking Out* (London, 1972), p.234 and *The Tribe That Lost Its Head* (London, 1959).
3. Anthony Sillery, 'Working Backwards', [Draft Autobiography], Rhodes House Library, Oxford (hereafter RHL), Mss.Afr.r.207, p.226.
4. *Cape Argus* (Cape Town), 8 March 1950, citing London *Daily Mail* correspondent. Michael Dutfield, *A Marriage of Inconvenience: The Persecution of Ruth and Seretse Khama* (London, 1990), which takes the story from 20 Sept. 1948 to 17 Aug. 1950, renders this as 'Tribe and I', p.159, source unknown.
5. PRO DO 35/4120, High Commissioner, Pretoria/Cape Town (hereafter HC) to Commonwealth Relations Office (hereafter CRO), 10 March 1950.
6. *Cape Times* (Cape Town), 7 March 1950, quoting London *Daily Mail*.
7. PRO DO 35/4115, copy of High Commissioner for SA to Prime Minister of SA, 25 March 1950; copy of Secretary External Affairs, Cape Town, to High Commissioner for SA, 27 March 1950; Patrick Gordon Walker to Prime Minister Attlee, 28 March 1950.
8. See, '2,000 Women Condemned the Decision', *Cape Times*, 9 March 1950. (For comment on International Women's Day as Soviet-inspired see PRO PREM 11/26 (1952), RHL, Fabian Colonial Bureau Papers 91/3, 'Resolution of Seretse Khama Fighting Committee', 12 March 1950; *The Friend* (Bloemfontein), 13 March 1950; also Oxford University West African Students' Club and West Indian Society, *Seretse Khama: A Background Study of the Southern African Crisis* (Oxford: University Socialist Club, 1950).

9. PRO DO 35/4120 and DO 35/4125.
10. PRO DO 4125, Seretse Khama Fighting Committee to Secretary of State for the Colonies, 17 March 1950. His reputation as negrophobe dated from his period as a British delegate at the United Nations defending South Africa over South West Africa. He had been promoted by Attlee, who had known him as a schoolboy in India, because of his British Indian background; see Churchill College, Cambridge, Attlee Papers, ATL 1/17, p.15.
11. PRO DO 35/4125, Note of a meeting with the Seretse Khama Fighting Committee, 17 March 1950.
12. 'MacKhama', South Africa (London), 25 March 1950, p.227; George Shepperson to Author, 11 Nov. 1985.
13. Zimbabwe National Archives, Harare (ZNA), Huggins Papers, Ms.281/1/14; Kenneth O. Morgan, Labour in Power 1945–1951 (Oxford, 1984), pp.415–17; D.J. Goldsworthy, Colonial Issues in British Politics, 1945–61 (London, 1961), pp.157–62; Miles Kahler, Decolonization in Britain and France: The Domestic Consequences of International Relations (Princeton, NJ, 1984), pp.238–41; Ronald Hyam, 'The Political Consequences of Seretse Khama: Britain, the Bamangwato and South Africa, 1948–1952', The Historical Journal, Vol.29, No.4 (1986), pp.291–47; Sunday Times (Johannesburg), 19 March 1950; Cape Times, 20 March 1950; PRO DO 35/4120, Harold H. Robertson, 'From Protectorate to Republic: The Political History of Botswana, 1926–1966' (unpublished Ph.D. thesis, Dalhousie University, Nova Scotia, 1979), p.304, citing Churchill to Smuts, 15 March 1950 (University of Cape Town, J.C. Smuts Private Letters, Vol.93/108) and Smuts to Churchill, 16 March 1950 (ibid., Vol.95/179).
14. Cape Argus, 14, 23 and 24 March 1950; also report on SA press in PRO DO 35/4120, HC to CRO, 27 March 1950.
15. RHL, Mss.Brit.Emp.365, 91/3, Fabian Colonial Bureau Papers.
16. PRO DO 35/4125, David C. Williams to Gordon Walker, 28 March 1950. The British Ambassador in Washington noticed the (white) establishment in Washington was 'strangely silent' on the Seretse issue, but that direct evidence from a black college in Virginia suggested that 'the case had had a very bad effect on Negroes generally who felt much moved and almost personally affected by it'; Dutfield, Marriage of Inconvenience, p.181. A Rhodesian agent in Britain, on the other hand, felt that 'The Americans paid an enormous amount of attention to the ['appalling reaction' to the Seretse Khama issue in the] West Indies' papers'; Arthur Benson to Hugh Parry, 30 July 1950 (ZNA, Huggins Papers, MS. 281/1/14).
17. South Africa, 25 March, p.230; PRO DO 35/4121, HC to CRO, 13 June 1950; The Star (Johannesburg), 22 March 1950.
18. PRO DO 35/4121, HC to CRO, 26 April 1950. Referred to by journalists as 'The Clinch'; John Redfern, Ruth and Seretse: 'A Very Disreputable Transaction' (London, 1955), p.137; Dutfield, Marriage of Inconvenience, p.195.
19. Redfern, Ruth and Seretse, p.143; Author's interview with Lady Khama, 29 Sept. 1985.
20. PRO DO 35/4131, Lewis notes on meeting with Seretse and Ruth Khama, 31 Jan. 1951.
21. Mary Benson, Tshekedi Khama (London, 1960), pp.215–45; Mary Benson, A Far Cry: the Making of a South African (Harmondsworth, 1989), pp.94–6.
22. 'Labour Split on Tshekedi Issue', Rhodesia Herald (Salisbury), Tues. 26 June 1951, p.7; Parl. Debs. Fifth Series. Commons, Vol.489, 26 June 1951, cols.1190–318; Parl. Debs. Fifth Series. Lords, Vol.172, 27 June 1951, cols.380–447.
23. 'Many from Home Village see Tom Driberg Married', Essex Chronicle, 6 July 1951 (clipping in Tshekedi Khama Papers, Serowe: TKP-57); Francis Wheen, Tom Driberg, His Life and Indiscretions (London, 1990), pp.251–3, citing Tom Driberg, The Best of Both Worlds: A Personal Diary (London, 1953), p.57.
24. PRO DO 35/4136, HC to CRO, 22 Oct. 1951; CRO briefing paper for new Secretary of State, 29 Oct. 1951; 'Notes for Secretary of State', 5 Nov. 1951.
25. PRO DO 121/151, W.A.W. Clarke minute, 25 March 1952; draft minute by Lord Salisbury to PM, 26 March 1952; note from 5 p.m. press briefing by Lord Salisbury, 26 March 1952; record of Lord Salisbury's 3 p.m. interview with Seretse Khama,

26 March 1952.
26. *Rand Daily Mail* (Johannesburg), 2 Oct. 1956, also quoted in Lawrence Peter Frank, 'Khama and Jonathan: A Study of Authority and Leadership in Southern Africa', unpublished Ph.D. thesis, Columbia University, New York, 1974, p.73.
27. PRO DO 121/151, Note on UK press reactions, *c.*28 March 1952.
28. PRO DO 35/4145, DO 35/4146 and DO 35/4147, Representations re exclusion of Seretse Khama from Chieftainship, Parts I, II and III. For Human Rights see PRO DO 35/7008.
29. PRO DO 35/4135, Miss A. Gladson to Lord Salisbury, 2 April 1952.
30. PRO DO 35/4145, DO 35/4146 and DO 35/4147.
31. PRO DO 35/4145, Arthur R. Kaladow to Winston Churchill, 5 April 1952.
32. PRO FO 371/966649, Oliver Messel to Anthony Eden, 2 April 1952.
33. PRO DO 35/4146, Archbishop of Canterbury to Lord Salisbury, 24 April 1954, record of meeting between Lord Salisbury and British Council of Churches, 9 May 1952.
34. PRO DO 35/4139, W.A.W. Clark minutes, 8 and 10 April 1952.
35. PRO DO 35/4139, Miss Booker's report on meeting at Caxton Hall, 6 May 1952; John Redfern, 'Peggy Cripps's Marriage to a Native Lawyer', *The Star* (Johannesburg), 30 Sept. 1959.
36. *Daily Worker* (London), 3 May 1952.
37. *Birmingham Post*, 12 May 1952.
38. *The Times*, *Daiy Herald*, *Daily Express* (all London) and *Manchester Guardian*, 12 May 1952.
39. See PRO DO 35/4469, 'Notes on Recent Public Activities over Racial Issues'; (Canon) L. John Collins, *Faith under Fire* (London, 1966), p.185ff. See also RHL, Fabian Colonial Bureau Papers and Africa Bureau Papers.
40. PRO DO 35/4469, Note on Recent Public Activities of Seretse Khama, pre-23 May 1952.
41. *Private Eye* (London), No.592, Aug. 1984, p.7.
42. PRO DO 35/4469, Minute by Mr Joyce, 23 May 1952; Tshekedi Khama Papers, Serowe (TKP) 52, Douglas Buchanan to Evelyn Baring, 19 July 1950.
43. TKP 58, Canon Collins gto Tshekedi Khama, 16 July 1952; Rev. Michael Scott to Tshekedi Khama, 22 July 1952; W.S. Pela 'to the Bamangwato tribe', *c.*July 1952.
44. RHL, Fabian Papers, Mss.Brit.Emp.s365/92/1, Fenner Brockway to Labour Party constituencies, 17 Sept. 1952; PRO DO 35/4279, Fenner Brockway to Lord Swinton, 15 Dec. 1952, and CRO to HC, 16 Feb. 1953; PRO DO 35/4469, Minute by Mr Bickford, 22 Sept. 1952; 'Defending Seretse Khama', *Manchester Guardian*, 18 Sept. 1952.
45. PRO DO 35/4279, Minute by Miss Booker, 10 March 1953.
46. *Seretse Khama and the Bamangwato People* (London: Seretse Khama Campaign Committee, 1953); *Parl. Debs. Fifth Series. Commons*, Vol.515, 1952–53, cols.2246–47, 2410–51; Vol.533, 1953–54, cols.259–60; Vol.525, 1953–54, col.850; Vol.535, 1954–55, cols.1961–62; Vol.540, 1954–55, cols.1878–89; Vol.542, 1955–56, cols.725–26; Vol.545, 1955–56, cols.361–62 and 1179–81; Vol.557, 1955–56, cols.1421–548; Vol.558, 1955–56, col.821. *Parl. Debs. Fifth Series. Lords*, Vol.186, 1954, cols.1214–19.
47. *Parl. Debs. Fifth Series. Commons*, Vol.515, as above; also PRO DO 35/4282, DO 35/4283, DO 35/4290.
48. *The Star* (Johannesburg), 11 Jan. 1954; TKP 52, Thomas Fox-Pitt Anti-Slavery Society) to Tshekedi Khama, 12 July 1954; Tshekedi Khama *Bechuanaland and South Africa* (London: Africa Bureau, 1959), p.14; ZNA, Huggins Papers, Ms.281/2/PM21.
49. Montserrat, *Life is a Four-Letter Word: Book Two*, p.234.
50. PRO DO 35/4339, Minute by P.J.S. Moon, 8 Aug. 1955; Minute by Mr Fowler, 9 Aug. 1955; Minute by G.H. Baxter, 23 Aug. 1955.
51. PRO DO 35/4289, Draft Parliamentary answer for 27 Oct. 1955.
52. Written by Gene Sharp, published in *Peace News* (London), Nos.1039–41, 25 May–8 June 1956.
53. PRO DO 35/4315, Letters from public. PRO DO 35/4329, South Africa House news release, 25 June 1956; Record of conversation with J.G. Strijdom, 26 June 1956.

54. *Parl. Debs. Fifth Series. Commons*, 1 Aug. 1956, cols.1490–548; PRO DO 35/1182, Home to Eden, 27 July 1956.
55. 'A Private Citizen', *South Africa* (London), 4 Aug. 1956, p.97; PRO DO 35/4302, CRO final draft memorandum, *c*.21 Aug. 1956; Benson, *Tshekedi Khama*, p.271.
56. *News Chronicle* (London), 26 Sept. 1956; CRO Press Release, 26 Sept. 1956 (copy in RHL, Fabian Colonial Bureau Papers, 92/4); Benson, *Tshekedi Khama*, pp.271–2.
57. Part III of this essay is based on drafts by Willie Henderson for a biography of Seretse Khama (1921–80) being written in collaboration with Thomas Tlou and Neil Parsons.

Doubly Elite: African Rhodes Scholars, 1960–90

ANTHONY KIRK-GREENE

This contribution investigates the African element among Oxford University's prestigious and unique Rhodes Scholars – the 'doubly elite' of the title. Set within the context of African students at British universities since the 1930s, the development of the Rhodes Scholarships and the criteria for selection lead into an examination of the presence of black African Scholars among this elite. Because such awards closely followed the independence of Commonwealth African states, the focus is essentially on those men and women selected since 1960, though there were, of course, many Scholars from South Africa and Rhodesia elected earlier. Out of approximately 5,000 Rhodes Scholarships awarded between 1903 and 1990, no fewer than 900 went to students from Africa. What is believed to be a basis for the first databank of all the black African Scholars elected is now established. The paper concludes with a discussion of the need for further prosopographical analysis of the achievements of this African double elite during and after their Oxford experience.

African Students at British Universities

Readers of Evelyn Waugh's *Black Mischief* will recall the opening scene, where the ruler of the fictitious African empire of Azania is discovered dictating to his patient Indian secretary a series of proclamations and patents of nobility, ordinances, decrees, and invitations to his forthcoming coronation: 'We, Seth, Emperor of Azania, Chief of the Chiefs of Sakuya, Lord of Wanda and Tyrant of the Seas, Bachelor of the Arts of Oxford University, being in this the twenty-fourth year of our life, do hereby proclaim . . .'.[1]

In the event, of course, Seth is firmly a figure of fiction as well as of fun. Whereas throughout the 50 years up to their abolition in 1947, many

The author wishes warmly to acknowledge the support received from the Warden of Rhodes House, Oxford, Sir Anthony Kenny, on researching this contribution, and the help given by his assistant, Mrs Kebble-White. While he was generously given privileged access to certain files and the text has benefited from scrutiny by the Warden, the interpretation of any errors therein remain his own responsibility.

of the rulers of India's 562 Native States could legitimately 'do a Seth' and inscribe the prestigious BA (Oxon) or BA (Cantab) after their name, thereby signifying their graduation from one of the acknowledged premier universities in the pre-MBA/Law School world – and in the process often adding to the lustre of their alma mater, or least in the eyes of the great British public, by even more spectacular success on the cricket or the polo field: remember the champagne-like grace of such 'England' sportsmen as K.S. Ranjitsinhji, the Nawab of Pataudi and the Maharajah of Baroda? – Africa's royalty was, almost, up to the 1960s, conspicuous by its absence from the lecture halls and playing fields of British universities, let alone the colleges of Oxbridge. Like Waugh's Seth, Joyce Cary's Louis Aladai, an 'African Prince' and heir apparent to the throne of Rimi in Northern Nigeria, was but a figure of Oxford fiction in the 1930s.[2] It was not until 1945 that Seretse Khama, the royal future head of Botswana, came up to Balliol College. At Cambridge, the Kabaka of Buganda was an undergraduate from 1945 to 1948, though he was mystified how the decision could have been made by the Oxford men who surrounded him.[3] Nor was it Africa's royalty alone that eschewed an Oxford education: the House of Windsor has consistently shown an unexplained preference for educating its scions at Cambridge (other than the future King Edward VIII, momentarily and unmemorably at Magdalen College, Oxford),[4] all the way from George VI and his brother Henry to the present Prince of Wales and his brother Prince Edward.

Not that the African presence beyond royalty was all that greater among the future generation of Third World nationalist leaders at Oxbridge. Whereas several of the 'founding fathers' of South Asian nationalism were often, to coin a phrase, 'Cambridge before they were Calcutta' or as 'Oxford' as they were 'Oudh' (Jawaharlal Nehru, Solomon Bandaranaike, Zulfikar Bhutto), those representing emergent Africa's inaugural generation of premier and president in the 1960s were, when they were university graduates at all, likely to have been either alumni of institutions other than Britain's two elitist universities or, of course, of the RMA Sandhurst. Julius Nyerere graduated from Edinburgh and Jomo Kenyatta from the LSE, while Kwame Nkrumah and Nnamdi Azikiwe both went to college in the USA. Latterday Sandhurst graduate Yakubu Gowon took a BA and a Ph.D. at latterday Warwick (exceptionally, *after* having received an honorary degree from Cambridge). Hastings Banda was educated at the Universities of Chicago, Nashville and Edinburgh, while Robert Mugabe acquired half a dozen first degrees, most of them while he was otherwise occupied. Among the also-rans in the head of state stakes, Obafemi Awolowo studied at the Inns of Court; Tom Mboya attended Ruskin College at Oxford; and Emeka Ojukwu followed up his days of fast sports cars at Lincoln College, Oxford,[5] with a course at the Officer Cadet School at Eaton Hall.

When we come to the third component of Africa's leadership cadres, the professions (education, bureaucracy, medicine, law, diplomacy, etc.), it is still universities other than Oxford or Cambridge which can point to the majority of alumni, Edinburgh and Aberdeen being two outstanding parent institutions in the field. True, at the Ph.D. level, Oxbridge began to register African students in the 1950s – for instance, Kofi Busia, Kalu Ezera and Ali Mazrui in the humanities at Oxford, Iya Abubakar and Muhammadu Dikko in the sciences at Cambridge. But, possibly because of the rewarding and respected link with the University of London (reinforced by the international reputation of such constituent colleges as LSE, the School of Oriental and African Studies, University College London and King's), whose degrees were conferred at every one of the new University Colleges in anglophone Africa until they became degree-awarding institutions in their own right – other than Fourah Bay, where the degree was Durham's BA (Dunelm) – many of the pioneer generation of African professors went to London: for example to take the founding fathers of African history alone, Kenneth Dike, Ade Ajayi, Adu Boahen, E.A. Ayandele, Bethwell Ogot and A.J. Temu. Davidson Nicol at Cambridge (Christ's) and W.E. Abraham at Oxford (All Souls) were among the first African scholars to be elected to College Fellowships, respectively in 1957 and 1959, along with the memorable Atiyah brothers, Michael and Patrick. Come the second academic generation, it was conspicuously North America, and to an extent the USSR and Eastern Europe, that began to compete in attracting Africa's doctoral candidates. If, in an approximate decennial periodization, the next wave (1970s) added other commonwealth countries to Britain's new as well as its provincial universities, that of the 1980s has featured a reduction in the British and, to a lesser extent, the American Ph.D.s, compensated by the need, the wish and the ability of African universities to establish and nurture their own Ph.D programmes back home. Sadly – in intellectual terms, however understandable in terms of economic, even human, survival – the 1990s threaten, over and above the conventional international faculty exchange, to be characterized by a one-way brain drain which the African universities cannot afford, for every year sees more and more disenchanted top-class faculty migrating from Ibadan and Makerere, Legon and Nairobi, to Amherst, Austin and all points west . . . and now to South Africa, too. In the university world, it is hard to persuade the African faculty how, as it were, Los Angeles' temporary gain can atone for Lusaka's longer-term teaching loss.

African Students at Oxford

None of these educational trends means, of course, that, while universities like Edinburgh, Aberdeen and London have a long record of African students (the Nigerians James Horton and William Davies graduated M.D. respectively from Edinburgh and from St Andrew's in 1859, well after the Sierra Leonean William Fergusson's M.D. from Edinburgh), there were no African students at Oxford before the Second World War. Oxford admitted its first African female student in 1933, when St Hugh's College (the Africanist Margery Perham's college, too)[6] offered a place to Kofoworola Aina Moore, member of an eminent Lagosian family, at a time when B.A. Mayanja from Buganda was already at University College and the Kikuyu Parmenas Mockerie was soon to follow to Ruskin College.[7] Another Kenyan, Eliud Mathu, came up to Balliol College in 1939.[8] Fifty years later, African alumni abound. In the 1990s, it is as commonplace to find Oxford graduates among Africa's academics, bureaucrats and diplomats (Lagos and Lusaka even have their own Oxford and Cambridge Club!), though fewer among the political class, with a handful of traditional rulers – real-life Seths and Aladais – such as the King of Lesotho and the son of the Crown Prince of Ethiopia, as earlier it was to find them among the politico-administrative elite of emergent South Asia and the Caribbean. By today, out of 15,000 students in residence, there is hardly an African country – francophone, lusophone and arabophone included – which cannot point to having had a representative at Oxford. Most of these are at the post-graduate level: whereas, for a variety of reasons (often economic), Oxford has only 769 (7.5 per cent) undergraduates from overseas out of a student body of 10,507, out of the 4,045 graduate students as many as 1,694 (42 per cent) are from 98 overseas countries, nearly 200 of them from the African continent (Table 1).[9]

The Rhodes Scholarships

Within the totality of student life in Britain, there is one aspect which is unique to Oxford. This is the Rhodes Scholarship Scheme. The burden of this article is to analyse the African component of what is arguably the most prestigious of Britain's multiple student awards at what is widely perceived as one of Britain's two, and the world's half-dozen, most distinguished universities. Hence the rationalization of the title of double elitism for this contribution to the 'African Presence' in Britain. To quote the conclusion of a recent analysis of the West African dimension to the Rhodes Scholarship Scheme: 'Holders of a Rhodes Scholarship carry an aura of distinction attached to few if any other student awards. Rhodes Scholars are – well, Rhodes Scholars; and that, in universities throughout the English-speaking world (and a goodly number besides), is in itself at once an achievement, a qualification, and a signal.'[10]

TABLE 1

AFRICAN STUDENTS AT OXFORD BY COUNTRY OF ORIGIN 1990-91

Country	U/G	P/G	Total	Country	U/G	P/G	Total
Algeria	-	2	2	Nigeria	6	16	22
Cameroon	-	4	4	Sierra Leone	-	2	2
Egypt	1	2	3	Somali Rep.	1	-	1
Ethiopia	-	4	4	S. Africa	15	48	63
Ghana	1	5	6	Sudan	-	1	1
Guinea	-	1	1	Tanzania	-	1	1
Kenya	11	9	20	Uganda	2	1	3
Malawi	2	-	2	Zambia	1	7	8
Mauritius	1	-	1	Zimbabwe	3	8	11
Mozambique	-	2	2				

Notes:
1. Because of the University's Foreign Service Programme for Third World diplomats, which recruits a good proportion of its students from Sub-Saharan Africa each year, the geographical spread of Africans studying at Oxford is considerably enhanced. For instance, over the past years, Oxford has uniquely admitted students from Benin, Burkina Faso, Chad, Congo, Gabon, Guinea, Ivory Coast, Madagascar, Mali, Niger, Senegal, Togo and Zaire, all francophone countries.
2. Overall, there were 2,463 students (17 per cent) from 98 overseas and EC countries, including 509 from USA, 185 from Canada, 177 from Germany, 143 from Australia, 104 from Hong Kong, 92 from India, 86 from China PR, 65 from Ireland, 63 from South Africa, 62 from Singapore and from Greece, 61 from Japan and from Malaysia, and 36 from Brazil.

1. Distribution

In 1893, through the fifth of his many wills and codicils, Cecil Rhodes, Bachelor of Arts of Oriel College, Oxford, millionaire mining magnate, founder of Rhodesia, Prime Minister of Cape Colony, imperialist extraordinary, and the subject of over a hundred biographical studies[11] and a dozen memorials in Oxford, decided to foster education as the best means of providing unity among the English-speaking peoples. He endowed 60 'Empire Scholarships' tenable at his old university (of which, if no scholar, he must surely rank among the greatest benefactors: in 1980 the Rhodes Trust was worth £35 million). Their allocation was, in geographical terms, three for Rhodesia, five for South Africa (these were tied to four named schools in the Cape Colony and one for the Colony of Natal); six for Australia, one per Colony (subsequently State); two for Canada, one for Ontario Province and one for Quebec; and one each for the Colonies of New Zealand, Newfoundland, Bermuda and Jamaica. To these, by his last will in 1899, were added 32 scholarships for the USA and, through a 1901 codicil, five for Germany, thereby breaking the Anglo-Saxon mould on the grounds that the Kaiser had recently made the study of English compulsory in German schools.[12] Rhodes died in 1902, leaving an estate worth £4 million. There were two pre-will Scholars, both from Diocesan College, Rondebosch. The Rhodes Scholarships came into full operation in 1903.

Over the years, the allocation of Scholarships has changed with the times. Additional Scholarships were soon made available for the rest of the Canadian Provinces; extra ones were given to South Africa after the First World War and a second was provided for New Zealand in 1926. Still in the Commonwealth, a triennial Scholarship was established for East Africa in 1933, and in 1942 the annual Malaya Scholarship was raised to two. In 1946, the Caribbean Scholarships were doubled. Two annual Scholarships were inaugurated for India in 1947, soon divided into one for India and one for Pakistan, and one every three years for Sri Lanka from 1959.

Further allocations were made in the 1960s to provide Rhodes Scholar- ships for the new Commonwealth countries, and it was now that the rest of anglophone Africa was given the chance to make its mark. Awards were introduced for Ghana and for the Malayan region (including Singapore) in 1960, for Nigeria in 1962, and for the British (later Commonwealth) Caribbean in 1965. Nigeria advanced from a triennial to an annual Scholarship in 1981, while Kenya has been allocated one Scholarship a year since 1986. The conversion of Northern Rhodesia into Zambia in 1964 and of Southern Rhodesia into Zimbabwe in 1980 brought further changes in the spread of the regional allocation of the Scholarships to what the Trust defines as 'the geographical area known as Rhodesia in 1899', so that today two Scholarships are given to Zambia and one to Zimbabwe, and *vice-versa* in alternate years. The term 'South Africa at Large' was introduced in 1972 to cater for a Scholarship from Botswana, Swaziland, Lesotho or South Africa, itself additional to the five founding South Africa awards. Conversely, allocations have been dropped or suspended ('a few constituencies are no longer represented' in the cool phraseology of the Trust) when the selection process or calibre of student steadily falls away, for example East Africa after 1953, Ghana since 1975, and more recently, Sri Lanka and Zambia. It must surely be on the cards that Western Germany will be expanded to Germany. Thought has yet to be given to Namibia, and Hong Kong's position may have to be recon- sidered after 1997. *Per contra*, eight European Rhodes Scholarships (three for Greece, two for Ireland, and one each for Denmark, France and Italy) have just been created.[13] Out of the nearly 90 awards now made annually, the 52 Scholarships originally identified in Rhodes' will continue to take precedence over those established since. The number of Rhodes Scholars has risen from 2,336 in 1945 to approximately 4,600 in 1987, and is now approaching 5,500.[14] Funding permitting (and each Scholar costs the Trust some £20,000 a year, for a maximum of three years), the total could reach the 6,000 mark by the centenary year of 2003.

In summary, the annual election of Rhodes Scholarships has typically reflected the following pattern of allocation:

TABLE 2

GEOGRAPHICAL DISTRIBUTION OF ANNUAL RHODES SCHOLARSHIPS (1980s)

U.S.A.	32	India	3	Malaya	1
Canada	11	New Zealand	2	Singapore	1
South Africa	9	West Germany	2	Jamaica	1
Australia	8	Bermuda	1	Kenya	1
Hong Kong	1	Pakistan	1	Commonwealth Caribbean	1
Zambia & Zimbabwe	3	Nigeria	1		

2. Criteria

How are the fortunate few, our doubly elite, chosen? Four principal criteria for selection were prescribed by Rhodes and have been scrupulously observed down the years. First come the candidate's scholastic and literary attainments. Next, their qualities of 'manhood', defined in the Rhodes context as subsuming the virtues of truth, courage, devotion to duty, sympathy for and protection of the weak, kindliness, unselfishness, and fellowship – no mean list of attributes to possess and display! A third requirement has been the exhibition during their schooldays of moral force of character, and evidence of instincts to lead and take an interest in the well-being of their schoolmates. Fourthly, but by no means finally, comes their fondness for, and proven success in, main outdoor sports.

Such have been the basic principles for the selection of these young paragons. Over the years there has been a tendency to de-emphasize athletic excellence, without in any way dropping it from consideration. Indeed, referees are still enjoined to take note that physical vigour remains one of the fundamental criteria, evidenced by 'fondness of, or success in manly outdoor sports' – though 'manly' has now necessarily become optional! Candidates must be between 19 and 25, and unmarried at the time of selection. There is no written examination. Superior academic record, frank confidential testimonials, and, above all, searching personal interview form the inflexible basis of selection to Britain's most prized scholarships.[15]

Rhodes himself once said that he was not seeking bookworms. What he wanted was 'the best men for the world's fight'.[16] To him this could be assured either by distinguished intellect founded upon sound character or by exceptional character based upon sound intellect. The key, then, to the Rhodes Scholarship lies in the exhibition of intellect, moral character and leadership. Significantly, these attributes were, in Rhodes' assessment of his scholars, the ones which would 'be likely in after-life to guide them to esteem the performance of public duties as their highest aim'.[17]

Apart from the extension of the catchment area, notably with the transformation of so many former British colonies into independent member states of the Commonwealth, two further changes of substance have taken place in the second half of the Trust's existence. One has been the eligibility of successful Rhodes Scholars to read for a postgraduate degree instead of the hitherto *de rigueur* undergraduate degree – often, as with the case of most North American Scholars before the war, allowing them to take the Oxford B.A. (there is no B.Sc.) in a concessionary two instead of the mandatory three years. The other came about in 1976, when for the first time women became eligible for Rhodes Scholarships: 24 came into residence in October 1977. Today, with a total of 166 awards in the first 15 years, women Scholars make up something like 30 per cent of the annual awards.

Rhodes Scholars from Africa

In analysing the 'African Presence' element among our doubly elite cohort of Rhodes Scholars, we encounter a set of definitional constraints. First, where recognition of the colour of its scholars is concerned, the Rhodes Trust is completely blind. By contrast, of course, the Trust has, because of the inviolability of the criterion of geographical allocation, to be critically concerned with the nationality of its candidates. Secondly, it is common knowledge that the scholarships set aside *ab initio* for South Africa and Rhodesia were at that time, and in the event for years to come, envisaged as being taken up by white students. The same outcome, if not the same assumption, was reflected in the subsequent East African awards. Nor has the abolition of the Rhodesian quota and its redistribution to Zambia in 1974 and Zimbabwe in 1982 *ipso facto* ruled out white applicants from either state. Merit remains the ultimate criterion. On the other hand, a very high assumption must be that the Scholars elected from Ghana, Nigeria and Kenya will be black.

Within these parameters, the identification of the 'African' element among Rhodes Scholars within the context of this collection consists of a selecting-out exercise. First, in order to accommodate the imperative underlying the fundamental interpretation of the 'African Presence in Britain', this contribution essentially excludes, in addressing itself to 'African' Rhodes Scholars among the total of approximately 900 Rhodes Scholars from Africa between 1902 and 1990, any analysis of scholars elected from the designated 'geographical area known as Rhodesia in 1899', that is to say present-day Zimbabwe before 1980 and Zambia before 1964. It was in 1982 and 1972 that the first black African Scholars were respectively elected. Secondly, by convention, if not by literal definition, yesterday's 'Black Americans' and today's 'African-American or Caribbean' Rhodes Scholars do not constitute part of this database. To re-define the corpus in positive terms, we believe that, for the purposes of 'The African Presence in Britain', we have successfully identified all the black Rhodes Scholars elected from Africa. The fact that our research data correspond with what is broadly accepted as the first quarter of a century of the new states of Sub-Saharan Africa lends a neat historical symmetry to the analysis.

We can now present the pan-African data in a series of tables. Table 3 summarizes the distribution of all the African awards since the inception of the scholarships nearly 90 years ago. In Table 4 we tease out from Table 3 a complete list of what may be called African Rhodes Scholars within the spirit of the terms and the title of reference of this special issue between 1960 and 1990.[18] Incidentally, not only were five of the 16 black African Scholars elected women, four of them are the first women from their respective countries: Mss Lucy Banda from Zambia, Lekalake from Botswana, Adhiambo Odago from Kenya and Catherine Onyewenjo from Nigeria. What is more, Monde Muyangwa and Wendy Nkuhlu have contined the Zambian tradition of women scholars. Table 4 may be expected to expand interestingly with the anticipated growth of awards to black South African students in the 1990s.[19] Table 5 goes on to illustrate the preferred disciplines of the West African Scholars.

A trend has emerged in the last decade for African Rhodes Scholars to move away from the traditional disciplines of history, politics, law, literature, and, especially when a postgraduate degree is involved, to study more 'relevant' subjects, for example, agricultural or development economics, linguistics or management studies. Taking the research wider than the West African cohort, among the Zimbabweans, for example, one read history, one law, and the third computation. The South African, 'one of the few blacks from South Africa ever selected',[20] came up to do research in sociology, in which he had already taken a B.A. in the USA, while the sole Botswana Scholar read for a higher degree in law, in which she had previously graduated in Canada. Of the Kenyans, three took

TABLE 3

RHODES SCHOLARS FROM AFRICA, 1903–90

Yrs.

	(1) S.Africa	(2) Rhodesia	(3) E.Africa	(4) Ghana	(5) Nigeria	(6) Zambia	(7) Zimbabwe	(8) Kenya
1902	2	-	-	-	-	-	-	-
1903-1917	76	31	-	-	-	-	-	-
1918-1941	211	68	4	-	-	-	-	-
1945-1959	117	42	4	-	-	-	-	-
1960-1980	160	52	-	4	5	8	-	-
1981-1990	72	-	-	-	7	14	16	5
TOTALS	638	193	8	4	12	22	16	5

Notes:
1. The South African and Rhodesian Scholarships were suspended from 1942 to 1945 but in 1946 were doubled in compensation. The South African intake averaged five a year up to the end of the First World War, rose to 9 between the wars, and averaged 8 after the Second World War until, with an extra 'South Africa-at-Large' award, it again rose to nine in the 1980s.
2. The pre-war average of two rose to three from 1918 and remained at that figure until 1973 when it dropped to two or one a year until 1979. Thereafter Scholarships were allocated two from Zimbabwe and one from Zambia, and *vice-versa* in alternate years.
3. One was awarded triennially for a candidate from Kenya, Uganda, Tanganyika or Zanzibar from 1933 to 1953.
4. A Scholarship was established in 1960. No award has been made since 1975.
5. A Scholarship was established in 1962 and became annual in 1985.
6. & See note (2). The first black Zambian award was made in 1972 and the first black
7. Zimbabwean award in 1982.
8. An annual Scholarship was established in 1986.

higher degrees (geography, management studies, human biology) – one having earlier graduated in North America – and two read for a first degree, one in modern languages, and one in politics and economics. Among the most recent Zambians, two registered for the M. Stud. in linguistics, two were accepted for the M.Sc in development economics, two for law, and one each for management studies, sociology, geography, and politics.

Finally, two points require to be made in respect of these tables. First, while a Rhodes Scholarship cannot be held for more than three years, a number of scholars who read for a B.A. during their tenure go on, with other sources of funding, to read for a higher degree, often (but not

TABLE 4
BLACK AFRICAN RHODES SCHOLARS 1960–90

Year	Zambia	Ghana	Nigeria	Zimbabwe	S.Africa	Kenya
1960		L.Hesse				
1962			P.Mbaeyi			
1964		J.Benneh				
1966			F.Okole			
1972	O.Ncube	F.Tsikata	S.Braide			
1975	E.Kalula	C.Ahwol	O.Osunboro			
1976	R.Mushota					
	N.Puta					
1977	E.Ngandu					
	D.Hatenda					
1978	L.Banda					
1979	O.Saasa					
1980		T.Williams				
1981	T.Banda					
1982				S.Samkange		
1983	S.Kopulande		T.A-Raheem			
1984	H.Mpuku					
1985	M.Chilufya		Y.Aliyu	P.Nherere	L.Lekalake (Botswana)	
1986	V.Mpepo		O.Akinboade			A.Odago
	N.Namoonde					
1987	M.Muyangwa		C.Onyewenjo			S.Liti
1988	M.Musande		A.Bello			K.Kamoche
	C.Ng'andu					
1989	M.Mutukwa		I.Chioke	J.Manyika	I.Shongwa	P.Kinguru
1990	E.Chipimo		A.Adebajo			D.Olago
	W.Nkuhlu					

TABLE 5
WEST AFRICAN RHODES SCHOLARS, 1960–90

Year	Name	Country	Previous University	Subject Studied
1960	L.W. Hesse	Ghana	Legon	Politics/Economics
1962	P.M. Mbaeyi	Nigeria	Ibadan	History
1964	J.G. Benneh	Ghana	Legon	Politics/Economics
1966	F.I. Okole	Nigeria	Nsukka	Mathematics
1972	F.S. Tsikata	Ghana	Legon	Law
	S.P. Braide	Nigeria	Ibadan	Geology
1975	C.K. Ahwoi	Ghana	Legon	Law
	O.A. Osunboro	Nigeria	Nsukka	Law
1980	T.O. Williams	Nigeria	Ife	Agricultural Science
1983	T.A. Raheem	Nigeria	Kano	Political Science
1985	Y. Aliyu	Nigeria	Kano	Agricultural Econ.
1986	O.A. Akinboade	Nigeria	Ife	Agricultural Econ.
1987	C. Onyewenjo	Nigeria	Ife	English Literature
1988	A.L. Bello	Nigeria	Ilorin	Applied Statistics
1989	I. Chioke	Nigeria	Ife	Management Studies
1990	A.Adebajo	Nigeria	Ibadan	Int. Relations

always) at Oxford. Secondly as with graduate students everywhere, not all Rhodes Scholars complete their higher degree: one such instance currently in the news has, of course, been that of President Bill Clinton.[21]

Conclusion

If this contribution has presented an initial anatomy of the growing 'African Presence' among Rhodes Scholars at Oxford University over the past three decades, it nevertheless singularly fails to achieve what the writer originally had in mind: namely, a survey of what became of them, in subsequent career terms, once they had left Oxford, together with a tentative valuation of the impact of this doubly elite on their country of origin. Although the Rhodes Trust has compiled three biographical *Registers* (1950, 1972, 1981), covering over 4,500 Scholars, and a further volume to mark the Scholarships' centenary is planned, no prosopographical analysis of 'who was who and who did what' has yet been undertaken. Even where the data do exist, that is, in the 1981 *Register*, they are of limited help to my original objective, since two-thirds of the African Rhodes Scholars identified did not come into residence until after the publication of that *Register*.[22] Now that the basic 'who's who' component has been established for African Rhodes students, the next stage is to set about compiling the 'what's what' data: to document not only what these notable African students achieved before and at Oxford (the schools they attended and their grades, the subject they read at the university and the class of degree obtained or the higher degree taken, their sporting, social and personal contributions to University and College teams, clubs, and societies), but also what, with the private and personal triumph of a Rhodes Scholarship behind them, they achieved in and for the public common weal of their country when they went home.

Only this kind of follow-up can put us in a position to undertake the final stage, calculating the influence of Rhodes Scholars on their respective polities and national economies . . . beyond, that is, some of the *prima facie* patina of Oxbridge tradition transplanted to the new African universities which inescapably came, and has inevitably gone, since the milestone Asquith and Elliott Commissions half a century ago – one recalls the disbelief of the stereotype American professors as they first came to teach on African campuses in the late 1950s and were confronted by grace and gown at Legon, halls of residence and sets of rooms at Ibadan, dons and cosy tutorials at Makerere.

However, in this collection, our focus is on the 'African Presence in Britain', not on the British academic values exported to Africa nor, in particular, on the effect of Oxford overseas, a topic which has been so informatively treated by Richard Symonds. As he rightly concludes of Rhodes Scholars in general, 'the influence of Rhodes Scholars on Oxford is perhaps easier to try to assess than the influence of Oxford on them'.[23] All that can be assessed so far is a matter of achievement 'over here', not yet (in the absence of the data) of impact 'back there'. It is in this preliminary respect that this article has addressed itself to the formation of a double elite in Britain, black African students who not only gained admission to the University of Oxford but who at the same time secured one of the coveted, limited and prestigious Rhodes Scholarships.

The record is impressive, relatively far more so than, say the recruitment of only 320 members of Britain's ethnic minorities (who today constitute 5.5 per cent of the total UK population of 54.8 million)[24] into the Armed Forces in 1990. Among them, the black community provided a mere 142 for the Army (out of 16,526 recruits) and 22 each for the Navy and the RAF (out of respectively 4,766 and 6,102 entrants). Or, again, more so than that of only seven black officers commissioned into the Navy and Marines in 1990, two into the RAF in 1989 (none in 1990), and one into the British Army in 1990 – the first since ethnic monitoring was introduced in 1987.[25] Or, yet again, and nearer home, more impressive than the fact that 86 per cent of black pupils scoring the equivalent of two As and one C or higher in 'A' levels gained a university place in 1990/91 against 90 per cent of white and 93 per cent of Asian pupils.[26]

The emphasis of this contribution has of necessity been limited to the historical: the fundamental identification of who the African Rhodes Scholars were and where they came from.[27] To track where they went and what they accomplished after the Rhodes experience remains the challenge for subsequent socio-economic research, in the same way as in due course it will rewardingly be for tracking Oxford's new Rhodes European Scholars. Only then shall we be in a position fully to measure how far the founder's search for 'the best men [and women] for the world's fight', endowed with all those formidable attributes which Rhodes believed would 'be likely in after-life to guide them to esteem the performance of public duties as their highest aim', has been realized by the beneficiaries of the Rhodes Scholarship Scheme.

In the meantime, it may well prove that all that the available documentation so far allows is for this particular aspect of the African Presence in Britain, however original it may be as a topic, to provide more a matter of immediate Oxford pride and purpose (of which, outside Oxford, one may already have had enough!) than of longer-term African practical significance. At the very least, my guess is that the answers are unlikely to echo that given to young Peekay, the South African schoolboy hero of Bruce Courtenay's recent novel, who, waiting for the result of his application for a Rhodes Scholarship, put, 'my' kind of prosopographical question to his grandfather about his Oxford-educated Uncle Arthur, 'the clever one in the family':

> What happened to him, Granpa?
> 'I don't know what went wrong. He rose to be Lord Chief Justice
> of Appeal . . . A miserable life, really, made a lot of money and

a lot of misery for himself and everyone else . . .

He died rich and lonely . . .

Funny thing about Arthur, he never could get things in their right perspective.'[28]

Yet, if it is widely accepted, as I believe, that the winning of a Rhodes Scholarship is at once a laudable achievement and a signal to the future, now that we at last know who Africa's Rhodes Scholars are, and what their achievement has been at Oxford, may we not justifiably search for the signal too, and, echoing President Kennedy, ask what they have since done for Africa following on what they did so distinguishedly for themselves at Oxford?[29]

NOTES

1. Evelyn Waugh, *Black Mischief* (London, 1932), p.9.
2. Joyce Cary, *The African Witch* (London, 1936). Cary's first draft bore the title *The Black Prince*: see A.H.M. Kirk-Greene, 'The Oxford Novel and the Third World', *Oxford*, Vol.XLIV, No.2 (1992), pp.76–79.
3. The Kabaka of Buganda, *Desecration of My Kingdom* (London, 1967), p.91.
4. See John Grigg's assessment in the *Dictionary of National Biography, 1971–1980* (Oxford, 1986), p.273, and Philip Ziegler's sorry and sterile portrait in *King Edward VIII* (London, 1990), p.41.
5. See Frederick Forsyth, *Emeka* (London, 1982), p.15ff.
6. For a view of her pre-eminence in African Studies, see Alison Smith and Mary Bull (eds.), *Margery Perham and British Rule in Africa* (London, 1991).
7. See Margery Perham (ed.), *Ten Africans: A Collection of Life Stories* (London, 1936), Chs. X and VII.
8. Jack R. Roelker, *Mathu of Kenya: A Political Study* (Stanford, CA, 1976), p.59.
9. However, in his political novel *A Man of the People* (London, 1966), Chinua Achebe devises a partisan newspaper editorial denigrating the dismissed Cabinet on the grounds that 'We are proud to be Africans – our true leaders are not those intoxicated with their Oxford, Cambridge and Harvard degrees' (p.4). Nevertheless, the less educated incoming minister, Chief the Honourable M.A. ('M.A. Minus Opportunity') Nanga is proud to introduce the fact that 'My Private Secretary has B.A. from Oxford' (p.13).
10. A.H.M. Kirk-Greene, 'Eighty Years of Mobility', *West Africa* (3 Sept. 1984). For a less enthusiastic view, from a former African Rhodes Scholar, see Tajudeen Abdul-Raheem, 'Cecil Rhodes: Robber – Philanthropist', *Africa World Review* (May–Oct. 1992), pp.11–12. When this was first published in *Africa Events* (Dec. 1988), it was unsigned: the author was holding a Rhodes Scholarship at the time.
11. The most recent, Robert I. Rotberg's *The Founder: Cecil Rhodes and the Pursuit of Power* (New York, 1988), runs to over 800 pages.
12. The German Scholarship was suspended in 1916 by an Act of Parliament; revived in 1929 but reduced to two Scholarships; suspended again in 1939; and restored in 1969 for West Germany only.
13. *Oxford University Gazette*, Vol.122, No.4252, p.1049.
14. Of these, the majority are American Scholars, of whom 2,628 have been elected since 1904. Approximately, 1,200 applications are received each year for the 32 Rhodes Scholarships available to Americans.
15. See *Cecil Rhodes and Rhodes House* (Oxford, 1982), p.9; the advisory *Memorandum to Selection Committees*; and the annual applicant's guide, *Scholarships at Oxford*

Memorandum for . . . [Nigeria, Kenya, etc.].

16. Quoted in *Cecil Rhodes and Rhodes House*, p.9.
17. *Cecil Rhodes and Rhodes House*, p.9.
18. See David P. White, 'To Be a Black Rhodes Scholar', *The American Oxonian*, Vol.LXXIX (Oct. 1992), pp.243–8. Despite his rationale that, 'there is no such thing as a *Black* Rhodes Scholar – there are only Rhodes Scholars', nevertheless 'being Black and a Rhodes Scholar is an issue worth talking about' is predicated on his also being an American; some of his sentiments (though not all his arguments) are endorsed by black African Scholars. For a valuable note on the first black American Rhodes Scholar, Alain Leroy Locke, who was up at Hertford College in 1907–10, see Jeffrey Green, 'A Black Edwardian Rhodes Scholar', *Oxford*, Vol.XI, No.2, (1988), pp.71–6.
19. Chris Landsberg (1991) and Omphemetse Mouki (1992) are two of the first examples.
20. *New York Times*, 14 Dec. 1988.
21. With the prospect of being its first alumnus in The White House, Oxford and the Rhodes Scholarship Scheme attracted a high degree of attention in the British press during the run-up to the Presidential election. *The Times* talked of how 'the discreet dons of Oxford' were bracing themselves for 'a fresh round of muck-raking amid the dreaming spires' (15 Oct. 1992), while *The Sunday Times* (25 Oct. 1992) carried a special feature on 'A Yank at Oxford'. Subsequently, *The Times* imaginatively reported 'Dons Glory in Their Boy as Head of The Western World' (4 Nov. 1992), and, even more colourfully, 'Dons Pop Breakfast Corks for Clinton' (5 Nov. 1992). The student newspaper *Cherwell* in 'Running for Rhodes', examined 'Bill Clinton's free ticket to Oxford and political success' (16 Oct. 1992), with the reflection by a Caribbean Rhodes Scholar how 'Cecil Rhodes . . . felt if he picked all the prospective leaders of the British Empire and sent them to Oxford to be educated, they would go on to rule the world'. In due course the Campaign for Oxford's *University News* led off with a triumphant 'First Oxonian in the White House' (No.11, No. 1992). While in general the British press did not find it necessary to dwell on the statistical significance of the Rhodes Scholarship Scheme, in America, a lot of factual comment on the Scholarship Scheme was generated, for example, 'The Rhodes to Leadership', *USA Today*, 3 Dec. 1992. The same pun appeared on the cover page (but not in the title of the article itself, p.8 of *Oxford Magazine*, No.89 (Hilary 1993), to describe Colin Matthew's regular *In Vacuo* piece 'The Rhodes that Led to Washington'.
22. The same handicap attaches to Lord Elton's, *The First Fifty Years of the Rhodes Trust and The Rhodes Scholarships* (Oxford, 1956). Even the official 1981 *Register* prematurely 'killed off' the first Ghanaian Rhodes Scholar, L.W. Hesse – see the letter from Cameron Duodu, *West Africa* (10 Sept. 1986) p.1856. As a possible precedent, The Association of American Rhodes Scholars (AARS) regularly compiles a list of addresses and occupations of their Rhodes Scholars, as part of *The American Oxonian*.
23. Richard Symonds, *Oxford and Empire: The Last Lost Cause?* (London, 1986), p.167.
24. The 1991 Census gives a figure of 207,000 black Africans – *The Times*, 30 Nov. 1992.
25. Figures from the *Daily Telegraph*, 10 July 1991.
26. Figures from the *Daily Telegraph*, 13 July 1991.
27. In view of the response of the American professor of African history to whom I outlined my research project in 1991, 'I didn't know there were any', even the establishment of their existence may be regarded as something of an achievement.
28. Bruce Courtenay, *The Power of One* (London, 1989), p.573. An earlier novel, focusing on the race relations aspect of Rhodes Scholars at Oxford (one a Caribbean, one a Ugandan graduating from Makerere) was Tom Stacey's *The Brothers M* (London, 1960). This was written before any black African Rhodes Scholars had been elected.
29. David Alexander, American Secretary of the Rhodes Scholarship Trust, unwittingly endorsed the appeal for this direction of research when, following the Clinton election, he explained to the press that 'Rhodes wanted to find people who were willing to do things not just for themselves, but for their society'; quoted in *USA Today*, 3 Dec. 1992.

Notes on Contributors

Hakim Adi teaches in London and has completed a Ph.D. thesis on the West African Students' Union and the political activities of West African students in Britain.

Ian Duffield teaches at the University of Edinburgh. He has written extensively on aspects of Afro-British history and especially on Afro-British convicts in Australia.

Paul Edwards held a personal chair in English and African Literature at Edinburgh University at the time of his death in 1992. He had edited the eighteenth-century Afro-British authors Ottobah Cugoano, Ignatius Sancho and Olaudah Equiano. His last book, jointly edited with David Dabydeen, was *Black Writers in Britain 1760–1890*, Edinburgh University Press, 1991.

Diane Frost is a Research Fellow jointly with the Department of Economic and Social History, University of Liverpool, and The Merseyside Maritime Museum. Her doctorate on Kru maritime migrant workers during the nineteenth and twentieth centuries, completed in 1992, was based on fieldwork in West Africa and the Toxteth area of Liverpool.

John Hargreaves is writing a short study of the overseas connection of Aberdeen University since 1860. This will be a contribution to the quincentennial history of the University where he was formerly Professor of History. He also continues to explore some general themes of his last book, *Decolonization in Africa* (1988).

David Killingray, Reader in History, Goldsmiths College, University of London, has written on various aspects of African, Caribbean, and British history.

Anthony Kirk-Greene is Emeritus Fellow of St Antony's College, Oxford, having recently retired as Lecturer in the Modern History of Africa, University of Oxford. He has published widely on the history, politics and sociology of tropical Africa and is currently working on the history of Britain's overseas civil services.

Roger Lambo was born in Kaduna, Nigeria, and studied at the Universities of Ibadan and Manchester. From 1982 to 1988 he worked for the External Relations Sector of UNESCO. He is currently working as an airline pilot.

Neil Parsons is at the Centre for African Studies, University of Cape Town. Previously he was at the Universities of Zambia, Swaziland, and Botswana and from 1988 to 1993 at the Institute of Commonwealth Studies, University of London. Co-editor (with Robin Palmer) of *The Roots of Rural Poverty in Central and Southern Africa* (1977) and author of *A New History of Southern Africa* (1982), he is now working on a biography of Seretse Khama 1921–80.

Marika Sherwood is a freelance historian currently researching Black political organizations in the United Kingdom in the 1930s and 1940s. She expects her book on *Nkrumah: The Years Abroad, 1935–1947*, to be published early in 1994. She is secretary of the Association for the Study of African, Caribbean and Asian History and Culture in Britain, and editor of its *Newsletter*.

Index

INDEX